Alfred Hitchcock's Silent Films

Alfred Hitchcock's Silent Films

MARC RAYMOND STRAUSS

McFarland & Company, Inc., Publishers

Jefferson, North Carolina, and London

Library of Congress Cataloguing-in-Publication Data

Strauss, Marc.
    Alfred Hitchcock's silent films / Marc Raymond Strauss.
        p.   cm.
    Includes bibliographical references and index.

    ISBN 0-7864-1901-6 (softcover : 50# alkaline paper) ∞

    1. Hitchcock, Alfred, 1899– — Criticism and interpretation.
2. Silent films— History and criticism.   I. Title.
PN1998.3.H58S76   2004
791.4302'33'092 — dc22   2004020169

British Library cataloguing data are available

Cover image: *Blackmail*, 1929 (BFI Collections)

Manufactured in the United States of America

McFarland & Company, Inc., Publishers
    Box 611, Jefferson, North Carolina 28640
    www.mcfarlandpub.com

To my father, Guy Armand Strauss,
who learned English and began his own love
for the arts from watching movies,
a universal language art form

Acknowledgments

First and foremost, I want to thank Dr. Harvey Hecht, professor of English at Southeast Missouri State University, for his thoughtful contributions to this book by discovering and collecting all of the film stills from the British Film Institute in London. Secondly, I want to thank my colleagues in the faculty, administration, and staff at Southeast Missouri State University for granting me a full year's sabbatical in 2002–2003 in order to finally organize over twenty years of written work in dance, film, and aesthetics into useful (and, I hope, interesting) texts.

Contents

Preface

Aficionados of Alfred Hitchcock who pick up this book will invariably be looking for something new — anything — to learn about the Master of Suspense. I believe they will be happily surprised and richly rewarded, for Hitchcock's silent films are indeed golden and full to the brim with innumerable examples of the "pure cinema" so greatly relished by this director throughout his career.

Still, one continues to wonder, if we might not be nearing a saturation point. (I began to wonder about this question a full decade ago.) As of this writing (fall 2004) and by my count, a full half-dozen new books about the director have been or are being published in this year alone, with no end, apparently, in sight. According to Jane Sloan's impressive if already dated annotated bibliography of writings by and about the director, *Alfred Hitchcock: A Filmography and Bibliography* (1993; G. K. Hall), well over 75 books in half a dozen languages and nearly 1000 articles had been written up until 1990. Dozens more books and articles have since been published, of course.

On the flip side, novices coming to a book with this title, *Alfred Hitchcock's Silent Films*, after seeing or hearing about, say, the ever popular *Psycho* (1960), *North by Northwest* (1959), or *Notorious* (1946), will more than likely ask, "He made silent films? I never knew!"

Both ends of the Hitchcockian continuum should find many morsels of interest to nibble on here. In this book I contend that, like an increasing number of critics, if you want to understand the later Hitchcock of his English and American periods, you must watch and study his "silents." Far from tentative or amateurish, these nine extant films reward repeat viewings with a richness of virtuosity and complexity as effective and exciting as his talking films— if not more so! Hitchcock's silents contain the very first appearances of many of his greatest technical and thematic achievements: the vertigo-inducing crowd scenes; his stair, chair, and other inanimate object symbolism and iconography; powerfully audacious and

1

startling camera movements, cuts, montages, and *mises en scènes*; unapologetic and transparent in-your-face manipulations of the audience's emotions and thoughts; and a charmingly self-conscious, always macabre wit. All of these elements comprise what Hitchcock himself referred to as the essence of pure cinema, an essence that he had already mastered and which is embodied in these still largely unseen and only moderately critiqued films—until now.

Fortunately, all but one of the director's earliest screen gems are laid out in the nine silent films produced and released in just five years, from 1925 to 1929. Sadly, the tenth, his second full-length feature (from 1925, but released in 1927), *The Mountain Eagle*, seems lost forever, although many of us continue to wait patiently year after year for it to surface somewhere. Also fortuitously, all but two of the remaining nine — *The Pleasure Garden* (number 1; produced in 1925, but released in 1927) and *Downhill* (number 4; released in 1927)—are readily available today for purchase or rental on video and DVD. To see these two rarest Hitchcock films, one must visit the British Film Institute (BFI) in London, where the originals (or prints from the originals) are stored, travel to but a handful of cinema archives sprinkled around the world (such as the Academy Film Archive Center for Motion Picture Study, at the Margaret Herrick Library in Beverly Hills, California), or dig around on the Internet like a pig after truffles.

I owe a tremendous debt of inspiration and insight to so many of the writers on Hitchcock who have come before me, all of whom (I trust) are listed in this book's bibliography. And, because all books have (or should have) a clear and interesting point of view presented by their *auteurs*, my own particular perspective evolved from some of these very critics and their writings:

• Stefan Sharff's *Alfred Hitchcock's High Vernacular: Theory and Practice* (1991; Columbia University Press), through his difficult-to-achieve, nearly objective descriptions of the filmmaker's popular (movie) and artistic (cinema) "structured languages," is a shot-by-shot analysis of three sound films: *Notorious* (1946), *Frenzy* (1972), and *Family Plot* (1976). Of particular value for me was Sharff's understanding of the intelligent "active-creative" (p. 8) capacity of a film's audience, as opposed to the all-too-often passive, spectacle-seeking response they prefer. In other words, Sharff's focus on Hitchcock's engaging artistry, rather than an audience's desire for simplistic entertainment — especially his identification of the director's ability to provide an audience with "thinking time" (p. 9) during the films' length — helped me better contextualize the director's "orchestrated [shots of] separation" (p. 9) into more meaningful discourse.

- Similarly, in *Hitchcock — The Murderous Gaze* (1982; Harvard University Press), William Rothman painstakingly presents his own detailed shot-by-shot descriptions of five Hitchcock films (one of which, 1927's silent *The Lodger*, is covered in this book) in ways that treat the filmmaker's compositions as a "complex system of references" (p. 2). Both Sharff's and Rothman's writings were essential influences on my own theories, for they constructed their theses based on what formalist literary theorists would call "close readings" ("viewings") of the "texts" ("films") themselves, rather than working backwards toward primary source material in search of validation of previously constructed theories. Like Sharff and Rothman's books, similar shot-by-shot expositions of various sections of these nine silent films are presented throughout this book, providing the reader with the same kind of highly detailed descriptions and analyses.
- Years before Sharff's and Rothman's work, Eric Rohmer and Claude Chabrol wrote the groundbreaking *Hitchcock: The First Forty-Four Films* (1957; translated by Stanley Hochman, 1979, Frederick Ungar Publishing). Their book was the first major scholarly text to consider Hitchcock as a filmmaker of status, and their research permitted all subsequent theorists to approach Hitchcock's films not only as popular entertainment but also as serious scholarship.
- Another Frenchman from the *Cahiers du Cinéma* school, François Truffaut presented what many still believe to be the definitive interview book with the director, simply titled *Hitchcock* (1967; Revised English language edition first printed by Touchstone/Simon & Schuster, 1985). With the inestimable bilingual collaboration of Helen G. Scott, Truffaut went straight to the horse's mouth for illuminating quotes on all of the director's films, including the silents.
- In a sense sequels to Truffaut's interviews, the recent *Hitchcock on Hitchcock: Selected Writings and Interviews* (1995; edited by Sidney Gottlieb, University of California Press) and the current *Alfred Hitchcock Interviews,* also edited by Gottlieb (2003; University Press of Mississippi), are selective collections of words spoken or written by that same horse. Along with the films themselves, these three books comprise the richest lode of primary source material on and or by the director himself, from which I have drawn deeply and rewardingly.
- Maurice Yacowar's wonderfully incisive, frequently tongue-in-cheek *Hitchcock's British Films* (1977; Archon Books) is an often just repudiation of Raymond Durgnat's maddening, obscure, strange, and yet important *The Strange Case of Alfred Hitchcock, or The Plain Man's Hitchcock* (1974; Faber and Faber). These two books represent the most

detailed studies of Hitchcock's early films prior to Charles Barr's recent book of 1999 (see below), and include excellent — if occasionally flawed — analyses of sections of his "silents." (It is important for writers and readers of the 21st century to keep in mind that most authors who wrote before the 1980s did not have access to nor the benefit of video and DVD, especially the all important rewind button that later audiences have had, so they had to rely almost entirely on their own memories of rare screenings of these films for their examinations. For this reason alone, we owe both Yacowar and Durgnat a tremendous debt of gratitude for their groundbreaking contributions to the Hitchcock "discipline.")

- More than any other book, Donald Spoto's richly revealing (and often devastatingly despairing) *The Dark Side of Genius: The Life of Alfred Hitchcock* (1983; Ballantine Books) got my dander up — and, no doubt, that of so many other fans and aficionados— with his incredibly *negative* appraisal of the filmmaker's motivations, especially towards women. Spoto almost single-handedly inspired me to *disprove* his contentions by re-viewing with ever-closer scrutiny Hitchcock's entire catalog of films again and again. Thank you, Donald Spoto. To be fair, his research has always been impeccable and, along with his excellent *The Art of Alfred Hitchcock: Fifty Years of his Motion Pictures* (1976 and 1992; Doubleday), his writing remains an important source of much information on the director.
- Thomas M. Leitch's excellent close reading of — and enjoyable, not adverse, engagement with — Hitchcock's films, in his very clever *Find the Director and Other Hitchcock Games* (1991; University of Georgia Press), begins with the assumption that Hitchcock's audience is more than willing to cooperate in its suspension of disbelief in order to identify with the semi-absurd plots and characters regularly presented to us. (No doubt Spoto inspired Leitch, too!) Like Sharff and Rothman, Leitch and I believe the greatest pleasure one can have with Hitchcock's films involves a constructively active, not passive, involvement with the material. Hitchcock's characters are not just on the screen, but absorbed, thinking viewers in the audience —*us*!
- Lesley Brill's equally positive take on the director, *The Hitchcock Romance: Love and Irony in Hitchcock's Films* (1988; Princeton University Press), also kept me focused on the affirmative. As with Brill's assessment, I believe the director's films are more about the search for healthy relationships and one's emotional growth as an individual than about, say, the manipulative exploitation and objectification of women (usually blondes).

- Ken Mogg's recent *The Alfred Hitchcock Story* (1999; Taylor Publishing Company), while at first glance seeming to be just another oversized cocktail table summary of Hitchcock's work (by my count there are at least half a dozen such books on the market, as of this writing), shares some rather sophisticated — albeit brief — insights into his films, including the early ones both silent and sound. Proof positive that you can't judge a book by its cover.
- Concerning Robin Wood's *Hitchcock's Films* (1965; Castle Books) and his second shot at it, *Hitchcock's Films Revisited* (1989; Columbia University Press), I prefer the first version, finding it easier to understand and eminently more readable. His sometimes thorny but always pithy discussions in the first book are much more accessible and engaging than what are overly analytical, convoluted ones in the second version. To paraphrase Hitchcock's own comments on the two *Men Who Knew Too Much* (1934 & 1956), I feel that Wood is more the talented amateur in the former, and hence more "raw" and immediate, than the consummate professional in the latter. But you decide.
- Last but not least, along with an interesting discussion of the rarely praised screenwriter Eliot Stannard and his influence on Hitchcock's silent films, Charles Barr's recent *English Hitchcock* (1999; Cameron & Hollis) brings to light many fresh ideas on the silent films within the larger context of his British period — a kind of updated sequel to both Durgnat's and Yacowar's books. Privy to the advances in technology — and his ability to unearth slightly different Danish and German versions of some of the silent films — Barr rightly states: "[T]hey already contain many of the strengths, and many of the thematic and formal characteristics, that are central to our sense of Hitchcock, and help explain the extraordinary critical status he has achieved. These [silent films] are genuinely formative, seminal works" (p. 23). I couldn't agree more, and I hope that with this book, I may both buttress and further Barr's assertions.

In summary: close and personal analyses of the films themselves — focusing on the actual montages and *mises en scènes* on the screen wedded to Hitchcock's own words about his work — make up the bulk of the primary source material from which I developed the perspectives set out in this book.

Owning versions of all nine extant films on video and DVD certainly didn't hurt, either, but visiting the British Film Institute (BFI) in London to hand-spool 32-millimeter originals and copies of *The Pleasure Garden*, *Downhill* (1927), and the silent *Blackmail* — the first of which also, happily, exists in this country at the Southern Methodist University Media Library, in Dallas— made this research even more a labor of love. If you truly want to have a singular experience while watching a Hitchcock film, immerse yourself in archives that literally reek of both history and decomposing film nitrate and spend a few evocative hours in the BFI.

Introduction

In *Alfred Hitchcock's Silent Films*, I contend that these movies hold all the keys to Hitchcock's later ones, and are, in fact, *fully realized works of art*. Not surprisingly, these films were made during a time when the pure cinema of silence was just reaching its zenith. Hitchcock studied and worked for the early American production company Paramount Pictures when it opened its first British studio in London in 1920, and was in Munich working on his first two directorial assignments when F. W. Murnau (1888–1931) created his now classic *The Last Laugh* (1924), Fritz Lang (1890–1976) was soon to begin his monumental *Metropolis* (1926), and other German greats such as Ernst Lubitsch (1892–1947) were honing their filmmaking skills. (These last two directors, like Hitchcock, would eventually relocate to the United States.)

Then, literally overnight, talkies arrived and changed everything; but not Hitchcock, mercifully. Within these pages, I believe the reader will find descriptions and analyses of these nine rarely seen silent films to be as fascinating as they were (and continue to be) for me, and that one or more of you will go on to further mine Hitchcock's films, both silent and sound, for even more gems of genius— gems that miraculously seem to be unearthed daily with each new viewing and viewer.

One of the biggest challenges with these early films (and, in fact, most silent films by any director)— and one that may never be fully overcome due to time and access— involves actually finding authentic copies to view. The problem is that many of these films have several "versions" out in the world located in different archives, museums, and libraries— versions of various lengths with differing scenes and sometimes different subtitles. Charles Barr discusses this point in some detail: "It is important, in looking at Hitchcock's early career, to be conscious that texts were more fluid — 'silent' films were shown with musical and sometimes other accompaniment, their projection speed varied, and multiple versions, with various kinds of color toning or tinting, might have claims to be as authentic as each other —

and that, beyond this, there are significant gaps in the materials that we have" (1999, p. 18).

Unless someone can find a way to see *all* of the versions of each film and then *accurately* detail their distinctions (even *Strangers on a Train*, from Hitchcock's middle period, has been recently found to have two versions, an American Hollywood and alternate British copy, as seen in the 1997 Warner Bros. double-sided DVD release), readers and viewers alike must be relatively content to take each interpretation of the films with at least a few grains of salt. The vagaries of memory and the inevitable embellishments of authorship (including those of this writer) invariably impact the writing and reading of those interpretations, too.

Still, aficionados often gleefully agree that fascination with all of Hitchcock's films seems endless and will no doubt continue for years to come. Let yet another critic present his or her case, hopefully with rigor, accuracy, and passion.

In this book I have tried to share with the reader the closest approximation to watching these films as is possible via words, and with the same kind of accuracy and passion that I demand from others. Of course, film is a visual medium, particularly so in the silents, and words have little to do with moving images. To a large degree, as Arlene Croce so aptly said about dance critics but which can easily apply to writers of any art, including film: "[A] critic tries to train the memory as well as the organs of sense [so he can] make the afterimage that appears in his writing match the performance. But often it doesn't match literally because the senses are assimilating impressions and not recording facts" (1978, p. ix).

Regardless of how closely one tries to literally match one's responses to a film with the "facts" of the film itself, all writers of all film books necessarily reflect the varying effects on themselves that occur *as they assimilate* their impressions. Of course, unlike a live performance, one can return again and again to a film, and in these days of slow motion and rewinds, it is plausible to believe that it is possible to bring closer and closer together that elusive match between impressions and facts that Croce speaks of. In other words, if careful, with a lot of work, and with some good fortune, *words can come close* to "matching the performance." That is what I have assiduously tried to do in this book.

Throughout these ten chapters, I have primarily followed both William Rothman's and Stefan Sharff's estimable leads in recounting and analyzing large sections of each silent film *shot by shot* and *montage by montage*, in similar fashion to what formalist literary critics would call "close readings" of the text, in order for the film "text" to *speak as clearly for itself as possible*. In one case, *The Ring* (number six), I have treated the film in almost its entirety this way. In another, *The Farmer's Wife* (number seven) — what I believe to be the true masterpiece of Hitchcock's silent era — I have recounted, detailed, and analyzed the whole film.

The reader will notice occasional quotations sprinkled throughout the book, quotations excerpted from many of the same writers already mentioned in the Acknowledgments and Preface. Included at times are Hitchcock's own words, too, all of which are presented in *italics*, to more easily distinguish between writers on the director and the director himself. All of these Hitchcock quotes are excerpted from Sidney Gottlieb's two excellent collections (1995, 2003) and François Truffaut's one collection (the revised 1985 version) of interviews with the director.

I debated whether or not to add length and density to an already "thick" exposition, and have opted to beg the reader's indulgence with these quotes in the hope that more qualitative information — especially words that, in this writer's opinion, could be neither written nor spoken any better — might themselves stimulate repeat close viewings of these marvelous films.

Throughout this book I have used abbreviations for the names of those writers whom I quote frequently (their works are shown in the Bibliography on page 211), for commonly used cinematic terms, and for the eight most popular concise film review dictionaries on the market. Following are keys to these abbreviations.

Author Abbreviations
(see the Bibliography)

Charles Barr	CB	Lesley Brill	LB
Rohmer & Chabrol	RC	Raymond Durgnat	RD
Sidney Gottlieb 1	SG1	Sidney Gottlied 2	SG2
Alfred Hitchcock	AH	Thomas Leitch	TL
Ken Mogg	KM	William Rothman	WR
Stefan Sharff	SS	Donald Spoto	DS
François Truffaut	FT	Robin Wood	RW
Maurice Yacowar	MY		

Film Term Abbreviations

AC	Autonomous Camera
CU	Close-Up
ECU	Extreme Close-Up
MCU	Medium Close-Up
LDS	Long Distance Shot

(Film Term Abbreviations, *continued*)

ELS	Extreme Long Distance Shot
MLS	Medium Long Distance Shot
POV	Point Of View
SC	Screen Center
SL	Screen Left
SR	Screen Right
US	Upper Screen
DS	Down Screen
OSL	Off Screen Left
OSR	Off Screen Right
USL	Upper Screen Left
USR	Upper Screen Right
LSL	Lower Screen Left
LSR	Lower Screen Right
NBS	Never Before Seen shot
PAP	Proscenium Arch Perspective

Abbreviations for Eight
Concise Film Review Compendiums

Blockbuster Video Guide to Movies and Videos, 1996	BB
Halliwell's 2003 Film and Video Guide	HA
Leonard Maltin's 2003 Movie & Video Guide	LM
Video & DVD Guide 2003 (Nick Martin & Marsha Porter)	MP
1992–1993 Movies on TV and Videocassette (Steven H. Scheuer)	SS
Time Out Film Guide 11, 2003	TO
Variety's Movie Guide 2001	VA
VideoHound's Golden Movie Retriever 2003	VH

One

The Pleasure Garden

Produced late summer 1925, first screening March 1926,
released January 24, 1927

> *A film has got to be ocularly interesting, and above all it is the*
> *picture which is the thing. I try to tell my story so much so in pictures*
> *that if by any chance the sound apparatus broke down in the cinema,*
> *the audience would not fret and get restless because the pictorial action*
> *would still hold them! Sound is all right in its place, but it is a silent*
> *picture training which counts today.*
> — AH, "Close Your Eyes and Visualize!"
> 1936; in SG1, 1995, p. 247

In the 1925-produced *The Pleasure Garden*, Hitchcock's first complete directorial feature (he had directed an uncompleted two-reeler in 1922, *Number Thirteen*, finished directing *Always Tell your Wife*, also in 1922, when that film's director fell ill, and assistant directed five films with Graham Cutts between 1922 and 1925), American silent screen star Virginia Valli (1898–1968) plays Patsy Brand, the sophisticated chorus girl heroine with a heart that's true. Her actress friend from the States, Carmelita Geraghty (1901–1966), plays Jill Cheyne, an aspiring star who seeks and finds fame rather than friendship. Prolific Scottish-born actor John Stuart (1898–1979) plays Hugh Fielding, our eventual hero. Versatile British actor Miles Mander (1888–1946), who plays Levet, Hugh's sympathetic friend early on, eventually marries Patsy, turns evil, and goes mad — typical of his British, and later Hollywood, character portrayals of oily types. Nita Naldi (1897–1961) plays Levet's common law wife as a native girl, and tries to commit suicide near the end of the picture with Levet speeding the process by drowning her — Hitchcock's first of many vivid cinematic demonstrations of how difficult and painful it really is to kill someone, as we see her briefly and horribly thrash about as shot from *underwater*. Naldi was a famed Ziegfeld Follies vamp and had earlier co-starred with then heartthrob Rudolph Valentino (1895–1926) in his smash 1922 film *Blood and Sand*.

11

Only three of the eight film review compendiums referenced even mention *The Pleasure Garden*, that's how obscure the film is and has been traditionally treated. Furthermore, nary a one has much more to say about it than "boring" (HA), "forgettable" (LM), and "humdrum" (BB). But the audiences of the time seemed to have loved it, as both Spoto (1983, p. 105) and Hitchcock himself (FT, 1985, p. 39) recount, both highlighting the good press it received with the line about the director himself: "Young man with a master mind." Maurice Yacowar's reprint of London's *Bioscope* review from the time (March 25, 1926) concurs with this assessment:

> A powerful and interesting story, this has been well adapted to the screen, and admirable acting and masterly production all combine to make this a film of outstanding merit. The story is clearly and logically constructed, the subtitling is concise and to the point, and the dramatic interest is held to the last minute. The scenes during Patsy's honeymoon on Lake Como, photographed by Baron Ventimiglia, present enchanting pictures and assist the dramatic appeal of the story. As Alfred Hitchcock's first production, this promises well for future efforts [MY, 1977, p. 281].

The story, according to Ken Mogg, is by the English novelist *Mrs. Oliver Sandys* from her novel by the same name, although the credits in the film just say "Oliver Sandys," so one might easily think that a man wrote it (1999, p. 4). However, Charles Barr reveals (1999, p. 215) that the real name of "Oliver Sandys" was one Marguerite Florence Barclay (1894–1964), who published the novel under the Sandys pseudonym just two years earlier than the film's production, in 1923.

As we shall see, not one but four women either wrote or co-wrote the original novel or play upon which the first ten films of Hitchcock's oeuvre — all silents — were based on. In fact, out of his fifty-two features, women played a significant part in a large percentage of the productions, particularly the writing: Daphne du Maurier (1907–1989) wrote three of the stories (*Jamaica Inn, Rebecca,* and *The Birds*), Helen Simpson wrote or worked on three (*Murder!, Sabotage,* and *Under Capricorn*), Patricia Hightower wrote one (*Strangers on a Train*), and several others wrote or co-wrote the adaptations or scenarios to at least half a dozen other films. Of course, Alma Reville (1899–1982), Hitchcock's collaborator from *The Pleasure Garden* on and his soon-to-be wife (from the time of *The Farmer's Wife* on), contributed dialogue, scenarios, and/or adaptations to well over a dozen of the films officially, if not all of them unofficially.

In fact, even *before* we see Hitchcock's own name as director of *The Pleasure Garden*— handwritten in script with a flourish that includes his

middle initial "J," for Joseph (for the first and only time in his career)—
we see the name of Alma Reville appear as Assistant Director.

One can easily argue that *The Pleasure Garden* is no minor accomplishment as this director's first feature film, and has a number of scenes that are especially worth noting and detailing. In this first film we get the beginnings, figuratively and literally, of what would come to be known as the classic Hitchcockian juxtaposition of images—juxtapositions that are truly *audacious*, a term I use for the director in describing some of the most singularly startling, self-conscious and visceral shots ever created for cinema.

> [E]ven in his first film Hitchcock proves himself a filmmaker of wit, moral seriousness, and lively style. The film is a very impressive debut. It has excellent lighting, a sense of composition, character, and editing that is nowhere flaccid, and even as a straightforward story moves along briskly and entertainingly [MY, 1977, p. 29].

The first such shot is the very first image we ever see of Hitchcock's authorship, a frenziedly dancing girl seen lower screen right (LSR) alongside the opening credits. Across those credits shines a bright spotlight upon her which comes from beyond upper screen left (USL), while the rest of the frame remains in dark shadow. Highly erotic yet objectified by the light, the dancing girl wears a skimpy dress and seductively wiggles about with a "come hither" look towards no one in particular—as if she is dancing just for herself, alone (as our secondary protagonist Jill will act only for herself, ultimately). "[T]he dance is lonely, manic in its desperate movements, and mechanical in its repetition. There is neither audience nor partner for the dance, just loneliness pretending joy" (MY, 1977, p. 27). Seeming to be no more than an apparition, this dancing girl is clearly a premonition of the narcissistic Jill in this film, Julia in *Downhill*, The Girl in *The Ring*, Sweetland in *The Farmer's Wife*, and Kate in *The Manxman*— all characters who will have opportunities to grow emotionally in their films but will not get very far.

The first real scene in *The Pleasure Garden* is also quite striking, and immediately establishes the director's unique cinematic approach, one that he will use throughout his career. I include a somewhat lengthy exposition of this scene in order for the reader to get a clearer idea from the get-go of the director's intelligence and complexity.

A host of chorus girls are seen in medium shot (MS) running down a spiral staircase, all legs and undergarments (further sparking the male audience's libidinous attentions, if they needed any, after the dancing girl from the credits). We then see them scurry across a stage in a long shot (LS) that is taken from above and offstage right. Cut to a MS of them from head height as seen from the same wing. The theater manager is also visible just offstage in both shots, smoking away on a cigar. Sudden cut to a closeup (CU) shot of the chorus girls as seen from the audience, and a full frontal of the lead performer singing and gesturing in front of the dancing chorus line.

Cut to a reverse angle MS looking down and panning slowly left to right (L to R) across seven men's faces in the audience. The bodies of other onlookers are visible in the background, for the shot is taken from just above their headline (approximating the chorus girls' positions) as these men gaze directly into our eyes (the camera's lens). "The tracking shot against their variety of facial forms and movements is an aesthetically exhilarating one. Already the Hitchcock touch hints at a saturnine view of human beings as easily opportunistic and exploitative" (RD, 1974, pp. 67–68). We see that one man in particular is both transfixed by and ogling the proceedings. Still given little information except this slow pan of lechers, humorous irony is revealed to us as the eighth face turns out to be a girl, her head leaning to one side, asleep. Theater scenes such as these will appear in a host of Hitchcock's films.

Reverse angle cut again, this time to a MS focused slightly upwards towards one particular dancing girl in the chorus, the others visible alongside her. This person will turn out to be our heroine, Patsy. Reverse cut back to a MS of one man in the middle of the wolf pack wearing an absurd-looking monocle. Adjusting it for a better look, he sports a big, lascivious grin on his face. Hitchcock then reverse angle cuts for the fourth successive time to an out-of-focus MS of the same chorus girl, now barely recognizable. Because it is the next shot after the lecher shot, we immediately assume this is his view, but in retrospect we realize that, had this man *not* had a monocle in place as we had just seen, the *previous shot of Patsy* would have been the one out of focus, not this one. But that is not the case: *this shot* is the one out of focus.

Our first awareness of Hitchcock's unique cinematic sense is now occurring, however subliminally, for we suddenly see a huge pair of hands *holding binoculars* rise up from below the screen into the frame in extreme closeup (ECU), as if being held up to *our* eyes. If we had time to think about it we might wonder, "Who is doing that?" but Hitchcock immediately cuts back again to another reverse angle MS of the same lecher *without* his monocle, binoculars pressed to his eyes: a simple sleight of film, surely, but what Hitchcock has done is to deny showing us the man's *removal* of the monocle and his replacement of it with binoculars. Why does the director construct the montage this way? One possible answer suggests itself: to already begin to manipulate our sensibilities and knock our thinking off kilter a bit. At best, we may unconsciously begin to wonder why that earlier shot was out of focus, but in our consciousness, we are only aware that something "different," perhaps audacious, has been perpetrated on us.

Cut now to the binocular-clad view (presumably) of a CU of several of the chorines' knees (thighs to calves) as the camera (binoculars?) pans L to R, not quite as out of focus. The camera stops on one set of gams, then sharply focuses. Now in a medium closeup (MCU) a slight distance further back, the camera lingeringly and titillatingly pans up the chorine's body to stop on the brightly lit chest and face of our soon-to-be heroine Patsy, symmetrically framed between two dancing girls. A privileged view for us, Hitchcock's camera holds on this voyeuristic MCU for four seconds.

Reverse angle cut back to a CU now of the same dirty old man smacking his lips and removing the binoculars, returning to his monocle. Cut to an extraordinary *CU* of just Patsy's face and chest now, isolated from the other girls this time. This cannot be, in our understanding of actual reality, for binoculars assuredly can see "closer" than a monocle. We surmise, then (subliminally at best, once again), that this must be the director-as-artist's prerogative choice of shots, regardless of whether it can be "seen" via a monocle or a pair of binoculars. In other words, this shot is that leering character's *subjective* perspective and *imaginative* gaze amplified for *our* (Hitchcock's audience) identification purposes. This is filmic work of a very sophisticated kind composed by someone who knows how to get into his true characters' minds—*ours*—and manipulate them at will.

Back and forth cutting now occurs six times between a CU of Patsy looking past the camera (us and the man) slightly screen right (SR) and the man looking past the camera slightly screen left (SL). Patsy flirts anonymously for a moment with no one in particular and then seems to catch the lecher's eye. He reacts personally to her gaze now, sexually excited. She responds seductively at first (*à la* the title credits dancer, perhaps), lips pouting together and eyes peering out into the darkness of the audience. Reverse cut back to an even stronger reaction from the man. Quick reverse angle cut back to a CU of Patsy's face, her eyes suddenly open wide now, realization dawning that he is being invasively attentive and not just leering objectively from afar. Hitchcock has us firmly manipulated now as we begin to identify completely with both characters. "Perhaps a certain irony underlies the virtuosity with which Hitchcock can switch us from one identification or theme to another," says Durgnat (RD, 1974, p. 69). That author is speaking about the director's skill at manipulating his audience's identification with several characters in *Psycho* and *The Birds*, but he could just as easily be commenting on Hitchcock's engineering of our thoughts in this or any of the other silent films.

In the same shot we see Patsy frown a "No, that's not appropriate" kind of look, then turn her head away, still dancing. Reverse angle cut to a MS of the man, now standing and sure of himself (as if he's got a conquest), but this time the camera is set up from a new position, audience left (if facing the stage) and from further down his row. Heading away from the camera *upscreen left* (USL) towards the outside aisle on audience right (if facing the stage), we see him trip over another binocular-clad patron (or was this the earlier man, one now subliminally wonders?). We suddenly realize that all these dirty old men were sitting in the front row, as we can see the apron lip of the orchestra pit just SL. The two men exchange angry and then conciliatory words, each wholly immersed in their respective worlds.

Cut to a slightly longer *reverse angle* MS of the original lecher, now in a right-facing profile moving right after entering *frame left* to speak with an usher. The shot makes us a bit disoriented with this combination of reverse angles and reverse directional perspectives, and is a typical cinematic ploy Hitchcock will use repeatedly throughout his canon to challenge our attention. In less than three minutes of Hitchcock's premier film, our sense of space, direction, and perspective in this theater and on the screen has been brilliantly opened up to accommodate numerous points of view.

Cut to a two-shot MCU of the monocle-clad patron pointing out his chosen gamine OSL to the usher. Cut back to the earlier LS from offstage right in the wings (from the perspective of the stage itself, as if facing the audience from onstage and using conventional theater directions) looking back onto the stage — the shot with the manager smoking and foregrounding the chorus girls. Cut to a CU of the very first title of a Hitchcock film: "Oscar Hamilton, Manager of The Pleasure Garden Theatre — George Snell." (George Snell is the name of the actor playing Hamilton, and that name is included in the bottom right corner of this title frame, the words of which are superimposed over a drawing of a theater curtain.) Cut to a full-frontal MCU of Hamilton gnawing and puffing away furiously on a cigar, a sign reading "Smoking Prohibited" prominently displayed over his left shoulder. Look fast, for directly over his right shoulder is what appears to be a camera's eye staring back at us! Is this a coincidence, a result of poor editing, or a self-conscious plant? Who knows; but it's startling if you catch it.

Cut to a MLS of the offstage right wing and part of the stage taken from offstage as the usher and monocled man enter the screen from OSL.

Hitchcock's jarring juxtapositions between long shots and closeups have begun to accumulate already in this film, and are yet further examples of his complete understanding and manipulative skills at the beginning of his career. Cut to a disorienting MCU of the monocled man in profile right and the cigar-chomping manager in profile left facing each other. Cut to title number 2: "Your chorus, Mr. Hamilton, is certainly most tempting." No minced words here. Cut now to a two-shot of the men in medium long (ML) profile, chorus girls leaving the stage in the background SL. The two men turn their backs on the camera to gaze at the women leaving, and Hamilton gestures upscreen (US) towards them.

With the next cut to a MS of the receding backs of the chorines, now without wings or men onscreen, we may surmise that the camera has either just been moved forward onto the stage or the cut was to a zoomed-in view of the same shot. As the backs continue to move US in MS, Patsy surprises our view by emerging from the chorus to stand in place facing SL. Acknowledging Hamilton's gesture to come over, she hurries across and past the camera OSL. This is another audacious shot because our identification had been held on the men for a moment or two, and so seeing Patsy enter the screen startles us. (Woody Allen would come to employ this frame-expanding trick of cinematic offscreen space and presence many times in his films over half a century later.)

Patsy is next seen immediately entering SR into a CU three-shot. She is brightly lit and centered between both men. Dressed all in white and the men all in black in front of a black curtain, title number 3 announces: "This is Miss Patsy Brand." The name of the actress, Virginia Valli (as with George Snell earlier), is spelled out in lettering lower screen right. (In the twenties, audiences were still being educated as to who was playing whom in these films, and so their real names were often included in the titles.)

Cut back to the three-shot CU of the two men with Patsy. Hamilton walks OSR as Patsy looks the old monocled lecher over, open-minded yet with an alert cynicism written on her features. Suddenly the object of her gaze and not the voyeur, the older man acts nervously and self-consciously, recalling the effect that Manet's famous painting *Olympia* had upon its viewers in the museum at its unveiling in 1869. Still, he quickly steals a glance down at her bosom. Patsy looks back knowingly after Hamilton SR. Dead center screen, we see the old geezer lightly reach out (to fondle a breast?), but he grabs one golden curl dangling alongside Patsy's face. Title: "I've fallen in love with that charming kiss curl of yours." (Golden curls will again be featured shortly — and much more tragically — in Hitchcock's third film.) Cut back to a two-shot CU of both of them in profile facing center screen (CS), recalling the monocled man and usher's earlier two-shot.

The intensity of this short scene now becomes palpable. Patsy nonchalantly reaches up to the same curl, hesitates, and then quickly yanks it off her head and hands it to him, laughing. Title: "Then I hope you'll be very happy together!" Man, first incredulous, becomes crestfallen. He grimaces painfully and hands back the curl, stretched out now with no body. (The allusion is obvious.) Hitchcock next affords us one of those rare privileged shots, a two-second, lovingly rendered extreme close-up (ECU) of Patsy's face brightly lit and looking OSL (presumably at the man). Her face glows with self-confidence and dignity, and even a touch of wry irony plays upon it as we gaze breathlessly at this beauty. Title from Patsy to the lecher: "Your love wasn't very lasting, was it?" No, it wasn't.

The main theme of *The Pleasure Garden* is not so carefully hidden within such seemingly thrown-away lines as this one. As with all of Hitchcock's films, silent or sound, here is proof for the importance of dialogue, contrary to the conventional wisdom that the director marketed solely in "pure cinema" techniques. It is illuminating to remember that Hitchcock was a skilled title writer for the five years of his apprenticeship before directing his first full picture.

Cut back to yet another glorious, three-second ECU: Patsy smiles to herself, re-tying the curl into place. Cut to a two-shot MCU as Patsy walks OSR, leaving a now befuddled old man sadly alone in the wake of his burst bubble. Similar light and tender moments will recur throughout the remainder of this short and poignant sixty-eight minute film, but they will also begin to carry an ever-increasing weight of emotion.

Let me also share in detail the very next scene, our introduction to the film's other important protagonist, Jill Cheyne (played by Carmelita Geraghty), in order to demonstrate yet again how minutely rendered and rigorously controlled Hitchcock's cinematic technique and montages were so early in his career.

The director cuts to the exterior of the theater and the marquee walk in front of The Pleasure Garden theatre sign SL in a medium long shot (MLS). People busily mill about, walk by the building's entrance SR, and exit its door in this six-second stationary shot, the front part of a car visible downscreen right (DSR). Cut to a CU of a brunette woman standing CS and looking around. Rewind. Yup, the last person to walk by in the previous six-second shot was this woman, who will turn out to be Jill Cheyne. This kind of surreptitious information sharing is another typical Hitchcockian ploy for, while the director never *announces* his intentions, he always implants a great deal of information for his audience to see should they choose to notice (or not)—no overemphasis, but planted nonetheless.

Still in CU, Jill looks about, dazzled by the bustling energy around her. We immediately begin to identify with her, in part because Hitchcock films her looking lost in the crowd, but also because Patsy had just left a taste in our mouth for a less superficial experience than theatre districts such as these often call for. Of course, as we get to know Jill better, such an identification with her will be sorely tested, but for now, it is essential that we *do* identify with her so that our manipulated turning from sympathy to derision will be all the more powerful.

Cut to a two-shot CU of a couple of low-life thieves (stereotypical thugs) leaning against the wall next to the theatre door. Rewind. Yup, they were there, too, in the first six-second MLS of this suddenly rich scene. Hitchcock knows that if he does not give us any context, we will not know where to focus our attentions—a very telling point about his directorial approach—but it's in his use of subliminal information without any underscoring or accents that is most extraordinary.

Cut to *the thieves'* point of view (POV): an artificially staged, three-second CU of a woman's hands, partly in light—a self-consciously placed spotlight circle of light focused down onto a handbag dangling from one wrist. I say "self-consciously" because this is the first shot (of many subsequent Hitchcockian shots) that bald-facedly calls attention to itself as a movie "trick," and not merely an imagined cinematic scenario projected into our thoughts.* Both her clothes and the background are seen in black shadow, further highlighting the artificiality of this drop spot onto the handbag.

Cut back to the lowlifes, same two-shot CU as they mumble to each other about their easy mark. Cut to a medium three-shot as the girl enters their frame from OSL. She is still stunned by all of the street energy around her and remains unaware of the men. We suddenly see the theatre door open and people rush out; Jill gets pushed backwards towards the evildoers. Cut to another self-consciously staged CU of a man's hand going into her handbag and pulling out some money and a letter. Cut back to the two-shot MCU of the men matter-of-factly congratulating each other, hardly moving. We won't ever see them again, but they have quietly served Hitchcock's purpose as yet one more set of competent, minor character players doing their duty.

---

*One thinks of the patently false rear projections in Marnie *and other films, or even Hitchcock's own cameos throughout his career, as similar self-conscious examples. One could also think of Peter Sellers as Inspector Clouseau, or Groucho Marx as anyone, and even some of Hitchcock's characters at times, all of whom occasionally look straight out into the camera's eye for a moment, break the fourth wall, and directly engage us with their gaze— shades of *Olympia *again.* Woody Allen's 1985 film *The Purple Rose of Cairo *exploited this conceit as its entire premise, with characters literally stepping off of the screen into the "real" world.*

Rather than showing a reaction shot of Jill realizing (or oblivious to the fact) that she has been robbed, Hitchcock withholds this piece of information until much later—for greater effect, of course; we know about it, but she doesn't—and is so confident that we his audience will carry this knowledge with us that he does not even show Jill to us for some time. This knowledge, too, the director rightly surmises, is also firmly within our minds—she doesn't have to be shown—as our minds are the only place that sustained images matter.

The director himself said the following about *Psycho*, comments which can justly be applied to this film, too: *"as it goes on, there's less and less violence [or other overt associations] because it has been transferred to the minds of the audience"* (Sarris, 1967, p. 244). The power of the staged handbag shot, therefore, is that the scene has allowed its imaginary transference into our minds, right where it belongs.

A newcomer to the big city, we feel quite a bit of sympathy for Jill at this early stage in the film; we may even take her to be the heroine of our story now, and not Patsy, and this identification, of course, is intended. Typical of Hitchcock throughout his career, and contrary to romantic film convention, the director manipulates us into feeling for a character who will, invariably, turn out to be the "wrong" protagonist. So, naturally, when Jill does in fact become more than evil, selfish, snobbish, and shallow, our *rejected* identification with her will be all the more willing and "felt." As Yacowar states, "the sophisticated Patsy shows herself to be increasingly warm and sincere, while the supposedly innocent Jill develops airs and callousness" (MY, 1977, p. 21). More to the point, Durgnat, in his inimitably succinct fashion, presents both characters thusly: "[T]he waif turns out to be a bitch, [while] the other wins through only after her grit is tested by a hard tussle with life's disappointments" (RD, 1974, p. 66).

Equally fair, though, and aware that the game is afoot the moment one of his films begin, Hitchcock provides us with early hints of Jill's soon-to-be-revealed nature, hints that we can spot if we're quick, or have seen the film before — more reason to watch this director's films over and over again. Yacowar interestingly postulates (1977, p. 21) that Jill's ambiguous smile back at the lechers when she first enters The Pleasure Garden could reflect either a burgeoning coyness, or just her reflexive naiveté in trying to be nice. Early on we can't tell, of course, but a subliminal seed of uncertainty is planted in our minds by this one ambiguous glance.

Other seeds of doubt accumulate: Jill has a *huge* crate of clothes lugged into Patsy's flat, implying that she's come to the city to stay. If we are fast, we can see her frown derisively upon first looking over Patsy's humble lodgings, as if to say, "What a dump! I'll stay here a night or two, but only as long as I have to." Testing the bed for firmness, she again scowls, then roughly shoves Patsy's little dog off the covers and flings its bone to the floor. As Jill kneels to say her evening prayers ("What a charlatan!" we might mumble to ourselves), we laugh uncomfortably as she maliciously kicks the dog away from its innocent licking of her feet. Yacowar nails Jill eary: "No honest suppliant would kick a dog. The action playfully foreshadows Jill's hypocrisy and the callous soul she will reveal" (MY, 1977, p. 26).

All of these actions are important Hitchcockian markers, but we still ignore them at this early point in the story. Why? Because the director has manipulated us into feeling sympathy for this bereft, broke, leered over, and seemingly innocent newcomer to the city. We even let a final clue go by as Jill steals the covers from Patsy and falls asleep in the middle of their shared bed. "Oh, she's so tired," we think — as no doubt Patsy does, too — and we forgive her yet again. But we certainly *could* be aware of Patsy's consternation over Jill's actions by now, if we had a mind to. Whether or not we do, Hitchcock, ever-generous director that he is, gives us this juxtaposed, contradictory information anyway.

Thomas Leitch echoes this point — Hitchcock's skill at subliminally undermining our conventional expectations— by discussing this scene and others in relation to the way the director always "plays on the audience's … ability to follow and enjoy a story" (TL, 1991, p. 43). We are led to think, based on the romantic conventions that Hitchcock knows inside and out, that Patsy embodies the urban sophisticate to Jill's naïf. After all, she's got a job, knows how to deal with lechers, and has a working role in the chorus of the stage show Jill seeks to audition for. But, as Yacowar again rightly notes (1977, p. 21), Patsy herself will very quickly become the real "patsy" in this picture, before becoming its true heroine, and Jill will become the conniver.

As one can already tell this early in the film, Hitchcock was far from merely the talented amateur during his English period. We must remember that he had already worked on over half a dozen films before *The Pleasure Garden* in capacities as varied as title scripter, assistant director, editor, and art director. A healthy interrogatory attitude towards life is but one lesson Hitchcock explores here, as in so many of his movies. In point of fact, I believe that he was a true romantic at heart, too, and I gladly follow both Lesley Brill's and William Rothman's illuminating leads on this point, based on their positive and optimistic visions for the Hitchcock canon in their respective books.

By choosing such a course, therefore, I find Patsy's later toast to Jill and her fiancé Hugh (played by John Stuart) to be most hopeful and heartfelt, as a title reads, "I wish you something greater than fame — happiness."

I take this title at its face value, for by now, our sympathies for Jill have already begun to subconsciously turn; all of her actions have proven to be more than calculating, while Patsy's prove more and more sympathetic. For example, Jill alternately flirts and bribes Hamilton the house manager into giving her an apartment, and repays him by ignoring him and then milking the milquetoast Prince Ivan, her biggest fan, for all *he's* worth. Hamilton gets nothing for his troubles and we never see him again, while the Prince doesn't even get a kiss—all he gets is a cigarette burn in the face!

When Jill poo-poos Patsy's gracious prayer for their real fortune, we finally start to consciously wonder about these characters' true colors. Hitchcock's hopes for true happiness hinge on learning from and surviving emotional and physical suffering—not ignoring it.

Because Patsy had humorously tripped over Hugh earlier as he was playing with her knowing dog, we really should guess that it will be *Patsy* and Hugh—not Jill and Hugh—who will have the real chance for happiness by the end of the film. While the dog tried to like/lick Jill's feet earlier, and certainly likes/licks Hugh here, it now barks at Levet, Patsy's boyfriend, when he first appears (played by a temporarily sympathetic Miles Mander). As shall soon be discovered, Hitchcock is toying with convention again, for Levet comes across much too unctuously nice at first to remain sympathetic (and I dare you to believe he remains so).

I, of course, like so many Hitchcock lovers, have worked backwards to these silents from the director's later, more available films, and would have Mander's oily image imprinted in my mind from three years hence in *Murder!*—if, of course, I could have made such a correspondence upon first viewing *The Pleasure Garden*. Once again, such a connection remained subliminal, for while my first look at Mander as Levet in *The Pleasure Garden* felt strangely familiar, Hitchcock has him playing against type—at least early on—in this film.

To further that aside, another consistently rewarding approach towards Hitchcock films is in one's always-pleasurable search for identifying the regular roster of very capable character actors he employed throughout his career. They are especially fun to unmask and compare during his British Period, such as Leslie Banks' wholly contrasting roles in the first *Man Who Knew Too Much* (1934) and *Jamaica Inn* (1939), as Jill's (yet another reincarnation?) mild-mannered and sympathetic blackmailed father Bob Lawrence, and the nearly unrecognizable cutthroat pirate leader Joss Merlyn, respectively.

Mander, as the two-faced Levet in *The Pleasure Garden* and as the wholly despicable Gordon Druce in *Murder!*, remains one of a slew of highly skilled character actors Hitchcock used to play as and against type throughout his fifty-two features. And this discussion hasn't touched at all on the director's exploitation of the dark sides of his true celebrity stars, such as Cary Grant (in *Suspicion* and *Notorious*, particularly) and James Stewart (as the ambivalent character in his star turn as the Sartre-spouting professor Rupert Cadell in *Rope*, and the obsessive-compulsive ex-cop Scottie in *Vertigo*).

Back to *The Pleasure Garden*. Levet soon becomes Jill's own equivalent of evil, not Patsy's loving husband, as we infer through the howling of Patsy's dog on their wedding day (prefiguring the Caypor dog's howling in *Secret Agent* nine years later). His nasty chain smoking habit, his pushing away of a small girl (as Jill had done to the innocent dog earlier), and the throwing away of his spent fags (cigarettes) and roses also do not bode well. To his credit (few Hitchcockian characters are either completely bad or good), Levet does make a genuine effort later to show affection for and be the loving husband of Patsy, particularly over dinner, breakfast, and overlooking the glorious Italian Lake Como locale—but it's either misunderstood or completely missed by Patsy.

Yacowar elaborates on Patsy and Levet's marriage in an interesting way:

> Patsy marries Levet out of numbness, as Katie [*sic*] will in *The Manxman*, as the girl will in *The Ring*, as in *Blackmail* Alice will out of boredom drift into a dangerous and fatal romantic situation, and as young Charlie will summon up Uncle Charlie in *Shadow of a Doubt*. For all these women romance springs artificially in the absence of lively engagement, either moral or instinctual [MY, 1977, pp. 22–23].

I would add, too, that it is their lack of interest and engagement *with their own lives*, not in others and the world, that creates this boredom, and that fractured energy is what needs the most work. By the time of their marriage, we already know—even though Patsy doesn't, at least not consciously—that she is really pining for Hugh.

The location shots at Italy's Lake Como during Patsy and Levet's honeymoon scene augur well for Hitchcock's artistic filming of location scenery throughout his career. One shot in particular, a barely visible boat floating on the lake as seen in LS through some mist, recalls the magically suggestive impressions of a traditional Japanese landscape painting.

Concerning Levet's disregard for objects and people in his life, we will see that Hitchcock continues an association of visibly thrown away waste with the shallow, upper-class attitudes in Julia's actions in the later *Downhill*; even through that film's main protagonist Roddy's actions as he struggles with his own "place" in life. Class conflicts and insights into those conflicts run rampant through these silent films, at a time when America and, to a lesser but no less explicit extent, England, was still riding high on the hog (just prior to The Great Depression).

Jill, apparently, gets exactly what she wants but not needs by the middle of the picture, and then Hitchcock quite suddenly drops her character completely from the film. If the story of Patsy and Hugh didn't keep us engaged, we'd wonder where Jill had disappeared to. It turns out, of course, that she will be reincarnated with a vengeance in the fourth film of the silents series.

The remainder of the film plays itself out slowly and a bit melodramatically, I think, and there are, sadly, no other classic Hitchcockian montages to speak of after the few already discussed. Still, Charles Barr's discussion of Levet's leaving for the East by boat (not West Africa, as he repeatedly insists), and his accurate chart breakdown of the sixteen successive shots involved in that parting, gives the reader a good understanding

The Pleasure Garden, 1925: Patsy Brand (played by Virginia Valli) kneeling in stunned silence after her mad husband Levet (played by Miles Mander) is shot to death by the local doctor Carruthers.

of Hitchcock's frequent use of cross-cutting and alternating shots in order to tightly control the "perception of the spectator" (CB, 1995, p. 29).

And, certainly, Levet's DT-induced hallucination of the native girl's image stalking him is a powerful one, hard on the heels as it is of her malicious drowning at his hands. The suspense leading up to his attempted murder of Patsy, and his subsequent shooting and killing at Carruther's hands, clearly prefigures the deus ex machina ending of *North by Northwest*, as Roger Thornhill and Eve Kendall are saved by a state trooper's gun shot thirty-two years later. Even Levet's sudden sobering exclamation, "Hallo, old chap!" and nonchalant observation of the mortal wound in his gut, prefigures an almost exact same shot in the first *Man Who Knew Too Much* seven years later, when that man who knew too much was himself killed.

So, as early as Hitchcock's first film in 1925 (but not seen by the general public until 1927), we can perceive a host of technical and thematic tour de forces already in full flower.

By the end of *The Pleasure Garden*, it is Patsy and Hugh who will have the best chance for true happiness, as they bravely endure life's malevolent misfortunes. Hopeful yet humbled, these two survivors have clearly set the classic Hitchcockian tone for the next fifty-one films. Hitchcock is saying that mistakes and challenges, all too human ones, are absolutely necessary if anyone is to achieve real salvation and love — let alone start down a righteous path. He asserts such hope for all his characters, including his audience, from his first film on.

Two

The Mountain Eagle

Produced fall 1925, first screening October 1926, released May 23, 1927

The Mountain Eagle is the "lost" Hitchcock film, meaning there is no existing print as of this writing. To attempt a shot-by-shot analysis consistent with the tone and content of this book is, of course, impossible at this time. Perhaps, if the film surfaces, a revised edition of these writings will be both warranted and welcome.

The Mountain Eagle, 1925: "Fear 'O' God" (played by Malcolm Keen) trying to protect Beatrice (played by Nita Naldi) from Pettigrew (played by Bernard Goetzke) in his mountain cabin.

Three

The Lodger: A Story of the London Fog

Produced July 1926, first screening September 1926,
released February 14, 1927

The reader will recall from the Introduction that one of the difficulties in coming to a consensus on all the shots and montages being the same and in the same order and of the same length in these films is that there are so many versions of them in the world. Edited by distributors, cut to fit the local projector, sped up or slowed down due to time constraints, lost footage, and a host of other variables reflect what appears to be a never ending problem with "original" and "authentic" versions of films.

Such discrepancies with *The Lodger* are a typical case in point. Out of nine separate books referenced with film length claims for this film in their "fact" sheets, only three agreed on one length, 75 minutes (SS, MP, LM), two on *approximately* 100 minutes (KM and Jane Sloan), and one each at 65 (BB), 84 (HA), 91 (VH), and 96 (TO) minutes respectively. I timed the version I own, a VHS-format recording I picked up from a now-defunct company called "Now Showing," and *it* lasted 83 minutes. That's a range difference of 35 minutes—approximately one-third the length of most of these silent films and more than *half* the length of *The Pleasure Garden* itself—with the shortest duration 65 and the longest 100 minutes! Clearly, most of us are watching completely different films, so I say again that, as much pleasure aficionados take with Hitchcock, we all need to carry numerous grains of sand to throw over our shoulders when viewing them.

To his credit, as I hope I am with this book to some extent, Charles Barr in his recent *English Hitchcock* (1999) has begun the difficult, Herculean, and thankless task of comparing some of these versions for accuracy against earlier critics' descriptions and interpretations.

The cast of *The Lodger* includes the excellent character actress Marie Ault (1870–1951), who plays Mrs. Bunting, the landlady — an uglier crone would be hard to find. Arthur Chesney (1882–1949) plays her husband, Mr. Bunting, who, I kept thinking to myself as I watched him, bears more than a passing resemblance to another excellent character actor, Edmund Gwenn (1875–1959), whom Hitchcock would successfully employ once in each of the next three decades (*The Skin Game*, 1931; *Foreign Correspondent*, 1940; and *The Trouble With Harry*, 1955). In researching Chesney's biography, this thought turned out to be not as surprising as first considered, because Arthur Chesney *was* Edmund Gwenn's younger brother!

Malcolm Keen (1887–1970), who we may still see as Fear 'O' God in *The Mountain Eagle*, if the film ever surfaces (hope springs eternal), and who will return as the sympathetic if wimpy caught-between-a-rock-and-a-hard-place judge Philip Christian in *The Manxman*, here plays Joe Betts, the jealous detective. June — yes, simply June, that's her acting name, although her last name was Tripp (1901–1985) — plays Daisy Bunting, referred to in the credits as a mannequin, used here chiefly in its historical context from the French, meaning a young woman hired to model clothes.

The famous matinee idol, writer, and composer Ivor Novello (1893–1951), who will return in Hitchcock's very next feature, *Downhill*, as the tragic hero Roddy Berwick, here plays the mysterious lodger himself. Is he the never-seen Avenger, who kills blonde-haired girls *à la* Jack the Ripper, or someone else with a different role to play in this based-on-a-true-story in the London fog?

The film was adapted by Alma Reville and Eliot Stannard from the best-selling 1913 novel by Marie Belloc-Lowndes (1868–1947), which concerned the real Jack the Ripper murders — never solved — in 1888 London. Remade three times, in 1932, 1944, and 1954 — the middle time also starring Novello again — Hitchcock's version received between three and four stars (or, in the case of VideoHound, dog bones) — their highest praises for movies — in six of the eight film review compendiums that use such ratings (see the Introduction for book titles).

Contemporary accounts were equally glowing, with London's *Bioscope* raving: "It is possible that this film is the finest British production ever made.... The tempo of the whole film has seldom been equaled.... Mr. Hitchcock builds up his evidence against the lodger relentlessly and logically. It is a directorial triumph" (reprinted in KM, 1999, p. 7).

After the credits are over, we see a screaming girl (in silence, of course) brightly lit with her mouth wide open. One can suppose that she *might* even be singing. Her head tilted slightly towards SL, it's impossible to tell where she is and what is happening. Fade to black.

"To-night golden curls" flashes one word at a time four times, as *we* flash, if we've seen Hitchcock's films in chronological order, to Patsy's titillating hair curl scene with the lecher from *The Pleasure Garden*. Disorienting cut to a low MCU shot taken at ground level of a girl crumpled on her back, head towards camera. With just these first short shots and confusing angles, Hitchcock immediately makes us work hard to follow this second of his feature's scenario. The director is hammering home the fact that if we are to fully enjoy his films it must always be as an active participant, never as a passive viewer.

The ensuing melodramatic account of a murder by a bystander is punctuated with typical Hitchcockian black humor as a man is seen sarcastically mimicking a cloaked avenger with his hands. The director's famed documentary-style filming of the scene of the crime feels quite "real," just as *Blackmail*'s arrest and booking of a thief will seven films later. Cut to various news reporters sending their stories in, and then a bunch of men gathered around a teletype machine reading along as it types out the description of the murder. Hitchcock cuts just after it gets to "...scarf covering lower half of his face," and the director now makes his first of two unmistakable cameos *ever* in a film, a six-second MS of himself as a newshound sitting at a desk, back to the camera, gesturing wildly while on a phone.

The mechanics of newspaper production is now shown, finishing with a title saying "Murder — wet from the press," rather than our American "Hot off the press" phrase. Cut to cars delivering papers, with the also famous image (*The Lodger*, rightly so, was the first true Hitchcock suspense thriller, and boasted a host of classic directorial shots) of two eyes peering back at us in MS (shades of Manet's *Olympia* yet again; see Chapter One) from the oval windows of one car, both leering and incriminatory. They're actually the backs of the heads of the driver and a passenger rocking side to side with the car's movements as seen through those windows. Quite a startling and unnerving little shot, it works much better, I think, than Hitchcock's own detailed yet disparaging comment on it — complete with his hand-drawn picture — in the Truffaut book (p. 46).

A crowd presses in around a newsboy — masses of bodies, mindless, formless. (An analysis of Hitchcock's crowd scenes alone could easily fill an entire book.) Title: "Murder — Hot over the aerials." Cut to five individuated shots of faces rapidly superimposed over and replacing each other as they react to the story over the radio with various forms of exaggerated astonishment, fear, and stupidity. The fourth person, in fact, appears downright idiotic, his (or her — it's hard to tell which sex he/she is) mouth drooping grotesquely wide, eyes agog, and it is quite unsettling.

Cut to a MS of a bunch of golden-haired beauties from a Pleasure Garden-type chorus ruminating on the news of the murder in their dressing room. Theatres recur in Hitchcock films with almost as much frequency as stairs, food, and lamps. Most of the chorines wear outrageous-looking blond wigs, while the true blondes wear — and rightly so — genuine trepidation.

Cut to our heroine, Daisy, a ravishing natural blond who happens to be modeling a mink coat at the moment, strutting around what looks like a one-ring circus for horses, with the other mannequins. Up until now, everything has been lit in semi-darkness or partial shadow, but the modeling arena is brightly lit and cheerful looking, if artificially so.

Shortly, Hitchcock cuts to our other three main protagonists, all brightly lit inside the Bunting's house. Hitchcock goes for our jugular here as Mr. Bunting tells Joe, the detective who is wooing Daisy, that the cops are no help, for they let the masked avenger get away each time. After Daisy returns home, Joe tells her he's keen on golden hair, too. In this film, Hitch will rub salt into this wound of guilt and irony early and frequently, and uses an actor *named* Keen to triple the effect of this supposedly innocent statement. But nothing is innocent, sacred, or safe in a Hitchcock picture.

As the gas lights flicker, then go out, the lodger's foreboding shadow slowly approaches and looms outside their door, lucky number thirteen prominently displayed. Ivor Novello's eerie entrance, overly melodramatic yet effectively noirish and expressionistic, is sharply juxtaposed with Mr. Bunting falling off a chair as a cuckoo clock chirps its "cuckoo."

The lodger ascends the inside staircase towards his rented apartment flat and, upon being shown into it by Mrs. Bunting, spies nothing but portraits of golden-haired girls on all the walls. He crosses his room to look more closely at one in an extraordinarily composed, six-second MS: As he walks toward the camera SL, we also see him move *away from us* as reflected in a mirror on the mantle behind him. Both images approach the portrait, but the real picture is out of sight behind the camera to our left, while the reflected one is visible behind him in the mirror. This quick shot is simultaneously unnerving and disorienting, and we marvel over its clever and deft composition.

The lodger then closes a window, and the shadow lines of its panes perfectly split his face in half, clear precursor to Manny and Rose Balestrero's multiple images in the broken mirror from *The Wrong Man* thirty years later. The obvious message of this image, of course, is to duplicate (duplicitously?) the lodger's character in our minds. And, if watching this film for a second or third time and knowing how the story turns out, one watches

Novello very closely in all his scenes for any hints of culpability. Why? Because Hitchcock's camera consistently creates suspicion where there is none — in the lodger's case, where only sadness and heartbreak remain.

One of Hitchcock's neatest throwaway shots appears shortly. I call them "throwaways" because they seem to have no purpose other than to self-consciously demonstrate his technical prowess. The scene steeped in surrealism, we see the lodger turn over all of the portraits in his room to face the wall. Suddenly Daisy herself walks in, notices what he's doing, and begins to laugh hysterically.

Prior to her entrance, the lodger had been primarily shot in the flat from his right and from behind, in medium distance. With his head bowed against the mantle across the room near the door, he is still seen leaning in right profile. After we see Daisy's laughter, Hitchcock's camera cuts to her POV, a CU of Novello's upper back, neck, and head, shot this time from his left. Rather than following this shot with a reverse angle reaction shot of Daisy, the director holds his camera on Novello as he remains deep in thought. The frame is highly charged now with our projected expectations of whatever he will do. Sustaining that tension, Hitchcock has him slowly turn towards the camera, not the easy 90 degrees to his left to face us (Daisy) but the long way around, 270 degrees to his right.

The emotional plot thickens as Joe, Daisy's suitor, upon seeing all of the portraits taken down and being put away, remarks to Daisy and her mom that he's glad the lodger is not keen (like him, Malcolm Keen) on the girls. The actor Novello may not have been keen on ladies, as he was an avowed and open homosexual, but his lodger, after staring at a not unappreciative Daisy, more than refutes Joe's projected insecurities.

Empowered by the lodger's gaze, and her thoughts of disproving Joe's assumptions against him, Daisy holds her first bit of autonomous knowledge (and sexuality) over Joe who, up until now, had literally smothered her with his juvenile flirtations. A quick CU of Daisy's reaction to Joe's misrepresentation of the lodger reveals both her relief — at not being understood — and her silent but burgeoning assertiveness. Rarely obvious, his *mises en scène* more often challenging than simplistic, Hitchcock subtly imbues the characters in this short montage with a rich ambiguity.

The lodger is soon heard pacing upstairs, and the family and Joe turn their heads upward in unison from the living room to see the chandelier lights swaying. Superimposed in the foreground in yet another of Hitchcock's famous tour de forces, a glass ceiling is seen to reveal an audaciously skewered shot of the lodger's pacing on the other side of the glass. Shot from a tilted, oblique angle, his body is visibly foreshortened almost beyond recognition above his shoes— another remarkable, most singular shot in Hitchcock's canon. In rare, self-deprecatory fashion, Hitchcock shows us this marvelous shot for a short four seconds, which only heightens its unusual energy.

After Daisy brings the lodger his breakfast the next morning (the lodger remains nameless throughout the film, strengthening his association with any man, Everyman), she is briefly prevented from leaving his flat as he quickly crosses to block her, back to the door and a hand on its knob. We immediately suspect his intentions—as intended—and Hitchcock just as suddenly exposes and foils our thoughts through the flirtatious manner with which he opens the door for her—a true gentleman. Upon being revealed as an innocuous action, we are guiltily embarrassed—also deliberately intended—by our unfounded suspicions.

A note about the American designer E. McKnight Kauffer's title designs is worth mentioning at this point. All of them up until now have had a kind of geometric, art deco look about them—simple, painted triangles on a plain, black background. The wording, too, by budding filmmaker, author, and screenwriter Ivor Montagu (1904–1984), has been relatively benign and purely descriptive: "Later that day," "The next morning," that sort of thing. Now, superimposed over the gentle but more assertive "One evening, a few days later, the lodger made himself agreeable," we see a brightly lit variety of geometric shapes appear alongside the words and a circular target with two arrows piercing a bulls-eye SL. More convoluted and engaging designs like this one will begin to proliferate now throughout the film, paralleling the action.

Cut to a M shot of a chess game being played in the lodger's room between the lodger and Daisy, the semicircular shape of the fireplace in the background recalling the title's bulls-eye and subliminally hammering home their budding romance by visually linking the two. The director's ironies now begin to multiply rapidly. Our hero and heroine will never smile as naturally and warmly in this film again, as they banter across the board in privileged MCU profile. As he moves a chess piece, Novello intones, "Be careful, or I'll get you yet," and any audience member can read at least three meanings into that phrase at this point in the film.

The camera cuts to a M shot from behind Daisy as she knocks over a chess piece onto the floor in the direction of the fireplace. Both lean way over to retrieve it. Because the camera is set up behind Daisy, the shot imparts into our thoughts and feelings simultaneous suggestions of sexual tension and a threat of violence. Perhaps the lodger steals a peak down Daisy's dress during the next shot, we subliminally think, taken from a slightly closer position to her back, with Novello behind and US of her.

Hitchcock then cuts to an extraordinary ECU of the lodger's hand reaching for the fireplace poker. We see it being raised SR above her fore-grounded curls. "What is he going to do?" we gasp. Hitchcock will not tell us—yet—for he immediately cuts away to a LS of Joe coming down the outside stairs to enter the house. These last four shots—M to MCU to ECU to LS, with the first three at a laconic pace and the fourth swift—momentarily make us believe Joe is *actually seeing* this highly charged scene with us. Uncertainty and trepidation is rapidly building to a crescendo in our minds over the lodger's actions, now no longer on the screen. Is it the rhythm of Joe's LS walk downward left, in counterpoint tempo with the ECU of the lodger's raised arm SR, that compels us to make—and accept—the imagined fear we now feel for Daisy? Or is it Joe's naïve, unsuspicious hello to the family that smoothes Hitchcock's transition to this scene so cleanly and powerfully, retaining its emotional charge for us?

Hitchcock stays with the downstairs scene even longer, revealing the unassuming and simple act of Mrs. Bunting tying her husband's tie as Mr. Bunting tries to twist around and say hello to Joe. But he is yanked back to face his wife. By now the urgency that something terrible is about to happen upstairs is at a fever pitch.

Finally—*finally*—Hitchcock cuts back to the original neutral MCU shot of the chess players, both bent over with their backs and rear ends to the camera. We see the lodger calmly and innocently stirring the coals in the fire with the poker. Hitchcock had us convinced of his guilt but good and, because our expectations have now been dashed, we experience some guilt yet again for doubting his intentions—as intended. This is truly effective artistry of the highest order.

> [T]here should be a slogan, "Keep them awake at the movies...." I think that pace in a film is made entirely by keeping the mind of the spectator occupied. You don't need to have quick cutting, you don't need to have quick playing, but you do need a very full story and the changing of one situation to another.... Now so long as you can sustain that and not let up, then you have pace. That is why suspense is such a valuable thing, because it keeps the mind of the audience going [AH, "Lecture at Columbia University," 1939; in SG1, 1995, p. 270].

We believe, by now, that Daisy is quite young and naïve in affairs of the heart, and equally innocent of love and the evils of the world—Teresa Wright's (b. 1918) young Charlie in *Shadow of a Doubt* comes quickly to mind, as does Alice White in *Blackmail*. We also feel that Joe, too, is wholly untested in both love *and* detecting. Shamelessly waving his new handcuffs around in the kitchen, he cockily proclaims, "When I've put a rope round the avenger's neck—I'll put a ring round Daisy's finger." Turning away with a combination of embarrassment and revulsion, Daisy's flowering purity becomes sharply etched in our minds. In a prankish and ruffian manner (and a clear precursor to both Hannay's and Kane's similar situations in *The 39 Steps* and *Saboteur* respectively), Joe suddenly locks his handcuffs around Daisy's wrists, hurting her, all within the lodger's expressionistically shadowy and surreptitious gaze down upon them from the upstairs landing.

Daisy permits Joe to apologize to her with a quick kiss on the cheek and then, breaking with conventional film etiquette, she gives *us* a sarcastic "quick take" directly into the camera and runs upstairs, leaving Joe to "slow burn," *à la* Oliver Hardy (1892–1957; of Laurel and Hardy fame), also directly at us. Allowing a combination of hurt pride, rejection, stupidity and jealousy to build within, Joe now begins to suspect and transfer his pain to the lodger. It is important to realize that his suspicions, like our own, are wholly unfounded at this point in the film. Nevertheless, the odds against the lodger are beginning to stack.

Later that night, Mrs. Bunting awakens within her deeply shadowed, noirish bedroom (where's Daddy Bunting, we wonder?). In a MCU, she stares straight through her headboard at the camera, as we envision the lodger stealthily skulking down the stairs via her imagination — which, of course, we see on the screen. In yet another amazing shot, we view his descent through a disembodied hand sliding down the banister as shot from a dizzying height looking straight down the stairwell, prefiguring *Vertigo* by thirty-one years. This whole montage is straight out of German director Robert Wiene's (1880–1938) expressionistic 1919 film, *The Cabinet of Dr. Caligari*. We should recall that Hitchcock cut his teeth in film studying the great German directors on their own turf — Murnau, Lang, Wiene — having just returned to England for *The Lodger* after directing his first two features in Munich.

It's time for another murder by the Avenger. Shot in the same manner as the first girl's death, with her face facing the upper left corner of the frame, Hitchcock shows us the Avenger's calling card, the heavily portentous triangle (like the titles) etched upon it. Drawn upon this very pattern, by now we've seen several angles on the three characters of this romantic triangle.

Cut back to Mrs. Bunting at home, still unnerved. As she leaves her bedroom to tread softly down the stairs, Hitchcock cuts to a high overhead shot looking straight down on top of her head, just like "mother's" exit from her bedroom thirty-three years later as she rushes to stab Arbogast in *Psycho*. Clearly, Hitchcock's technical virtuosity did not wait for the sound era.

Exaggerated yawning lowlights the next morning's breakfast scene.

Apparently, both Mr. and Mrs. Bunting didn't sleep too well (if we cared to think about it, we still have no idea where Dad was last night and why *he's* so tired). He jumps up suddenly, reading about the previous night's murder.

Boredom gives way to fear gives way to somberness as Joe walks in like he owns the place (no wonder Daisy resents him, he assumes too much). He directs the Missus to pour him some tea. She complies, with no reaction from Mr. Bunting. He is more interested in the murder, but his ignorance, or at best allowance, of Joe's controlling audacity still says much about who the real man of the house is. Dad pulls up a chair as Joe, proudly and not a little cockily, launches into all the horrible details. All three are framed together, the two men jabbering, but the silent landlady has our attention, her imagination ours— residual identification from the previous night's visions still strong in our minds.

Three very quick and startling one-second shots occur next. They seem all the quicker due to the deliberately laconic pace of the breakfast scene, which had lasted nearly two drowsy minutes. In ECU, crash goes some food to the floor. Its suddenness and in-our-face proximity intensifies our confusion. Where has this occurred? In the kitchen, from the previous scene? Immediate cut number two to Daisy in CU profile right brightly laughing/screaming, another blink-of-an-eye shot. If we had time we might be able to flash on the murdered girl's scream at the opening of the film, or Daisy's own hysterical laughter upon first entering the lodger's room earlier. But no, another quick one-second cut shows a CU of a painting falling off a wall. Bing — bang — boom. Repeated replays reveal that no one knocked anything off the table in the kitchen, so the crashing food must have happened elsewhere, but one is so involved in the scene that I had to repeatedly rewind the shot to look for some disturbance there rather than presume it had happened elsewhere.

Hitchcock then cuts to a MS of all their eyes shifting upward again — the four-second glass ceiling shot from the previous night rushing into our minds— and we realize the crash must have occurred upstairs in the lodger's flat. As innocuous a narrative line as this short montage is, Hitchcock has facilely and powerfully created drama and tension in our minds out of seemingly nothing.

> Again and again, he presents a view we cannot interpret because he has
> withheld something about its context, or we misread because we take its
> context to be other than it really is. Sometimes Hitchcock makes no secret
> of cloaking his presentations in enigmas and sometimes withholds infor-
> mation without our realizing it. The process of following any Hitchcock
> film is one of continual rereading or rethinking [WR, 1982, p. 9].

Not having seen Daisy for a while, we also begin to wonder where she is located in the house. Last seen, she'd been laughing at her parents' yawning during breakfast. So, we rewind to the beginning of that scene again. It seems that Hitchcock *had* given us information on her whereabouts after all, without emphasis, for there she is in a medium three-shot preparing breakfast for the lodger. Her presence didn't register on us then, for her yawning parents, and especially Mrs. Bunting's thoughts, were our intended focus. We even ignored her as she picked up the tray and carried it OSL. In retrospect, the yawns now seem a deliberate directorial plant to lull us into not paying attention and mislead us, Hitchcock's real characters in this morality play.

Everyone is seen now running upstairs, Joe leading the rush, and when he opens the lodger's door, there are the two of them in MCU happily laughing in each other's arms—Joe's worst fears made manifest.

Even at this early stage of his career, Hitchcock had begun experimenting with his trademark cinematic cuts between a stationary camera showing a person moving towards it and its reverse angle, the camera dollying in (*not* zooming) as if the lens were the eye of a person's traveling point of view. Here, Hitchcock does this very shot with Joe as the camera approaches the lodger and Daisy, a foreboding sense of Joe's anger transferred from within him to within us.

Cut to a title: "What are you doing to Daisy?"—Joe's reflexive, accusing jealousy. While they do look completely innocent, almost naïve, and Daisy's explanation of the situation supports those facts ("A mouse scared me"), this is not wholly true, for they are surely "guilty" of genuine, mutual affection—something Joe will never achieve in this film. Hitchcock pounds this point home in this confrontational scene, only further inflaming Joe's irrational hatred. As we shall see, it shall very soon completely blind him to any sense of true justice.

Shot from the earlier reverse angle MS position of his entrance, we see Joe move between the lodger and Daisy. Once there, the camera reverses again, from behind the couple's earlier two-shot MCU position, empowering the scene once more by forcefully engaging our attention and making us shift rapidly between perspectives. A third cut is now shot from a medium distance via the proscenium-arch perspective (PAP; see it's earlier use in Chapter One), to allow the parents space to enter the frame as they finally arrive in the room.

Explanations begin. "I was silly enough to be scared by a mouse." Audacious and flimsy, Joe will have none of it. He presses on the attack, accusing the lodger of pawing at his girl. Cut to Daisy bending down, and we finally see the forgotten food tray in CU on the floor. Cut to the lodger moving towards the door, this time in a MS without camera movement.

His walk seems both out of place and artificial, but it nonetheless holds our interest, and he furiously waves his visitors out.

Just as Daisy passes the lodger, she stops, turns to face him, and apologizes. As we watch them in a two-shot CU profile, recalling the earlier intimate chess game, their genuine affection for each other jumps out at us from the screen, primarily due to Novello's emotionally charged and highly expressive features—another of the director's lovingly rendered, and poignant, moments. Daisy and Joe leave.

The lodger immediately closes the door and turns to berate the landlady, threatening to leave the boarding house if he is disturbed again. As extraneous as this brief shot seems, it acts as Hitchcock's reassertion of the lodger's determination and will, while also lending the scene a much-needed sense of credulity.

In an exaggerated, melodramatic scene highlighted by lengthy still shots of their pensive faces and furrowed brows, Mrs. Bunting is next seen sharing her suspicions about the lodger with her husband. Ignorance breeds misunderstanding and unfounded accusations, and Hitchcock goes to a blackout with their fears sharply etched in our minds.

Fast fade into a quick two-second shot of Novello in CU staring straight into the camera. "*Now* what's Hitchcock doing?" we wonder. The director loved to juxtapose shots and images from seemingly out of nowhere and with no context, thoroughly confusing his audience. Where is the lodger now, and why do we get the uneasy feeling he is looking directly into our eyes?

Because of Hitchcock's accusatory set-up with the Buntings in the previous scene, the accused now stares back at us (and them) accusingly. Confronted now with Novello's mesmeric, steady gaze, the shock of seeing him in CU out of time and space forces us to meet his eyes, thereby indicting our own dubious voyeuristic tendencies in this film through our suddenly guilty feeling of self-consciousness, no longer safe in our chairs at home.

And before even these thoughts can fully register, we see that Novello is not really staring at us at all (after all, how could he, really, being up on a screen that was originally projected nearly eighty years ago), but at fashion models strutting their stuff back at the one-ring circus. So now we ask, "Where did this scene come from?" Seemingly unaware of the two gorgeous gals sitting on both sides of him, his chair in an elevated position surveying the mannequins modeling in front of them, *Novello* is actually the one mesmerized by the proceedings, and not the one doing the mesmerizing. Our attentions and identifications are shifted rapidly about in this film.

In a hysterically absurd, straight-faced bit of business, we watch the

girl to his right flirt unabashedly with him, nonchalantly crossing a leg —
to no avail. The girl to his left now taps out a cigarette. We see Novello
hesitate in his gazing, eyes still riveted front, then reach into his vest pocket
for a lighter. He fires up her snurd without so much as a body pivot. As
viewers, this scene seems hilarious to us, so hard as it is upon the previous sinister machinations — a pleasant, humorous, and necessary release.

> *Comedy, too, does, paradoxically, make a film more dramatic. A play gives*
> *you intervals for reflection. These intervals have to be supplied in a film by*
> *contrast — and if the film is dramatic or tragic, the obvious contrast is com-*
> *edy. So, in all my films, about two-thirds of the way through, I try to supply*
> *a definite contrast. I take a dramatic situation up and up and up to its peak*
> *of excitement and then, before it has time to start the downward curve, I*
> *introduce comedy to relieve the tension. After that, I feel safe with the cli-*
> *max* [AH, "Women Are a Nuisance," 1935; in SG1, 1995, p. 81].

Daisy, it turns out, is one of the models in this scene. In a MS she circles towards Novello, where the camera is now standing in for him. For a
full, highly charged four seconds, Hitchcock cuts to a quick reverse angle
CU of Novello's face, eyes glowing and staring right at us/Daisy. Cut to a
two-second CU of Daisy staring right back at us/Novello, slyly walking
OSR while maintaining eye contact. If that look isn't a come on to both
him and us I don't know what is. Hitchcock's audacity is only exceeded
by the frequency of his titillating impudence.

At police headquarters, Joe has drawn out a map with small triangles
on it representing the ever-enclosing area of the Avenger's marauding. As
he points to a roughly made circle of the area in question, Hitchcock slowly
dissolves into a shot of another man leaning over his own map, a more
detailed rendering of the neighborhood and one large triangle before him
centered in the frame. "Who is this person?" we wonder. The Avenger
himself? The lodger? Are they one and the same? These questions are deliberately implanted in our minds.

Cut to the Bunting's parlor, where Daisy receives a lovely dress as a
present from the lodger, the one he had seen her modeling earlier. The parents, furious and fearful, refuse to allow her its acceptance, and Dad brings
it back upstairs. Novello is palpably disturbed by this overt rejection, as
our views of this montage and these characters are shot with particularly
expressionistic and oblique angles and CUs.

That night Daisy draws herself a bath — more titillation. The lodger
is seen in a MCU shot brooding upstairs and staring out his window at a
torrential rain. Hearing her singing, he moves toward SL, and then we see
a hand in ECU reach for a door handle — the bathroom's door handle. In

spite of its complete cliché quality, we're startled. In yet another sexual jerk out of our seat, Daisy's naked feet are seen through the clear bath water, patty-caking.

A note on Hitchcock's camera again: Regardless of the fact that the landlady's house is sizable, the placement and movements of the camera in this film are remarkably creative. One continually gets a sense of spaciousness, three-dimensionality, and roominess on the screen. We are frequently shown yet one more angle with which to look over the proceedings, as each scene is shot from not one, not two, not even three distinct perspectives, but more like four, five, six, or seven. Such grandness and awareness of cinematic and real space is not surprising, for Hitchcock actually had a

> three-sided [and three-floored] house ... constructed, with narrow walls and low ceilings in the exact dimensions of a middle-class home. The difficulties of lighting such a set were considerable, but with [director of photography Baron Giovanni] Ventimiglia's genial patience and Hitchcock's knowledge of how the Germans had moved cameras up and down a staircase (suspended, if necessary, from tracking or scaffolding overhead), the complex and sinuously evocative shots were all achieved with surprising economy [Spoto, 1983, p. 95].

Hitchcock's special attention to such detailed spatial considerations would continue throughout his career.

The lodger and Daisy go out on a date together, Mom freaking out. Their touching scene together under the street lamp confirms their love for each other to us. Joe, naturally, stumbles onto them while out on a prowl. Consistent with his juvenile and jealous behavior, he erupts. Daisy banishes him forever from her life, then takes the lodger back home. Joe sits down on the same bench, pouting. (Malcolm Keen's characters seem to get nothing but bad breaks with the girls in Hitchcock's films, as we shall see again in *The Manxman* two years later.) Staring at the ground with his fists on his cheeks, he puts two and nothing together and concocts a damning, hallucinatory scenario against the lodger.

Back home, the passion of their love is about to be consummated in Hitchcock's first-ever protracted love scene, an extraordinarily constructed montage. Shot in profile from first one side and then the other, in closeup and with medium shots, Hitchcock has the two lovers alternately face the camera directly—first Daisy, gorgeously lit, then Novello, also gorgeous (even then, Hitchcock knew how to exploit and work against types and stereotypes). In an incredible zoom, Novello's face comes closer and closer to the camera until just his nose and mouth are visible, blotting all else out. The shot would seem almost vulgar through its forced intimacy upon our eyes if it weren't also so daring and inviting, and it's an extraordinary, highly charged juxtaposition of image and emotion. Their kiss, all in slow motion and in ECU profile, now becomes deeply satisfying, for Hitchcock lovingly renders their sense of anticipation, the clinch, and Daisy's ecstatic reaction to us. This last shot is confidentially presented to us from just above her forehead, only her eyes and golden curls visible behind the lodger's hair. She opens those eyes and blissfully stares into heaven's gate — *our eyes* — then achingly closes them. It's quite a scene.

The lovers arise and turn, the lodger's protective arm around her shoulder, and face a wall with the dusty outline of a missing painting visible above two oval, eye-like miniatures "staring" back at them (we might flash on the police car's oval eyes from the beginning of the film). Sitting beneath those eyes, Novello suddenly pushes Daisy violently away and gets up to face the doorway, an inexplicably tortured expression on his features. Startled and physically hurt by his surprisingly rough treatment, Daisy grabs her shoulders in pain, but then turns to comfort him. They kiss again.

Enter Joe downstairs, gendarmes in arm. Wanna have a woid wit your lodger, ma'am. They rush upstairs, search his room and find a locked cabinet. Shot from a kneeling position (the inanimate *cabinet's* point of view), we see the lodger proffer its key to Joe, who lobs it just to the left of the camera towards a henchman. The key seems to jump out of the frame into our laps. Out comes the lodger's bag and, upon examination, Joe discovers the map of the Avenger's murders. Shot in a stunningly foreboding CU from above and in front of his *hat*, Joe slowly lifts his head and turns it slightly to the right. Seen by us, and revealed by Hitchcock, Joe is now the true evil party (besides the Avenger) in this story. He will be only slightly redeemed by the end of the film.

Falsely accused of murder, and after a brief tussle, the lodger lifts his wrists in helpless, limp innocence toward Hitchcock's beckoning handcuffs. Joe is shortly shot (by now, we wish he'd *really* be shot) starkly framed against the gray white of a door, and we become privy to his raw, hateful emotions. As he turns right to glance back at Daisy, we see all of his thwarted longing and emasculated yearning painfully etched on his face. Head bowed, he turns to face the camera, briefly self-pitying — and hence, pitiful — then, guilt-ridden. Realizing his duty, and with a renewed if somewhat cowed resolve, he determinedly stalks out of the room. Throughout even his forty-two sound pictures, Hitchcock could always command at will the purist and most potent of forces through such simple and silent looks.

As they descend the stairway, Daisy's stupid parents are not spared the director's accusatory camera. They, too, will not see what is plainly before them — innocence and love.

Before making a break for it, the lodger whispers to Daisy to meet him by the lamp where their earlier date took place. Mom faints, and Hitchcock shoots Daisy in CU as she wrestles internally with her demons: stay with Mom, or rush to her lover's side. With her dark hat and clothing, and filmed against a blank yet grayish wall (like Joe's earlier scene), Daisy is lit in her most mature, womanly manner yet. Gone is the frivolous, flirtatious gamine of less than a half-hour ago of screen time. One's thoughts jump forward to both the young Charlie and Alicia's similar maturations toward the end of their films, *Shadow of a Doubt* and *Notorious*, respectively.

Cut to the lodger alone and bereft on the bench. Pulling up his coat, he hugs himself close, manacled and despairing. Daisy arrives, and the lodger recounts the real reason for his actions. His sister was killed during her coming out party at the hands of the Avenger, his first victim. Daisy's love, not needing any proof, gets it anyway, even though we now know the lodger had intended to become his own avenger, a not particularly pleasing thought of ours

The Lodger: A Story of the London Fog, 1927: In handcuffs, the innocent-of-murder but vengeance-seeking Lodger (played by Ivor Novello) hangs helplessly in expectation of a lynching barely averted.

towards him. But we quickly shunt it aside (if it appears in our minds at all), our conventional need for a hero winning out. (Move deliberate Hichcockian ambiguity.)

Entering a bar, his handcuffs hidden beneath his coat (precursor once again to Hannay's and Kane's similar predicaments), Daisy feeds him a brandy. A drunk leers as women prattle, the mob readying itself in our minds. Discovered, Novello runs from what seem hundreds, thousands of pursuers, as Hitchcock shoots him in that inimitable traveling forward zoom of his, imbuing the camera — and hence, our sensibilities— with a real sense of panic. Flinging himself over a steel-spiked fence, his cuffs catch and the lodger hangs helplessly, Christ-like, as the mob pounces on him from above and below.

Meanwhile, Joe hears of the real Avenger's *deus ex machina* capture (flash forward to Hannay's look-alike capture in *The Wrong Man*) and rushes to save the lodger from being torn to pieces. Hitchcock makes his second cameo appearance as one of the senseless mobsters, wildly waving his arms at the defenseless, hanging man. In the same, tortuous manner with which Hitchcock demonstrated the difficulty of actually murdering someone in *Torn Curtain* nearly forty years later, he now shows us just how hard it is to take a hanging, handcuffed man off a fence.

A quick cut shows Joe —*and Hitchcock himself now*—freeing the lodger from his cross and the mob's clutches. And, after the director shows the latest newspaper account declaring the Avenger arrested, he cuts to yet another shot of *himself* still leaning over the fence, dead center screen, derisively yelling something to the crowd around him with an incredulous look on his face. All told, if we watch carefully, we are privileged to an additional eighteen seconds of screen time of our omnipresent director. Including the initial six seconds in the newsroom near the beginning of the picture, Hitchcock's onscreen time will turn out to be the second longest ever in his canon (see Chapter Ten for a description of his longest).

With fitting irony and a self-congratulatory sense of false pride, Joe says, "Thank God I was in time," all of us including himself knowing full well that he and he alone was responsible for the mayhem and the lodger's near lynching.

Daisy's kisses are most tender and healing. Lying in a hospital bed, the lodger (it is more than maddening by now that he still has no name — partly because he's been through more than one man should take in a lifetime, and partly because he really does represent Everyman) is hovered over by the doctor, Daisy, and an empty frame of a missing portrait above his bed!

All ends happily, a rarity for a Hitchcock film, but

...the theme of the innocent man being accused, I feel, provides the audience with a greater sense of danger. It's easier for them to identify with him than with a guilty man on the run. I always take the audience into account [AH in FT, 1985, p. 48; originally, 1962].

Shortly — in fact, in the very next film — we will see Ivor Novello's character wonder if he were not still trapped in this picture, for the film opens with him being chased again by a mob!

Four

Downhill

First screening the week after May 23, 1927

The film is based on the actress Constance Collier (1878–1955) and Ivor Novello's play (really a series of sketches), but they used the pseudonym David L'Estrange, noted on the opening credits. The main protagonists are: Ivor Novello as Roddy Berwick, who gets top billing above even the film's title; Isabel Jeans (1891–1965), who will also star in the next film, *Easy Virtue*, as the virtue-plagued Larita Filton, and who will make an appearance in *Suspicion* as Mrs. Newsham, here plays Julia, the money-grubbing reincarnation of Jill Cheyne, who disappeared halfway through *The Pleasure Garden*; Annette Benson (1895–?) plays Mabel, the fickle, hedonistic, conniving, vindictive and lying pastry shop worker, who gets pregnant by Tim Wakely but accuses Roddy of being the father, and is Jill's intermediary station stop from *The Pleasure Garden* on her transformation into *Downhill*'s Julia; Robin Irvine (1901–1933), who has a starring role in *Easy Virtue* as the virtue-less and lily-livered John Whittaker, here plays Tim Wakely, the virtue-less and lily-livered heel who will not take responsibility for his part in Mabel's pregnancy; and Ian Hunter (1900–1975), the South Africa-born British and Hollywood smoothie who here plays Julia's co-conspirator Archie, will next play the plaintiff's counsel, or prosecutor, in *Easy Virtue*, and Bob Corby the Champion boxer in Hitchcock's following film, *The Ring*. As with all of Hitchcock's early films, many of his character actors are used over and over again, in part because they were consistently good and in part because the British film industry was still quite small in the 1920s.

Hard upon the heels of, apparently, the greatest film ever made in British history, Hitchcock's highly praised *The Lodger*, *Downhill* couldn't have lived up to its predecessor even if it were an excellent film — which it's not. Only four of the eight film compendiums referenced even reviewed it, and none gave the film higher than a two-and-a-half star rating. Current

21st century comments such as a "creaky, early Hitchcock effort" (BB; p. 290) are barely offset by the half-hearted "lesser Hitchcock boasts the master's visual flair" (LM; p. 376) and "directed with imagination" (TO; p. 329). In light of this rather weak support, the May 26, 1927 *Bioscope* review in London was probably closer in truth to the period audience's response: "[I]f the plot is hardly plausible, Hitchcock's treatment is of great interest [and the] photography is admirable" (cited in MY, 1977, p. 42). Even Charles Barr found little of value to say: "*Downhill* is not a film with a strong claim to being rescued from obscurity" (CB, 1999, p. 46).

My own feeling is that, while it may be a generally weaker film in its totality than the extraordinary *Lodger* and the upcoming *Farmer's Wife* and *Blackmail*, there are many points of interest to be found, many of which have yet to be clearly identified.

In significant ways, *Downhill* begins where both *The Pleasure Garden* and *The Lodger* left off. In *Downhill*, the title for Part One, "The World of Youth," recalls the first film's entire struggle (and final title) by the youthful and naïve characters, while the same lead actor, Ivor Novello, who had barely escaped a lynching by a mob as the lodger in Hitchcock's previous film, here scores the winning rugby goal right at the start as yet another crowd comes rushing towards him. Novello stares directly into the camera with that deer-in-the-headlights look that seems to say, "Not again! I just left that film," and he would be right! But Hitchcock has gleefully thrust Novello into yet another nightmarish scenario, one that he may *never* escape from.

There is quite a bit of narrative banter and exposition early on in *Downhill* via titles, moreso than in any other Hitchcock silent — most likely due to Novello's input as both the co-writer and top star. We do see some nifty camera work in an early pastry shop scene ("Ye Olde Bunne Shoppe") with a begging street urchin, as Hitchcock's shot of the outside door is taken at the height of an average adult's head, humorously revealing just the door opening as if by magic. And the "ornamental eroticism" (MY, 1977, p. 45) of shopkeeper Mabel's nearly silhouetted, stolen kisses with Roddy among the shadows of her archly lit beaded curtains once again recalls the director's recent emergence from his training under of German expressionism.

But our first ever classic Hitchcockian dolly shot — his movement of the camera that makes us feel as if we're traveling with it and watching from *within* its eye — occurs when the boys (Roddy and Tim) walk into their headmaster's office to face their sentencing over playing hookey and flirting with Mabel, the shopkeeper, on school time. Hitch had already done some quick and clever camera pans in earlier films (see the description of the opening scene in *The Pleasure Garden* in Chapter One, and several others in *The Lodger*), but here the camera aggressively asserts its presence by *backing up* as the boys walk toward it/us, which at the moment represents the headmaster's point of view (POV) behind his desk. Hitchcock self-consciously keeps the boys centered and their image at a stable size in the frame during this smooth-traveling MS.

Whenever the director effects one of these extraordinary dollies, I always have the same two feelings: One, that I am actually on the tracks with him and the camera gliding backwards (or wherever his camera is going at the time), and two, my sense of reality feels strangely skewered. I believe that both feelings are intentional.

The first one is easy to explain. In this case, that's just where I am (or, better, where my vision *comes from*), in the camera's eye looking backwards towards the boys as they advance toward me. But my/the camera's backwards movement cannot actually be happening, because the headmaster (the camera/myself) is standing still behind the desk — hence my disrupted sense of reality. In other words, according to the logic of the film's montage up until this point, this movement cannot actually be occurring; but, it *is* happening. Its effect is both purposeful and palpable.

The second feeling is a little harder to explain, because if I *were* actually standing still in that room, like the headmaster behind his desk, the boys' image would be getting *larger* as they approach me. But it doesn't. It remains the same size because the camera is tracking backwards with the same focus at the same time that the boys are moving forward. This sense of arrested size *and* movement could just as easily be effected by having the camera's lens simply pull back as they approach it, but I believe that Hitchcock wants us to not merely sense or imagine this movement but to *actually feel the camera's movement from its inside*, as if we are looking from within the camera's eye while on his dolly. "Feeling the movement" of something on the screen is much more "real," and open to manipulation, than just "imagining" a movement, and so this is Hitchcock's intent for us — to literally feel these two-dimensional images on the screen as a three-dimensional, visceral experience.

Immediately following this shot, Hitchcock shows us its reverse angle, the *boys'* perspective of the headmaster, as they move towards him. But, lo and behold, as the camera moves forward with/as them towards the headmaster (once again, not a zoom in but an actual forward tracking shot), the headmaster's image gets *larger*, as it would if this were real life.

Both of these back-to-back camera movements can only mean one thing: Hitchcock is privileging and empowering the headmaster's character by fixing the size of the boys' image on the screen as they approach, while *his*

image increasingly looms before them from their perspective, thus impart-
ing to them an inferior position. Another way of putting this is that, as the
boys approach the camera and headmaster, their image in the camera
remains the same size and becomes *relatively* smaller while the headmaster's
image *actually* gets larger. All of this happens, of course, beneath one's
consciousness, but we cannot help but feel that something extraordinary is
happening on the screen and in our minds, and only repeat viewings can
bring an understanding of these extraordinary juxtapositions to the surface.

This same camera technique is repeated shortly as Mabel approaches
the boys to make her accusation, also in the headmaster's office, except
this time, *her* figure looms larger in their/our eyes, as it would in reality,
while the boys' image stays the same size yet again. The two montages
together have quite a visceral and psychological impact on the viewer.

From here on, *Downhill* aggressively takes up the theme that *The Pleasure Garden* began: A carefree life *will not* reap happiness, and a self-centered, greedy, and shallow one will fare even worse. As Patsy learned (and
benefited from) in the earlier film, one must suffer emotionally and often
physically in order to have a chance to grow and mature. Let us see if
Roddy can learn the same lesson. Such a moral, not surprisingly, was to
remain one of Hitchcock's most humanistic and hopeful themes throughout his career.

As discussed in the earlier chapters concerning Hitchcock's use of
character development from film to film, we see *The Pleasure Garden*'s Jill
becoming transformed into the evil Julia in *Downhill* by way of detour
through the malignant character of Mabel, the scorned and vindictive pastry shop worker. She's the one who gets Roddy thrown out of both home
and school for making her, as Raymond Durgnat incorrectly notes, "preg-
gers" (p. 74), for it was really Tim Wakely who was the guilty party, even
as Roddy kept stupidly silent out of his sense of misplaced friendship and
honor. As charmingly flirtatious as she appears early on, Mabel's downhill
flight occurs many times faster than even Roddy's will.

Yacowar and Durgnat correctly identify another of Hitchcock's classic motifs, the extreme long-distance overhead shot (ELS)—of which the
birds amassing above Santa Rosa in the film of the same name is but the
most famous of dozens—as Roddy leaves home, a miniscule, wholly unrecognizable figure far below the camera.

Sets of stair imagery also recur in this film more than even in *The
Lodger* (or, say, in those two most classic embodiments of stair symbolism,
Psycho and *The Birds*), but one of Hitchcock's minor motifs, chairs—the
tall-backed, solid, upper-class, cushiony kind—also stands tall. Hitchcock's first use of such chairs finds Roddy cowering in one while facing a

blazing hearth (which itself will reappear shortly) as he awaits his father's wrath, dwarfed and unnoticed. Upon discovery, he is summarily banished from the household by his father's false pride.

Yacowar also rightly highlights (p. 43) the very next descending escalator shot towards the underground (subway) as the obviously symbolic image that it is, but no one as yet, I believe, has noted *why* it is such a powerful moment: Hitchcock holds his completely immobile camera on Roddy's descent for an incredible twenty-three seconds of real time! In today's action packed films, directors would not dare hold such a shot any longer than, perhaps, one-tenth that time. Hitchcock's audacity, patience, and deliberateness with this one shot — something as simple as an immobile and steady camera focused on a figure descending an escalator, with the image clearly receding and getting smaller (as opposed to the earlier headmaster's looming dolly shot)—*forces us* to feel Roddy's sense of total loneliness, and that feeling is downright oppressive. "He may never be able to climb out of this hole, for all the time I show him descending into it," Hitchcock seems to say. For what is still in store for him, that thought proves more than prescient, especially based on the ambiguity with which the director will end this minor but increasingly interesting film.

At the beginning of Part Two, "The World of Make-believe," Hitchcock provides us with his very first fully realized — and highly sophisticated — montage in a film. In CU, we see Roddy stare directly into the camera's eye again (perhaps alerting us, like Manet's *Olympia*, that he sees us, too), then looks about as the camera dollies slowly back to a MS to reveal him at a job, apparently as a waiter. Placing down coffee cups and bussing around a bit, he finally fixes his eyes on something resting on the table before him. We then see two people in the foreground get up and cross towards USR. They will turn out to be two of the film's other protagonists— Julia and Archie — but at this point we barely notice them or whether they have any import. So far, in establishing this scene, a leisurely minute has gone by.

Still in CU, Roddy next reaches down and, glancing around again, this time in a way that seems furtive, he surreptitiously pockets what we can just identify as a cigarette case. "Has he stooped to thievery so soon in the film?" we ask ourselves. We shall soon find out. Then, as Roddy turns his head to look SR at the aforementioned couple, the camera slowly pans right with him and pulls back a bit to follow his gaze, and we suddenly see the couple begin dancing side by side and facing screen right. Beneath our consciousness, we think, "That seems strange," but we know not why, not quite yet.

The camera continues panning right and pulling slowly back, first to a MS and then to a MLS, so as to keep Roddy in the frame. Then *all at once* we see:

- A chorus line dancing *towards* the camera;
- Spotlights partially blinding us from an obviously offstage left position, US center;
- Parts of a music hall and an audience coming into view at the extreme SR;
- And Roddy, SL, beginning to bounce to the beat of imagined (silent) music.

This densely packed montage takes just twenty seconds and, immediately following the earlier unhurried minute of his work as a waiter, we palpably feel jolted by the realization that what we had been watching was not a scene in a café from a neutral frontal perspective but *a musical theatre number being shot from the privileged position of offstage right*! This is audacious cinematic manipulation of the highest order.

Hitchcock is far from finished with us though. Cut to a disorienting MS of the upper back and head of a man smoking (once again, he will turn out to be Archie, Julia's cohort and lover, but Hitchcock still deliberately withholds any identification of him, so as to make our eventual realization of who he is that much more startling), his face reflected in a mirror SR. His dresser works on him from OSL, just his hands seen behind the actor in the reflection. Quick cut to what we think is a CU of the actor's image in the mirror now facing us. Why do we make this assumption? Because we just saw his image in the mirror, SR in the previous shot, and cinematic convention tells us that Hitchcock has just moved his camera in for a closer shot of that image from a fresh angle. But remember, he used a *cut*, not a zoom or pan, so the "reality" that we *assume* to be sustained with those other techniques does not have to apply to a cut.

Looking him straight in the eye, we see the actor in CU take in a breath of smoke and blow it out. But instead of the smoke coming from behind the camera and moving towards the mirror, as we naturally assume it should, it comes *directly towards our face* as our view and the camera's image fogs up! Hitchcock is here teaching us a little something about film technique, I believe — now you see it, now you don't, and a cut is not the same as a dolly. This shot, just as surprising as the previous music hall sequence, almost makes us jump.

Now Hitchcock does a quick and humorous dissolve from Archie's exhale to *Julia* in CU, blowing smoke at us, her head turned to her right while her body faces screen right. Her dresser stands behind her to our

left fixing her hair (it's a strict parallel shot to Archie's earlier one). Turning back to face her mirror in right profile SR, she looks down onto her
dressing table and spies a photo of Archie. Cut to a CU of the photo with
him in the same pose we had just seen of him blowing smoke in our faces.
Cut back to the profile R shot of her as she sprays some perfume from a
bottle SR at the photo. As the camera zooms in this time for a CU of the
picture — *not a cut*— Hitchcock quickly dissolves back to his real face, only
this time, we notice that it has more age lines and grayer hair than in the
photo, his hair is parted on the left and not the right, and he sports a non-
airbrushed, unsightly mole on his cheek! Completing this extraordinary
montage, Archie gets up from his seat to leave and collects his overcoat
from his dresser, both of them seen now only in a MS reflection in his mirror.

But the director still isn't through with us. Cut back to Julia still smoking and taking off her make-up. Hitchcock quickly cuts to a CU of a hand

Downhill, 1927: The self-centered, gold-digging actress Julia (played by Isabel
Jeans) being languorously preened over by her Dresser (played by Hannah
Jones).

knocking on her dressing room door. Who are we supposed to think this is? Archie, of course. Well, the hand knocking on the door belongs to an actor alright, but it's not Archie. Remember Roddy, our so-called "hero"? Hitchcock's little scam with the smoke and mirrors was so engaging that chances are we had forgotten him already. The director was counting on that.

Cut to a MCU of Julia calling "Come in!" as she arches way back over her right shoulder to look towards both the camera and the door. This is another Hitchcockian ploy that occasionally occurs in his films, a shockingly risqué and private view just for us and us alone, his voyeuristic audience (precursor to *Rear Window*), of her swooping *décolletage*. The director always loved to humorously titillate us and heighten our pleasure at powerfully tense moments such as these by self-consciously intruding sexually suggestive shots.*

Quick cut to Julia's view, an upside-down MS of the door opening to reveal — you guessed it right now —*Roddy*. And, because most of us have worked backwards in time to these earliest of films, aficionados will recall a similar upside-down shot of an intruder entering a room in the form of Cary Grant as Devlin, insinuating himself into Ingrid Bergman's (Alicia) bedroom, in *Notorious* 19 years later!

But the director *still* isn't through manipulating us in this extended montage. Roddy comes in and says via title, "You left your cigarette case onstage again, Miss Julia." Aha, so *that's* what that earlier scene was really about, we belatedly and half-consciously realize. Hitchcock had deliberately implicated us into believing Roddy was a thief rather than merely a thoughtful, lovelorn young lad. Why Hitch, you naughty, naughty prankster, you! We just love this kind of thing, and he knows it. Deliberate manipulation of our sensibilities through an artwork that is only later revealed and realized is one of the most pleasurable and harmless bits of fun imaginable. If we had had (or made) time to think back to that scene during these last fast-paced four minutes, we might have figured out that Roddy was not slyly *stealing* the cigarette case (on a stage that we thought was a real café) but *retrieving* it so he could use it as an excuse to see Julia after the show. The director's brilliance in this, just his fourth full directorial assignment, is in the "when" and "how" he reveals information, all of it purposeful, and its effects on his audience — us— the true character "actors" being "directed."

---

*As similar examples of Hitchcock's love for injected titillation, one might think of Grace Kelly pulling Cary Grant into a convention-breaking, highly charged kiss outside her hotel room, much to the surprise of both Grant and us, in To Catch a Thief 28 years later, or the same actress seducing James Stewart in ECU at the beginning of Rear Window the year before — just two examples of unabashed, and pleasantly intrusive, eroticism.

Immediate cut to a MS of Archie sneezing, rapidly switching our attention yet again, in a reverse shot aimed back at where the camera had earlier set up shop in Julia's dressing room (OSL, we now realize). Archie had entered the room during their flirting and had walked OSL to sit in a large chair and smoke!

Another quick cut. Medium long shot (MLS) of Roddy and Julia flirting and holding hands, the cigarette case held between them, facing each other dead-center screen in profile, Roddy L, Julia R, with Archie sitting in the high-backed, cushy chair (motif alert) directly facing the camera from SR. Foregrounding both of them, he reaches to his right past center screen ("in front of" the couple) and pours himself a drink, his glass centered directly in front of Roddy and Julia, then squirts a solid shot of water from a spritzer bottle, the fluid spurting into his glass in a sharp torrent. Perfectly framed in front of Julia's pelvis CSR, this one-second blast of water is easily translated in our minds as a shot of liquid soiling Roddy's right pants leg CSL! Needless to say, Hitchcock's spritzer orgasm overtly and hilariously dampens their ardor.

So concludes this extraordinarily rich and long montage, a whole series of brilliant shots taking just under ten minutes.

The next one lasts but ten seconds.

Yacowar rightly acknowledges the audacity of this next shot (1977, p. 45), but only manages to impart a small sense of its powerful impact and technical virtuosity. Its intensity and compactness required a dozen viewings to unravel.

In MLS, a huge human figure fills the screen and moves away from the camera, shrinking in size. It takes the entire half-length of this scene (five seconds) for us to realize that the figure is actually a shadow, Roddy's, projected onto an upwardly angled stairway (motif alert) and the upper landing wall. As he walks toward the stairs away from the camera and the projected light, it begins to dawn on us that the camera is aimed up at him from below center screen (somewhere near *our* feet).

At the five-second mark, Roddy's *real* figure comes into view, and we see him actually start up the stairs. For these next five seconds, in a cinematic sleight of hand, Roddy's shadow miraculously appears to be going *downhill* as his actual figure walks *up* the stairs. How is this illusion possible? Because at the same time that Roddy's actual figure recedes from the camera (his image on the screen naturally looking increasingly smaller with its increasing distance from the camera), his shadow (created by the projected light above his actual figure on the stairs and upper landing wall), gets smaller with its distance from both the camera and the light. In other words, even though Roddy and his shadow are *ascending*,

Hitchcock has made them look like they're both *descending*! It's an extraordinarily powerful illusion, reminiscent of those impossible drawings by
Dutch graphic artist M. C. Escher (1898–1972), such as the kind that show
stairs circling a building going up yet arriving back at the beginning down
below (not surprisingly called *Ascending and Descending*, 1960). This ten-
second scene is one of the most singular pieces of screen imagery I've ever
seen.

Cliché of clichés, but a fitting portent of doom, a black cat scurries
nervously up the stairs between seconds nine and ten to follow Roddy into
his flat SR.

Cut to the inside of the flat. MS of Roddy opening an envelope, then
dropping it unconsciously to the floor in the typically arrogant and wasteful manner Hitchcock's wealthy characters often behave. We see him pensively read a letter. A title reveals that he's just inherited 30,000 pounds
from his grandmother. Roddy looks more thoughtful than at any other time
in the film up until now. The camera records him glancing down, still in
MS, to spy the cat lying at his feet and flicking its tail. As Roddy moves to
scratch his head in disbelief over the news, the camera quickly zooms in
to his face for a CU, jump-starting our attention again. Discovering he still
has his hat on, he grabs it roughly and swings it downward with a derisive motion. We're surprised by this gesture, in part because it comes out
of nowhere and doesn't seem consistent with how one might react upon
hearing such good news, but also because it is juxtaposed against the just-
seen calm thoughtfulness of his features. Hitchcock's camera quickly cuts
to a CU of the cat jumping in reaction, and so *that* shot amazingly becomes
a cinematic reflection and projection of our own reaction to his reaction.
Talk about across-the-screen manipulation!

Propelled once again into the film, we think Roddy has thrown his
hat to the floor (or at the cat), for it has dropped out of sight below the
bottom of the screen. We subconsciously think, "Boy, old habits die hard.
The rich have no respect for any objects, even their own." We could even
think, if we had the time (but, of course, only retrospect allows it), "Jeesh,
Roddy is acting just like Levet and Jill did in *The Pleasure Garden*, throwing everything away." But then we see with the very next shot that he's
still holding onto the hat. Another planted false assumption by the director to mess with our heads? No doubt about it.

Cut to a MS of Roddy sitting down in a high-backed, cushiony chair
facing a blazing fire in the flat's hearth. Holding the telegram in his hands,
it is foregrounded directly in front of the rising flames, overt symbolism
(like Archie's earlier water squirt) and premonition that the money will
soon burn up. The scene is an omen for us about Roddy's hopes for a

learning curve, one that may never happen in this film. Thinking the inheritance will take care of everything, Roddy temporarily inhabits the persona of both Jill and Levet from *The Pleasure Garden*, as now he surmises that he should be able to win or buy Julia's attentions, if not love.

The next CU hand we see knocking on Julia's door, of course, has Roddy's new tux sleeve attached to it. As he childishly and flauntingly displays the telegram for her to read in a MS, Hitchcock has her dresser accidentally but painfully prick Julia with the needle she's sewing her dress with as Julia stands in it alongside Roddy. He may be interested in love but we will never know, for Julia's true gold-digging colors come out now. As both get bubbly over his newfound wealth, Julia points towards the back of a chair (the same one in that room from the earlier scene, and in the direction of the camera — us — again), to where Hitchcock cuts to reveal cigar smoke curling up from behind it. We have forgotten *Archie* this time, not Roddy. But we will soon learn that Archie is a patient and understanding man, in more ways than one.

Shortly, feigning equality, he shares Roddy's cigars (and all of Julia's expensive bills) with this temporary interloper, both men spitting their respective bit tips onto the floor in another typical Hitchcockian display of shallow, throwaway excess. As he pours himself a drink, Roddy accidentally (ha!) knocks a rose out of a vase onto the floor, further reminiscent of Levet's similar derisive action towards the same love symbol in *The Pleasure Garden*.

As if this point were not hammered home enough, to further demonstrate their rich disregard for both life and objects, Julia's dresser helps Archie on with his heavy overcoat as he starts to leave the room, then extends her hand for a tip. Archie cruelly drops a hot ash from his cigar into it, precursor to the similarly thoughtless actions of Florence Bates (Mrs. Van Hopper) dropping a cigarette into cold cream in *Rebecca* thirteen years later, and Jessie Royce Landis (Clara Thornhill) putting one out in her uneaten eggs in *To Catch a Thief* twenty-eight years later.

After Julia and Roddy marry and she begins to take him for all he's worth (which takes, for Hitch, all of 30 seconds), Julia barely permits Roddy one half-hearted kiss on her lips — not much more than what Jill grants Prince Ivan in *The Pleasure Garden* — before we realize that she has now been completely transformed into the earlier power-hungry woman. The tawdry story of Jill's life that we were spared from seeing in the earlier film is now taken up with a vengeance.

Roddy and Archie's humorous fight scene over Julia is interestingly analyzed and accurately rendered by Yacowar (1977, p. 49), although he skipped mentioning a few funny shots straight out of vaudeville with

Roddy standing under a potted plant, Archie wryly surprised by a stuffed animal while lying prone, and Julia humorously running around saving expensive vases. This is the only bit of real levity left in the film, but Hitch so loved a good fight (see his similarly humorous one in the rarely screened *Waltzes from Vienna*, or the harrowing versions of them in the murder of Gromek in *Torn Curtain* and the rape/murder of Mrs. Blaney in *Frenzy*).

Needless to say, Roddy loses everything again and descends even further "downhill" (towards the Underworld?), in an elevator this time, for a painfully long twenty seconds.

Part Three, "The World of Lost Illusions," has our pathetic hero playing a Parisian dance-hall gigolo for 50 francs a dance. Between dances, a plain, bored-looking woman (the Poetess, played by Violet Farebrother) slowly builds interest in and passion for Roddy as he tells his tale of woe to her. Yacowar got it backwards, though — it is *Roddy* who tells her that she seems unique among all this artificiality, not her telling him (1977, p. 44). But Hitchcock perverts that genteel notion quickly for, as the dawn's "searching, relentless sun-light" (via title) shows these denizens of the dance-hall for the shallow riche that they are, it also exposes the Poetess as a frightening-looking vampire, dark circles under her eyes and black lipstick dripping down her mouth! With the words coming from him and not her, the irony of Roddy's descent becomes all the more tragic, for he truly has entered Hades' shadow world.

Anguished and broken-hearted thrice now, we next see Roddy even lower, if lower he can go, deep in the bowels of some lost Marseilles dockside. This whole scene is dull and a bit interminable — like half of *Vertigo*, but quite deliberate, I believe, for dull and interminable *would* be the feelings Roddy (and Scottie) must have had at those times— until he has his justly famous, vivid, and sharply etched hallucination, with all the women in his life pressing in on him. Mabel, Julia, the Poetess, the dance hall madam and even Archie are all seen in MS parasitically clamoring over his money on a table and pointedly laughing at him/the camera/us.

Slowly and pitifully, Roddy pulls himself out of this nightmare and staggers— via a shaky, hand-held camera *à la The Blair Witch Project* 75 years later — home to daddy, who asks his forgiveness in a wholly undeserved *deus ex machina* ending — unless one believes in the biblical story of the Prodigal Son's return. In fact, all three extant films we have seen of Hitch's silents have so far ended this way— saved by a last-minute force beyond our protagonists' control.

Or is this *not* the end? Cut to a short postscript of Roddy back at school scoring another rugby goal, smiling and dazedly looking around, just like at the beginning of the film. Is his look one of wonder? Two snobs boringly applaud in the crowd. What has he returned to? Has anything changed? Has he learned nothing from his travails? Perhaps we detect a look of consternation on his face as if to say, "Is this all there is?" to life. But we may just be projecting, as Hitchcock intends.

As usual, Hitchcock's endings are much more ambiguous— and far from wholly satisfying — than one might hope for in his films, in spite of our feelings that they are morality plays of potential catharsis. The director certainly holds out hope for his characters, which include us as audience members, before, during, and after he puts them and us through the ringers, and he feels these ringers are necessary for them/us to move towards happiness. How his characters respond to those challenges he leaves totally up to them (and us, his other "characters").

Why doesn't he end his films happily? Because, after all, the ends of Hitchcock's films are not meant to solve all the world's problems, or even his characters' within and outside of the films, but are merely pleasant and engaging queries to ruminate over and discuss afterwards.

Five

Easy Virtue

First screening August, 1927

Isabel Jeans, who just finished stealing Roddy blind as Julia in *Downhill*, here plays Larita Filton, a woman, as Donald Spoto accurately states, "with curled hair and curling lips" (1983, p. 109). Her first husband, an older man of nasty looks, is played by Franklin Dyall (1874–1950). The co-respondent artist Claude Robson is played by Eric Bransby Williams (c. 1900–?). The plaintiff's counsel, better known as the prosecutor, is played by Ian Hunter, fresh off his role as Julia's patient co-conspirator Archie in *Downhill*, and soon to be the heel and champion boxer Bob Corby, in *The Ring*. John Whittaker, Larita's second husband, is played "with suitable spinelessness" (Spoto, 1983, p. 109) by Robin Irvine, Roddy's spineless "friend" from *Downhill*. Fresh off her role as the vampire Poetess in the previous film, Violet Farebrother — with no sense of fairness about her and nobody's brother — plays the nasty Mrs. Whittaker. Sarah, John's real love, is played by Enid Stamp Taylor (1904–1946). His somewhat nondescript younger and older sisters are played by Dorothy Boyd and Dacia Deane respectively.

Of the eight popular film review compendiums referenced, five gave *Easy Virtue* two or two-and-a-half stars, ratings of poor to average (although Scheuer praised it with three stars), with such comments as: "Vapid social melodrama with minimal points of interest" (HA, p. 252); "Considering the directorial credit, this is close to dull" (MP, p. 327); and "A yawn" (BB, p. 304). *Bioscope* (September 1, 1927) had little positive to say about it, too, claiming its only virtues were the established reputations of the writer Noel Coward and the director.

Leonard Maltin, though, found it "imaginatively shot" (p. 396), while the British *Time Out* justly stated: "[T]he first half of the film … is pure Hitchcock, its combination of conciseness and idiosyncrasy demonstrating Hitchcock's master of silent narration" (p. 345). I must agree with these last two comments, for I found much of interest in the film that belies its generally limited praise.

Adapted from a play by the polymath Noel Coward (1899–1973), *Easy Virtue*'s credits are shot over a silhouette still of an old box photo camera facing SR. Opening title: "'Virtue is its own reward,' they say — but 'easy virtue' is society's reward for a slandered reputation."

The film opens on a CU of a divorce bill with the camera's focus on the words "Filton vs. Filton." Dissolve into a CU of something that looks like a round, white, spongy object, the outline of a sperm swimming towards it. The "sponge" tilts upward (or the camera tilts down) to reveal itself to be a man's wig, its part in the middle the "sperm." Continuing tilt reveals a CU of a nasty looking and stern judge's face presiding over a court. Staring directly into the camera, he raises his monocle (shades of *The Pleasure Garden*) to focus on a speaker in the courtroom. Field of view reverses as we see the monocle in ECU approach the camera, bringing speaker into larger and clearer focus. We recognize him as Ian Hunter, Archie from *Downhill*, and someone we will come to know as the plaintiff's counsel, or simply the prosecutor, in this film.

Bored and yawning, another reverse angle shot shows the judge rubbing his tired eyes. Monocle now removed, he turns toward SL (his right) to stare at a fuzzy image that we can't make out either. Raising the monocle again, we expect to see through it as it gains focus but, instead, Hitchcock just cuts to a MS of a woman in clear focus in the box defending herself. Cut to the prosecutor's viewpoint of her (we soon learn she is Mrs. Filton), arguing. From his angle we can see that she's quite wealthy, carrying a fox stole on her arm and wearing pearls above a lavish dress. Cut to the judge's MS POV of the prosecutor again, and then a quick cut to a disorienting long shot of the courtroom and the rabble in the gallery. It takes us a moment to realize this shot is taken from *behind* the prosecutor (hence the disorientation, for the shot is jarringly distinct from the others), for he is centered in the foreground directly between Mrs. Filton and the judge in the far distance, SL and SR respectively.

Cut to a CU of the prosecutor, once more from the judge's POV. Cut to a CU of Mrs. Filton, now from the prosecutor's perspective, denying being kissed by a co-respondent. Cut to a LS from the judge's POV of the gallery's reaction. It looks like derisive laughter from this distance, but one can't be sure. Cut to the CU of the prosecutor reaching behind himself and pulling out an object. He holds it and asks the defendant via title to once more "repeat your statement with regard to this decanter." Cut to Mrs. Filton beginning her comments.

Immediate cut to an ECU of the decanter held in a hand by someone.

Extremely slow and confident, Hitchcock now affects a thirty-two second camera tracking shot back from the decanter to a LS, revealing this to be a flashback scene of an older man, Mr. Filton, pouring himself a drink while frowning at Mrs. Filton, who is sitting and posing for a handsome young artist, Claude Robson. Cut to a CU of the handsome young artist from Mrs. Filton's perspective. MS of Mrs. Filton in a long flowing gown perched like a queen. She turns a furtive glance towards her husband. Cut to her view, his drink glass and hand in MS obliterating his face as he downs what seems to be one of many. He turns back towards the decanter, a bit wobbly now. Artist's POV of the missus reveals a fed-up, bored woman.

Now that all the facts of the case have been established, Hitchcock's confidence multiplies and he feels free to really play with our minds. Camera asserts its autonomy by showing the handsome young artist from no one's POV now, a neutral camera shot that simultaneously draws attention to itself and momentarily confuses our sense of perspective. Shot from the artist's left side in MCU (Mrs. Filton can be imagined far OSR), we feel ourselves as voyeurs of the artist in the same way as he must feel towards his model — privileged, close and personal. With such knowledge, we can see that his is a frustrated libido. Through this relatively quick and brazen five-second MCU, we are also jolted into a clear awareness of the three-dimensional space of the artist's studio (recalling the same sense of the lodger's digs).

Cut to a two-shot for the first time, husband and wife in MD. Hubby pours yet again from the decanter in question as his wife turns to look. Cut to a CU of the missus reaching out and imploring him not to have another. Cut to a reaction shot of hubby from her POV, also in MCU, and this one startles us, for he glares back at her over his shoulder from a twisted right profile position almost directly into the camera's eye. His impact on us is further enhanced, for he foregrounds in stark contrast the harsh blank wall behind him. This highly charged moment, so unexpected and odd, jumps off the screen.

In a long two-shot of the couple, he pours again and melodramatically drains his glass. Braced, he starts in on her, arguing, and slowly closes the gap between them. Sudden cut to an ECU of the husband's face staring straight into the camera muttering to himself, brightly lit and centered in the screen. Slow, fifteen-second *dolly backwards* reveals him to be wearing a lighter colored suit, and we suddenly realize he's sitting in court next to the prosecutor! Without bringing attention to it, Hitchcock had cut away from the flashback to the courtroom again. Rewinding of the DVD reveals he was there all along right beside the prosecutor, but we'd not noticed him at the time — nor knew who he was to even look for him, as Hitchcock intended — for we were focusing on the other three protagonists.

Hitchcock always surprises us in his films, and we have just experienced another wonderful example of the director showing us everything but only emphasizing *some* things.

Hubby jumps up out of his seat to protest something we will never find out about, for even though he could wield titles with the best of them, Hitchcock was also noted for his disdain for dialogue in silent films, and strictly limited explanations when he felt them unnecessary. So, while we certainly wish to better understand the cause of the couple's difficulties and why they're in court, the quieting retort of the prosecutor and the rather curious reaction on the face of Mrs. Filton reflects the relish, I believe, with which Hitchcock deliberately frustrates our desire and need for information. Such a withholding, of course, also insures our greater attention.

Fully back in the courtroom drama (but on alert for any other flashbacks, certainly), Mrs. Filton continues her self-defense. Title: "And so, for the next three days, I was unable to sit for my portrait. When I resumed...." Her comments cause several interesting reactions in us. First of all, we're still hoping for some kind of explanation for the previous untitled scene. There is still no answer for us to that one. If anything, we're even more confounded to hear her words (well, "see" them), particularly the first two, "And so," as if she *has* just given us the reason why (the courtroom audience and Hitchcock certainly know, but *we* don't). Second, with the information Hitchcock *does* give us, we are forced to wonder why it took three days for her to begin the portraiture again. Third, with the open-ended "When I resumed," we are set up to expect the next shot to reveal her back in the studio via flashback. All of these thoughts, I believe, are deliberately implanted in our minds by the director.

Cut to an ECU of Mrs. Filton in a bright light sitting for her portrait, right? Wrong. The cut is an ECU of Mrs. Filton all right, in flashback, but she's not in the studio, we sense. She's facing the camera, her eyes sad, and the camera dollies back from her for a very slow fifteen seconds— with that same languorous pace as the other two cuts between the courtroom and the artist's studio— to reveal her standing and toying with her hat in a boudoir. Turning in a MS, she moves to a vanity table and sits down, then reaches for something with her back to us in CU. Cut to a CU of a hand writing on a pad: "...was the maid always present when Larita Filton disrobed." We naturally (and wrongly) assume that Larita is the writer.

What the hell does *this* mean? Why would Mrs. Filton be writing such a thing? Cut to a MS of a maid and Larita (we are meant to begin identifying with her more now that her first name is used), finishing up touches on an outfit she is wearing. We then see her get up and walk through a curtain into ... the artist's studio!

So, let us recap: We first assumed we'd be seeing Larita resume her modeling in a second flashback, but then we didn't see that, and now we realize we were right the first time, in a way, but it was a flashback back to a few minutes *prior* to the place in the flashback we thought we'd be seeing! What an interesting way of playing with the screen time. Hitchcock's experiments with audience manipulation are multiplying geometrically with each new silent film.

Cut to a LS of the artist and his model seen chatting together USR and preparing to work, his easel foreground left. Artist walks towards the camera and turns around right to face the easel, then looks around to his left to view his object of beauty. This scene is shot from the privileged camera's perspective of the earlier flashback, and the power of his gaze comes hurtling in on our senses now. Cut to the artist's POV from this position, the model gazing back at us in a MS, immobile and statuesque. Why does this shot feel so strong? Because we realize (subliminally at first, but palpably) that Hitchcock had deliberately set the camera up for this shot during the earlier flashback as a clue, a plant, to prepare us for this later flashback! Representing the artist's private view of the model (remember, the husband is not in this later scene — yet), Hitchcock allows us privy information to his special view, which we will return to again even later. And the easel, because it is set in the foreground, becomes a metaphorical screen or curtain with its own private side reserved for only certain viewers— the artist and us— at special times.

The artist turns away from his view (a reverse angle, the original privileged shot) and moves US to adjust the lighting. He returns to Larita in a long shot (POV from the screen/curtain/easel now) and then, in MS, he adjusts her gown and calmly takes her hand with a familiar intimacy. Once again Hitchcock thwarts our expectations, for nothing he has shown us up to this point has overtly demonstrated one way or the other whether the artist and model have been having an affair. But the director knows his audience, and filmic convention. We come to a movie to be titillated, and we expect — no, demand — a certain amount of hanky panky. There *will* be an affair, so we look and wait to see when it will happen, not *if* it will, as we think ourselves oh so clever.

In this scene, Hitchcock turns this convention on its side and denies us our smug beliefs by not making a big deal out of this revelation at all. In fact, he does the exact opposite, exposing the affair in one quick, matter-of-fact act.

Not giving us any time (once again) to consciously appreciation his wily direction, Hitchcock flashes another double-edged title our way: "That hurts, Claude ... He bruised my wrist after he'd been drinking." This reality check pulls us up even shorter as Hitchcock shows us the real pain, both emotional and physical, that extramarital affairs, spousal abuse, and divorce can create. It also abruptly chastens our smug assumptions of and desires for an affair. We may even secretly blush after reading this title, slightly ashamed of our own fantasies and willing cynicism projected onto these suddenly not so imaginary, struggling characters onscreen.

Larita looks away, her gaze taking us back to the decanter of liquor on the table. The artist swears her husband will not be given another drink while in his studio, and grits his teeth disapprovingly for effect (it's really his first truly assertive act in the film, and our first glimpse of his own strong character). Cut to the decanter on the table in the studio—no, not the studio's table, but back on the prosecutor's bench! (Our conventional thinking still makes us believe in the continuity of a scene in spite of this cinematic cut, which, the reader will recall from a similar discussion about *Downhill*, does not require consistency of image.) Camera slowly dollies back for ten seconds, gently breaking us out of this second intense flashback and giving us a brief chance to rest. Whew, we need it.

Prosecutor: "Do you suggest that your husband is an habitual drunkard?" Cut to the defendant looking away, not willing to answer. It's become clear she is of several minds about the whole proceeding, further complicating the issues in our mind (just like Hitchcock wants them to be). Her gaze turns left again, this time to the blank faces of the jurors. Surprising cut to a CU of the writing tablet again, a hand scripting "The artist and the woman he pitied <u>alone together</u>" (her underlines), and "Pity is akin to love" written below that. If Larita is not the writer, as we assumed earlier in the second flashback, then who is? We will not be told or shown the answer to this question for yet a while longer.

Cut to the judge (remember him?) asking, "Are all these details necessary?" We think, "he himself may have a mistress of his own waiting at some hotel," and we suspect the prosecutor believes so, too.

Cut to a four-second, CU profile of Larita facing SL talking, which immediately fades into a four-second CU shot of the prosecutor facing SR. Alternating four-second CU of Larita, five-second CU of prosecutor, five-second CU of Larita, quick LD shot of the rabble in the gallery, and then a five-second CU of the judge's monocle swinging from its line like a clock's pendulum, impatient. Cut to a seven-second CU of an actual clock's pendulum swinging, then back to seven seconds of the swinging monocle. Due to its obviousness and redundancy, the sequence is at once an obvious, redundant, clever, funny and sardonic commentary on the stereotypically luxurious and wasteful lifestyle of the rich—and the pace of justice—both common Hitchcockian themes.

The prosecutor pulls out damning evidence, a letter from Claude the artist. Cut to a CU of the letter: "Why suffer that foul brute when you know I'd give everything I have in the world to make you happy." Cut to the letter turns out to be *yet a third flashback* of Larita reading it, and we are tipped off to a sense of impending doom now by yet another slow, ten-second dolly backwards— with that same dreamlike languor of the other slow dollies— to reveal Larita in her living room with the artist. Claude makes his loving move towards her in a two-shot CU, and ... guess who walks in?

Cut to the husband's POV in MCU from slightly above the couple (he's standing on the inside door landing). One of Hitchcock's extraordinary architecturally staged shots is now presented to us for the very first time — that of a MS of Claude twisted around to look in the camera's (Mr. Filton's) direction, his back and head blocking all but the left eye of Larita (which effectively disembodies Larita's figure for us onscreen), the both of them peering directly into the camera back at us. This kind of shot will find its greatest fulfillment and perversion in Norman Bates' reaction shot to Marion Crane's murder in *Psycho* thirty-three years later, as he simultaneously covers his mouth with one hand and reaches towards us and the camera with his other, revealing only one of his eyes. (Perkins' image remains an iconic marker to this day for all of Hitchcock's work, and continues to appear on posters and book covers year after year.)

Cut to the laughing husband in MCU, triumphant. This shot alternates twice with an ECU of the artist twisting around to his left, still blocking all but one of Larita's eyes, both of them completely startled, aghast, and trapped. The power of these alternating shots jumps out at us, charged and unnerving.

Staged and deathlike in appearance, and yet tense and alive, the husband is next seen from a point blank position staring SR (at the artist). Hitchcock then quickly cuts to the hubby's POV, the camera catching the artist staring wide-eyed, angry, and confrontationally defensive back at us. The camera slowly turns to the right to reveal Larita even wider-eyed, mannequin-like, and frightening-looking, and then we feel the camera move slowly backwards to focus on the husband, his eyes now directed SL. Hitchcock's camera has never been more mobile and bold in any film up to this point.

We see the husband walk in a MS between the two lovers, and the camera cuts to the artist's POV now, another startling, architecturally-structured shot showing the hubby replacing Claude's earlier position that blocked out almost all of Larita's face, just her left eye again peering eerily over her husband's shoulder this time. The entire sequence has been filmed brilliantly, and Hitchcock has wrung and sustained tremendous tension out of the scene.

The plot thickens even more. In a quick M two-shot, the husband now moves menacingly forward, but we suddenly see the artist rush towards a drawer, draw a revolver, and shoot him. Rather than dropping to the ground immediately (as it's supposed to happen in real life and the movies, convention tells us), the husband continues to charge right at the camera, arm and walking stick raised menacingly above his head. In a MS from Larita's POV, the husband gets off a good ten whacks with his walking stick on the cowering artist before his adrenalin can no longer delay the shock and pain of the bullet. Even this early in his career (and, of course, culminating in the justly famous murder scene of Gromek in *Torn Curtain* almost forty years later), Hitchcock shows his audience just how messy and difficult any real violence truly is. It takes time to kill someone, and nothing is or should be what one expects.

When the husband does finally fall, the camera stays on the artist as he searches his mind for what to do next. Gun still in hand, he watches the wife run to her spouse. The maid comes in, then rushes out. Ditto the butler. With the camera shifting towards SR, we're shown the artist's profile in a MS, immobile and staring hard towards something in lower SL. Cut to what he sees: outside a window, two people, one a policeman, hurry towards the house two stories below. They are sharply lit in the glare of daylight. For three reasons this shot is yet one more jarring surprise for our eyes. One, we've not known where and at what time of day this studio shot had been located up until this moment, although we may have subliminally assumed it's evening due to the darkly lit interior. Two, we're suddenly given information detailing its position on a second floor of what we can assume to be a large apartment building. Three, the brightness of the outside pierces through and disrupts the dark, dreamlike interior of the studio and our acclimated mind.

In CU, the artist raises his fingers to his mouth and turns to face the camera, justifiable paranoia springing to his features. Staring down at the gun still in his hands, he looks up again right into our eyes (this gaze is more than a little disconcerting), almost seeming to ask us, "What do I do now?" We cannot help him, and we do not realize until much later that that was the last time we would see him in this film.

Cut to a cop blindly questioning Larita (he never raises his head from his notepad) while the husband, obviously still in pain, stirs helplessly at their feet in a twisted CU. His pose — alive, though — is reminiscent of the golden curl girl in her death near the beginning of *The Lodger*. Rushing to her husband's side, Larita helps him sit up and longingly searches his eyes for forgiveness. Shot, defeated and exhausted, he lifts the artist's letter in front of his face as Hitchcock cuts back to the prosecutor's hand holding the letter. Leaving this final flashback, the director begins that now familiar slow and languorous dolly shot back on him (twelve seconds). If we had a mind to—but we don't, that's how caught up we are in Hitchcock's scenario by now—we might wonder, "What happened to Claude the artist?"

We see more discourse ensue, shots of the courtroom visible from high overhead. Surprising cut to a CU of a woman in the gallery, smirking. She looks down, and another mystery is suddenly cleared up. Larita wasn't writing any of the notes we had seen in the previous scenes, this smirking woman is a reporter writing her story! Cut to a CU of her notepad with the last line written earlier repeated: "Pity is akin to love," this time followed by "Nearly 2000 a year" (the artist's money, apparently, was left to Larita in his will). Wait a minute. *The artist is dead?* When did that happen?

Once again, Hitchcock gives us no time to ponder this question. Cut to a static MS of the jury deliberating and arguing among themselves. "The Verdict" appears superimposed over the old camera still from the credits. Hitchcock draws the verdict out, too, in order to sustain our tension, as he shows the jurors walking slowly back to their box and seating themselves. Quick successive cuts to a CU of a very nervous Larita, an ELS of the gallery waiting with baited breath, an ELS of the judge entering, an ELS of the gallery rising, a CU of Larita rising, an ELS of the judge sitting, an ELS of the gallery sitting, and finally a MS of the bailiff rising and asking the foreperson to give the verdict.

"We find Larita Filton guilty of misconduct with the late Claude Robson." Hitchcock has done it to us again. The artist *had* died, not the husband! How? And if he is dead, why is she only being tried for misconduct, not murder (which, if we're quick, we're already thinking)? And, if *she* didn't kill him, who did? Was it suicide? Probably, but Hitchcock never will let us know the answers to these questions. Why? Because they don't matter. They are all MacGuffins, what Hitchcock called red herrings that plot lines may hinge on but his characters (and audiences) don't really need to know much about, because the films are more about their emotional and physical struggles and growth. In fact, by never or hardly ever revealing them, our curiosity remains and becomes increasingly piqued!

So, Claude is dead, but before we can even ask any of these questions, which startle us so rapidly due to Hitchcock's deliberate withholding of key information, the director speeds the narrative even further along. The judge reads the penalty, Hitchcock denying us even that information by refusing an explanatory title. Fade to black. We, his main characters, are hooked, line and sinker—end of Act One, apparently.

But no. Fade up on an ELS of the courtroom nearly cleared out, Larita almost the last to leave. Once outside, the camera focuses pryingly on her downturned head in a LS from behind a phalanx of reporters. This is the true coda to an extraordinary ten-minute-plus montage full of flashbacks, red herrings, withheld information, and a host of clever cinematic twists and flourishes.

Divorced and broken hearted, Larita takes off for the "tolerant shores of the Mediterranean" (title) in an effort to relax and forget. Ah, the rich. They can always fall back on a little travel to soften their emotional pain. Entering a hotel, she begins to sign the register "Larita F---" but stops, then turns to look directly into a CU of a box camera—as if aware of someone looking over her shoulder (perhaps us)—then changes her last name to read "Grey," like her mood.

The next title poetically reads straight out of Coward's play: "Larita could hide her scarred heart, but not her magnetic charm — and soon came attentions which she most desired to avoid." Both the hotel lobby and, particularly, Larita's room hallway are designed by Hitchcock's art designer to resemble theater stages. As Larita crosses the former she is recognized but, in another typical Hitchcockian red herring, nothing comes of it. Every shot of this director is calculated to create the greatest effect on his audience. Knowing our appetite for slander has been whetted through the introduction of Coward's quote, Hitchcock teases us with what we know he must fulfill—some sort of payoff consistent with the play and film's conventions. This does not mean he won't delay that fulfillment as long as he can, however.

Cut to a LS shot of a tennis match as seen through one of the competitor's racket strings in the foreground. After a bit of volleying back and forth in ELS, Hitchcock cuts to a MS of Larita watching the match from a chair on the sidelines. Suddenly, *Hitchcock himself* strolls by in front of her, carrying a walking stick and wiping some sweat off the back of his neck. He unlatches the court door and walks through it, Larita briefly turning to notice. Cut back to a MLS of the game in progress, but we soon see that the holder of the earlier racket, John Whittaker, is graciously apologizing to Larita in a MCU profile. He had just hit her in the head with a tennis ball, an abrupt and funny shot that came into our view from OSR.

It turns out to be quite a welt, actually, for shortly we find our young lovers *tête-à-tête*, John still fawning over her face, as they overlook a picture-perfect Monaco (a 1920's shot, just as breathtaking, of an early 1950's eight-millimeter film of my parents' honeymoon). The whole scene, also typically Hitchcockian, feels simultaneously absurd yet plausible.

Larita points OSL requesting something from that space with the cocky, self-satisfied arrogance the director specially reserves for his derisive accounts of the rich. What she points to turns out to be a wet bar, where John touchingly fumbles through a procurement of said cocktail. He splashes dashes of two separate liquors rather heavy-handedly into a shaker and adds their assorted condiments, a sense of both innocence and sexual desire accompanying his movements. Awkwardly mixing up the concoction, John's hands go limp during his half-hearted shaking, transfixed by Larita's beauty.

She laughs at his naiveté. They drink. Nothing else happens, our conventions delayed yet again. John spies some flowers sent her by another admirer, and has his own idea. He arises and moves toward her, and Hitchcock slows the action to a crawl, charging John's CU kiss of her hand with a voyeuristic insistence and intensity. Cut to a MS reverse profile of this same action repeated in her hotel room, fresh flowers on the table from John. With typical visual economy, Hitchcock has condensed this last scene — lasting all of thirty seconds— with his trademark parallel efficiency. Closing in on a MCU of the soon-to-be lovers, then an ECU, Hitchcock heightens their sexual tension through jump cuts, building our expectations to a steamy pitch.

Now is a good time to mention that, from the moment these two young lovers met, Hitchcock has surreptitiously placed surrogate erection symbols in the background of several shots: At the tennis court a tall and narrow pitch pine could be seen in the background; penile-looking pillars in the hotel lobby were prominently displayed; and an erect statue in Larita's room have all been not-so-subliminal, humorous erotica for our senses.

Cut back to a MS of the lovers. Larita turns her head away from John to gaze at what might be described as the design of vaginal openings in the creases of a plush chair. Slowly moving towards it, Larita slips sensuously into its folds and opens her arms towards John in a simultaneously expansive, playful, and come-hither gesture. The erect statue with one large ball supporting it hovers directly above her head in the background of the screen frame. John turns, fleeing (just kidding — he must be loving this). Head intently bent towards her, he approaches ever closer. Cut to a two-shot CU, and Hitchcock finally treats us to an extended and exaggerated fifteen-second, tension filled shot of the clinch we've long been anticipating. And it's all the more sweet — we can almost taste it, it's so palpable — because of its long delay. Like an Astaire-Rogers duet we know is coming, Hitchcock grants us the greatest pleasure by taking his time getting (us) there.

As she succumbs ever so slowly to his kiss in a tight CU, their sexual tension is sustained through our extraordinary view of the yielding but

firm pressure of Larita's hand against John's chest, her lower torso twisting away from him even as her upper half arches back into him. This is a
truly gorgeous and potent screen moment. His lips slowly and achingly
approach hers, but when they finally touch, Hitchcock fades to black. A
lovely afterimage, however, remains.

Fade in to another Coward title: "Larita found something re-assur-
ing in John's devotion.... It was like a cool breeze sweeping away the ugly
memories of the past." Fade out.

Fade in to an ECU of a swaying horse's head as he chews his cud. Cut
to a MS revealing the head to be at the front of a horse drawn carriage.
More poignant scenes occur in the carriage as John admits that all that matters is that he loves her. Their open-hearted gazes into each other's eyes,
in CU profile, are quite touching, and reminiscent of his peering under
her hat into her eyes at the tennis court, except now *he's* wearing a hat,
and we can just see her right eye (the private one?) peering back at him.
This is quite a different shot from, one recalls, the earlier artfully composed one-eyed gazes.

Cut to an early example of the classic Hitchcockian ELS of a carriage
crossing a bridge (one can already *think back* to Hitchcock's similar shot
of Roddy's lonely walk away from his home in *Downhill*), miniscule in the
distance. But the ELS in *this* film functions as an important break in the
action, a partial respite and relief from the scene's immediate predecessor.
By releasing us from his hold, albeit briefly, Hitchcock allows us a necessary and intentional breather, giving us a bit of time to reflect upon and
appreciate all that has occurred up until this point.

> There are very few— astonishingly few— people who can write a screen
> story. There are no chapter headings, no intervals between the acts. The fad-
> ing in and fading out are so quick that they do not give the audience time to
> discuss and work out and think over what they have seen and why they have
> seen it [AH, reprinted in SG1, "Life Among the Stars," 1995, pp. 48–49;
> original 1937].

Cut back to a medium high shot looking down on the couple, both
of their hats now prominent. We are still only permitted to see one eye of
each lover. Might this mean that either we or they or all three of us have
limited vision in life, and are privy to only so much of another's existence?
Or is it just one more audacious shot from this master of cinematic technique?

Vertiginous shots of scenery with annoying foliage cover the foreground, deliberately delaying more love payoffs. Cut to the same high shot
of the lovers with John leaning in for another kiss dead center frame, his

hat now completely obscuring his face. Larita's left eye and partial profile are barely visible behind her hat. Shaking her head "No," Hitchcock quickly cuts to the carriage driver wearing a bored countenance, the director's subtle commentary once again on the dull nature of the dallying romances of the rich in the eyes of the poorer service workers.

John, beginning to win Larita over, says via title: "We could get married right away, and go straight back to my people — they'll love you." An odd way of speaking, we think, but again pointing up the artificial separation of class systems. Quick cut back to the nearly asleep driver as he pulls up alongside another horse and carriage.

Tight CU of John and Larita's approaching kiss, hats blocking all but their noses and mouths. As their lips touch, Hitchcock cuts to an ECU of the huge, looming heads of the two horses in similar pose and profile. One is even wearing a small hat with a flower in it, just like Larita's! Cut to the clinch. All we see are hats now in MCU, their faces totally obscured, Larita's long string of pearls the only thing visible as it dives down into her *décolletage.*

Immediate cut to a medium distant, static camera shot of a moving car pulling up behind them and entering the scene of horses and carriages. Cut to an ECU of a disembodied, nervous hand pumping a bulbous car horn (think about it). John prods the catatonic driver to move on, but Larita opts for a stroll. As they disembark, we see just how vulgar her wealth and attitude really make her, for her preposterously long scarf nearly catches on the carriage upholstery. (Though it occurred a month after the film's first screening, this image turns out to be a not-so-subtle eerie premonition of the modern dancer Isadora Duncan's tragic death in the south of France, her scarf getting caught in the open wheels of a car.) Obligatory silent screen fast-forward argument (*à la* the Keystone Kops) ensues between the two irate drivers, alternating with shots of the sauntering couple climbing steps. Fade out.

What seemed a sure thing is, in Hitchcock's hands, once again not as it appears: We learn this this time via title, "As the evening wore on, so John's patience wore out, until — ." Cut to yet another justly famous scene, this one readily acknowledged by a number of film critics, of that remarkably expressive switchboard operator (played by Benita Hume) reacting to Larita's marriage acceptance over the phone. Without showing the lovers at all, her one-minute cameo fully captures all of the apprehensions, hopes, uncertainties, and final consummatory agreement between them through just her mobile facial expressions. Pure Hitchcockian cinema at its finest.

MS of movers loading tons of luggage onto a car dissolves into a MS of those same tons of luggage piled high, this time with a toy poodle (representing France) atop the pile staring directly into the camera. Dissolve into the pile in a train cabin now, a smallish bulldog (long live England) panting atop it. Fade to black.

We next see a train pull in towards us in a LS SL, cut to more luggage transfers to a car, and now a small retriever is happily circling the vehicle. In one minute, Hitchcock efficiently and humorously portrays the big move.*

Cut to the interior of the car, John pointing at something (where they're going?). Both have hats on again and, while Larita's is smaller than its predecessor, it still obscures her eyes from our view. "How blind love can be," we perhaps hear the director proclaim. In a MS the car moves OSL. We see it enter the screen in a LS heading down a country road directly towards us, nothing else around for miles, and then it moves toward SR. Cut to a slightly vertiginous LS of the road and countryside from behind the driver's head. Larita, peering out from under her hat, dangles a lit cigarette in her mouth. She is smiling and all seems carefree, but we may detect some hidden trepidation behind her features. More confusion in our minds as we see the car seemingly head back up the same road away from our view towards SL, but we are not given any explanation for this shot.

In LS the car pulls up in front of a palatial country estate. A butler enters the frame from OSL and opens the car door. Cut to a similar-looking LS of the house interior and Larita's introduction to John's father Colonel Whittaker and his younger sister. The little sister gets an obligatory kiss from Larita, then says via title: "It's funny, I thought you'd be dark and foreign-looking!" This throws our heroine a bit and gives her pause via a brief subjective aside to us in a privileged CU towards the camera. Not since the trial scenes have we seen one of these fourth wall breakers, and it pointedly reminds us of her earlier troubles.

In LS Sis runs upstairs to fetch her mother, whose first view of Larita is taken from the high vantage point of the upstairs landing. Also seen in LS looking down at a sharp, oblique angle, it is one of Hitchcock's favorite shots of imminent foreboding. MCU of Mrs. Whittaker (played by Violet Farebrother, the vampire Poetess from *Downhill*) reveals a severe looking, stern profile, and she is a clear precursor to Bruno and Marnie's emotionally cold mothers. Camera holds on her in MCU as she menacingly descends out of the frame. Cut to a MS of Larita's POV from below, the mother still descending towards the camera. At the bottom of a second

---

*For a brief but interesting discussion of Hitchcock's use of dogs as characters in his early films, see Charles Barr's "Postscript: Hitchcock & Dogs" in his English Hitchcock, 1999, pp. 186–189.

set of stairs, Larita proffers her outstretched hand. Mrs. Whittaker keeps her own close and shakes Larita's brusquely. Momentarily disorienting, the camera cuts in mid-shake to a startling reverse angle MCU of the two women. Again, the slow pace of the mother's descent coupled with the steadiness of her bedrock stare abruptly jars us with this sudden cut.

These two shots still do not prepare us for the truly audacious and disturbing cut to a CU of Mrs. Whittaker's face staring right at us and exclaiming, in monotone (we can almost hear it spoken, her face is so rigid and her mouth so sharply etched): "I trust you won't be bored by our simple family life." Irony drips from her mouth like the blood did from her Poetess. Cut back to the earlier reverse two-shot MCU, relieving the pressure a bit on this woman's direct confrontation of our sensibilities.

More introductions all around as the older sister is now met. Cut to a CU of a farcical-looking dinner gong being gonged. The family now prattles over Sarah, apparently the spurned bride hopeful, who just happens to be staying for dinner at Mrs. Whittaker's request! Hitchcock quickly slips *that* piece of information in under our radar, upping the ante of Larita's problems.

Hitchcock gives us a little time to think these new developments over by cutting to a PAP shot of Larita's upstairs bedroom bed, which is facing SR in foreground. It is framed theatrically with the headboard against SL, footposts to the right. Larita lolls frustratingly on a chair in the background. As the maid unpacks her clothes in the middle of the frame, it begins to dawn on both Larita and us that she's made another major mistake in her life by marrying this boy.

Whoops, there goes that dinner gong again (quick CU). John hurries to finish dressing in another upstairs room. Down the stairs he comes and, along with his father, not one, not two, not three, but four women await him below, all draped over the lower banister. Let's see, from left to right that would be John's mother, Sarah (the *other* woman), the older sister and the younger sister (these last two do not have names in the film). Sarah rises onto the lower stairs to greet John, and we see that they are standing much too closely together to be mere friends. The younger sister runs upstairs to see how Larita's getting along at her makeup table.

We see Sis enter the bedroom in MS as reflected in the oval eye of Larita's vanity mirror, Larita's CU image doubled in the glass. Puffing away on a snurd, she is marveled over by the little sister as she puts on her face. The girl seems a younger, more innocent version of Lil in *Marnie* as she tries to throw a monkey wrench into the works, blurting out "Sarah's here," and waiting to see how Larita reacts. She is more gossipy than threatening, however.

After Larita comes downstairs, we see John standing between the two women in his life in a three-shot CU. He introduces them to each other, glancing inquiringly side-to-side to see how each takes it. Happily small talking, Larita spews more cigarette smoke about. Everyone heads toward the camera in a MLS, then veers off SL toward the dining room, Dad leading Larita, John, and Sarah while the other three (Mom and her two girls) take up the rear. We see Mrs. Whittaker get in a shrug over the whole proceedings.

The "humble" household dining table is shot theatrically in PAP via a Last Supper motif, a huge chandelier splitting images of two Christ-like figures that tower presidingly over the affair above a mantel. Even at this distance, the room seems full of people, which also includes a maid and butler standing frozen at attention in their proper places. Close in on Mrs. Whittaker dictating seating arrangements, making us feel even more claustrophobic and stifled by her oppressive personality in this darkly lit room. With the narrative slowing to a crawl, soup is served, and Hitchcock mercifully *dissolves* to the main course. The first of its type in the film, this small technical trick helps us keep interested even now.

Sarah, who is sitting *between* John and Larita (!), is coolly startled by Larita's interruption of her conversation with John. Immediate cut to that disturbing, full-frontal subjective CU shot of the mother staring hard at the proceedings.

Cut to a MS shot of the trio from just over mom's right shoulder. This is another first in the film, a Hitchcockian over-the-shoulder shot where the camera seems almost connected to the character, and it's a clear foretelling of Devlin's introduction to us in *Notorious*. (See the description of Crewe's attempted rape of Alice in *Blackmail* for another example of this signature shot.) Cut to an autonomous camera (AC) POV CU shot of the three of them, a PAP vision from the "front" of the table *à la* this scene's introduction. Cut back to a CU of the suspicious mother, a nugget of recognition momentarily brightening her features. Title: "I've seen your face somewhere, Larita.... I wonder if we've any mutual friends?" A look of predatory gloating flits across her nasty face. Gamely, in a MS centered alone in the frame, Larita shoots back a matter-of-fact, casual comment (untitled), but it looks and feels studied and too tightly controlled, in spite of her nonchalant holding of the ever-present cigarette in her hand.

Release cut with a long shot of the table as the women get up to leave. Mom returns, though, to confront her son: "John — who is this woman you have pitchforked into the family?" Cut to a MCU left profile of her accusation as she glares downward towards her son OSL. In a highly charged visual, we see John rise out of his seat to enter Mrs. Whittaker's frame from below. Cut to a CU of John glaring directly at us and saying, "My wife, mother!" Now mom faces *us*. "But what do you know about her? Where does she come from? Who *is* she?"

John quickly deflates and is now suddenly seen as the same lily-livered milquetoast that actor Robin Irvine played in the previous film. In MS he drops into his chair, the frame showing his father sitting SR, son and mother SL. Dad gets up and harrumphs uselessly. Mom flicks him a withering, contemptuous glance. She turns back to her son: "If only I could remember where I've seen her face before … I'm certain she wants to conceal something from us!"

Shortly, we see a MS of the father serving Sarah and Larita some after dinner sherry. John crosses to the settee and hunkers down between the two women in his life. In a tight three-shot MCU he sulkily crosses his arms on his chest, little-boy like. Cut to a CU of mom and dad sharing conspiratorial, suspicious glances. Cut to a CU of Larita noticing, holding back a response, and then downing her drink in one gulp. Sisters in CU react in a humorous aside, instantly speculating on Larita's drinking habits. Suspicions lie heavy in the air as Larita excuses herself and heads upstairs.

Cut to the upstairs. Hitchcock shows us Larita's weary sadness from behind her for a nearly thirty-second static MD camera shot. She opens her bedroom door, shoulders slumped, walks towards her bed, and leans her head against the tall bedpost, defeated. The entire scene is shot theatrically through the archway of her door, until the maid, asked to leave, closes the door behind her in our face. Cut to a closer MS shot of Larita sitting on her bed, also nearly thirty seconds long, as she leans against the post again, the camera holding on her shallow breathing. Slow revelations from her past are sneaking up on her. Fade out.

Title: "During the days that follow, Mrs. Whittaker made Larita's life a burden to her — in private…. But she was all smiles and sweetness with her — in public."

Cut to bright long shots of polo ponies frolicking in a field. Everyone's now out at the track, playground of the rich. Cut to a MS of John and Colonel Whittaker facing SR pointing out towards the (unseen) horses in the field. Cut to a MS of Mrs. Whittaker and Larita looking off SL, presumably at the same scene.

Here is another typical Hitchcockian ploy in which we're fooled into believing nothing of import is happening, when in fact something is. In CU Larita suddenly clutches at her chest, in what we assume is fear over a horse falling or something. Cut to a MS of the crowd facing SL, between Larita's view and the polo field. Due to Hitchcock's matter-of-fact insertion of this same-sized MS as its two predecessors (John/Colonel Whittaker and Mrs. Whittaker/Larita), we wonder at most what might be making Larita jumpy over something so innocuous looking. However, trained as we are by Hitchcock to look for things of import in all shots, we quickly scan the scene, but see nothing to clue us in.

The next shot only begins to help, even though Hitchcock had actually just shown us exactly what had caused her fears, dead center frame in the earlier MS! Cut to an ECU of Larita staring hard and breathing heavily as she peers OSL from under her hat. Next shot takes us a second to realize it's an ECU of the same man who was sitting frame center in the MS of the crowd. Cut back to the ECU of Larita, hammering home her recognition of this man — the prosecutor from the trial (actor Ian Hunter)! MS shows Larita getting up and splitting fast, Mrs. Whittaker unaware of any of this (she's still staring OSL). Cut to a MS of the prosecutor getting up himself and heading OSL.

Cut to a MS of John and Dad, both SC, John staring OSL (after Larita, we infer), Dad staring SR towards the prosecutor, we assume (an old friend?). These inferences are automatic due to the camera's very clear directional focuses up to this point — the three MS scenes with the crowd looking left, Larita's and Mom's gazes left, etc. But Hitchcock has deceived us once more. As John hurries to meet "Larita" (OSL, ostensibly), the director's next shot reveals the person to be the *prosecutor*, not Larita, whom he greets! Our directional assumptions were deliberately thrown out of whack (precursor to *Vertigo*) with what turns out to have been a *reverse shot* of John and his father, taken from *behind and to the left*, not in front of them and to the right. Hitchcock had wanted us to think John was going to see Larita so that, when he meets up with the prosecutor instead, it's a shock to our system. It's especially surprising because this is the first time in the entire film that we even knew that the two men knew each other! (Another entire book could be written about Hitchcock's vertigo-inducing crowd scenes alone!)

We now see the prosecutor walking straight towards the camera, John's POV. Cut to a CU of them chatting in profile. MS allows Colonel Whittaker to enter the frame from behind and to the right, consistent with the actual directions we have been deceived into misreading.

So, where *did* Larita go? Cut to a MS of her staring towards SL, which after all of this directional subterfuge totally confuses us now. She turns around and slinks off SR. We may now correctly surmise that she did *not* want to meet up with the prosecutor.

We now see the trio of men in MS, the camera now slightly off to the left from its earlier two-shot profile position. They pass right past the stationary camera, inducing subliminal tension in us by suggesting they are moving after Larita, or at least in her direction. By now, Hitchcock's control of both the cinematic and real space is playing brilliantly upon our emotions. With the camera now behind them and slightly to their right, they arrive near the tree and outdoor chairs where Larita had just been standing. They look OSL.

Cut to a ML shot of Larita meeting up with Mrs. Whittaker SC, Larita having just entered the frame from OSR. This is a typically disorienting Hitchcockian crowd scene, though, so we have to look fast to spot them. On video and DVD, it is often necessary to rewind the film just to make out which characters are which, although I venture to say that the initial big screen audience had to work just as hard to keep up with the director's clever and quick directional changes, and with all his characters.

This shot of Mrs. Whittaker and Larita is also a reverse shot of their earlier one. Larita throws a glance back over her left shoulder, presumably at the men. Cut to the men back at the tree shaking hands all around. Prosecutor leaves OSL as John and Dad look around for their mates. Even with all of these directional changes, it's clear that the director's sense of continuity is impeccable. We are forced to work hard to keep up with his narrative line, all the while being encouraged to appreciate his self-concious cinematic technique.

MD shot of Larita and Mrs. Whittaker chatting, then deciding to leave with the crowd flowing behind them. They head off diagonal right in the screen towards the background of the frame. MD shots of various crowd members get into their respective cars.

Let's keep in mind that, by now, Larita has spotted the prosecutor but has managed to elude him. She feels safe — temporarily.

We see two cars coincidentally (ah, but there are no coincidences in a Hitchcock film) idle side by side (like the earlier horses), then see a CU of the prosecutor from behind the wheel of one car smiling OSL at what turns out to be a MCU of John at his steering wheel. We are just aware of a darkly shadowed back seat window SR behind him. Suddenly, Larita's brightly lit face pops into view in that window to see whom he is talking to. Quick two-second cut back to the CU of the prosecutor, immediately recognizing her. Cut to an ECU of Larita recognizing him, then a cut immediately back to the CU of the prosecutor, unnerved, as he puts his car into gear. Note the power of Hitchcock's alternating image sizes. Quick fade to black.

CU of a handwritten invitation: "Colonel and Mrs. Whittaker request the pleasure of Mr. and Mrs. Greene, Company at their dance at 'The Moat House' on 22nd June 1926. R.S.V.P." The film is fast becoming a quagmire of choking reeds in the moat of our drowning victim. Wonderful three-dimensional MD shot of Larita, with her ever-present cigarette and smoke, centered behind the older sister and Mom in the foreground as they work on the invitations. CU of Larita wryly smiling to herself. Either she knows she is soon to be exposed or she is valiantly trying to put on a good face, or both.

Shortly we see Larita hurrying to catch up to her husband outside as a car pulls up beside the house. In MS, out steps the prosecutor with his wife — Mr. and Mrs. Greene! Cut to a CU shot of Larita realizing she's about to be exposed, and we see her fingers reflexively curl around her throat in a stranglehold. Cut to an ECU of the prosecutor staring hard directly at us, black eye sockets accusingly burning a hole in the camera. Hitchcock quickly cuts to an ELS of the gathering party, though, deliberately delaying and preventing us from the intimate, privy knowledge of their first encounter since the trial — a meeting we had been willingly made to anticipate even more by the earlier shots at the polo field and in the two cars. Small talk and the meanderings of a group of partygoers further delay us for another frustrating twenty seconds. Finally Larita, the prosecutor, and our voyeuristic needs have that promised moment alone. With his use of alternating close-ups, long shots, reverse angles, and camera set-ups from a myriad of directions, this scene, as with so many of Hitchcock's others, carries a strong sense of three-dimensionality — and, hence, realism — with it.

We watch Larita and the prosecutor talking together briefly in medium profile, but no title is forthcoming. Hitchcock once again goes against convention by denying us information, and we see Larita gesture the prosecutor away towards SL. She then turns up the walk herself and heads OSR to leave the frame completely empty, Hitchcock leaving us with nothing but our own thoughts to fill the screen. A long shot reveals Larita walking up the path alongside the mansion away from the camera.

Cut to an inside-of-house MS, Larita entering the study. Soundtrack quiets as she drops herself onto a sofa in futile resignation. CU as she raises her head, lost in thought. Music springs alive as she sees something. (We know that soundtracks were created for this video and the DVD, but we cannot know how the original accompaniment was played in the 1927 movie theatres, of course.) We presume what she sees is in her mind, for her gaze seems to fix on something imaginary; but she looks startled, so we wonder what she can be thinking. Then, at first, we think she arrives at some bright idea, but the camera cuts to a medium shot of a box camera sitting on a bookshelf across the room aimed right at her, the very same camera we saw over the opening credits! Now we wonder if what she had been thinking about has miraculously materialized.

We next endure a painfully long, twenty-two second, immobile camera MD reaction shot of Larita. This extended shot causes several things to occur in our minds: 1) We feel Hitchcock's camera and this little box camera powerfully hold Larita in their voyeuristic grips; 2) All her feelings and thoughts are clearly revealed and framed dead-center, as if she cannot move away from or escape either camera's (and our) gaze; 3) We feel as if the box camera stands in for the camera of her mind, a private place where she will never again find any peace, it seems.

In addition, the way Hitchcock directs actress Isabel Jeans in this scene, with her knees pressed together but her skirt almost riding up above them, arms held stiffly by her side, hands clutching at the sofa pillows upon which she sits, and the camera filming her in an insistently invasive, full frontal shot, he makes us see her as the highly vulnerable, helpless subject she truly is at this moment. The shot is almost painful for us to watch, not only on Larita's behalf—after all, she's only a character in a film — but as a distanced audience member encroaching upon this woman's privacy for such an extended time.

The moment coalesces not only in her sudden springing to consciousness over this emotional intrusion (at our, the prosecutor's, and the director's hands), but also in our *own* self-consciousness as her simultaneous surrogate. From Day One in this director's oeuvre, he was the master of suspense, all right — but of *our* feelings, not his screen characters'. Seizing a book, she hurls it at the box camera, knocking it off its perch. Cut to an ECU of her heavily blackened eye sockets, their whites insanely aglow, as she stares panting and unnerved OSL at both the camera and her past. Fade to black.

Fade up on a MS of Larita brightly lit, asleep in a bed facing SR. Head lolling, she suddenly awakens and calls John to come to her. Why he's not sleeping in the same bed is a mystery to us, although certainly the prurient conventions of silent British films must have had something to do with it. (Remember, Mrs. Bunting had also been sleeping alone, without Mr. Bunting, in *The Lodger.*)

Shot from diagonally left in front of the bed, we first see not John but his shadow appear in MLS behind Larita on the wall as he enters the room, rushing to her side. Cut to a title: "I was dreaming—horrible dreams!" and then we see her gorgeously shot in left profile for five blissful seconds. Hitchcock denies us any lingering, though, and lightly brushes off her nightmare without any titled explanations. We next see Larita stretch out her arm towards John SR, and Hitchcock immediately cuts to a MCU of her reaching out directly towards *us*, yearning and pleading via title: "Wait, John — I'm miserable — this place is getting on my nerves."

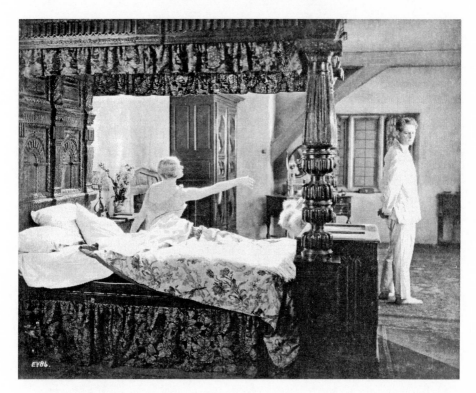

Easy Virtue, 1927: The apparently virtue-less Larita Filton (played by Isabel Jeans) plaintively appealing to her lily-livered second husband John Whittaker (played by Robin Irvine).

The next short montage is one of those incredible Hitchcockian pieces of assembled film that literally jumps off the screen to grab us, occurring as it does so hard upon the extremely poignant, five-second CU profile of Larita.

After the title, we are blessedly granted three more seconds of her desperate appeal directly at the camera/John/us, followed by a quick cut to a MS of her POV, John standing at the door at attention. He is powerfully and doubly framed by both the vertical lines of the door behind him and the borders of the gray walls further beyond that. The right footboard of the stark, black bedpost can be seen in the foreground. Cut to John's POV, a MS of Larita jumping out of bed and rushing towards us/John, and then Hitchcock cuts to an extraordinary MS from behind John's left shoulder back towards Larita, our identification with him suddenly complete in spite of ourselves.

Cut to a MCU of Larita and John facing each other in profile. Cut to the same shot in CU. Tenderly, with hands on each other's shoulders, she says via title: "Take me back to the South of France — we were happy there." (As Hitchcock always was, beginning with Levet and Patsy's honeymoon in nearby Italy in the director's first film, and culminating in his postcard paean to the region in *To Catch a Thief* nearly 30 years later.) "But Larita, why can't you be happy *here*?" Larita turns her head towards the camera (prepping us to pay attention), then back at John: "Because your family have hated me from the first — and they're teaching you to hate me!" More silent exposition is shown, but John will not — or more likely cannot — accept her entreaties.

Reverse angle shot from behind Larita's left shoulder as John turns to leave the room. This is another amazing image for, because Larita's back is now seen in strong shadow and John is filmed in blinding light, we "see"/imagine Larita's front to be similarly blinded. Cross hatches on the door behind John look like a jailer's cell. Cut to an ECU of Larita, thoroughly defeated, her left lip curling up into that wry smile of hers again, only more cynical now, forlorn. Fade to black.

Title: "So Larita remained — and suffered." Cut to a CU of a cigarette in a hand. We see Larita reading an oversized book outdoors. Cut to a MD shot, a large hedge in the center of the frame obscuring Larita on a chaise lounge SL from seeing John and Sarah strolling SR. Larita turns her head, however, to eavesdrop. CU of a two-shot of Sarah speaking to John: "John — you're neglecting Larita — and it's not fair to her." Cut to Larita, reacting. John's confession: "It's all been a terrible mistake ... Mother made me see that." Sarah smiles sympathetically, exultant. Larita frowns. Sarah: "If only you'd realized — before it was too late." A second divorce — let alone a first — would not do in polite society. Hitchcock condemns such hypocrisy, I believe, by showing Larita's all-too-knowing reaction as she gets up to exit SL. "If you only knew just how wrong this whole thing was," she seems to say by her body language.

The really sad part of this whole affair is that none of these people are intrinsically good or evil. The social conventions of the time are what are forcing them to be so pathetic. Hence, the film's title is truly reflective of the matter and Hitchcock's real subject, not these miserable, nondescript people. One might perhaps also conclude that the director is saying that social conventions *cause* people to become lazy, character-less, and indistinct — an interesting thought.

This is a good time to mention Hitchcock's singular and consistent perversion of the filmic conventions of "good vs. evil." We find out quickly and right from the beginning of his features that nothing and no one is *ever* all good or all bad.

Cut to a profile of the younger sister inside ogling and exclaiming over a newspaper article. We can and do guess at her discovery. Naturally we're wrong, for when she brings the paper to show Mom, all we see in CU is a picture of all of them at the polo field. Mom and sis appear to have a healthy and easy love for each other (the only such relationship in the film, actually), and it shines through clearly in this scene. Look for it quickly, though, as they smile and laugh naturally together. But ... boom! Mom stares long and hard thinking, "...photo ... photo...."

Her head jerks up, eyes bright and knowing, and in a CU straight into the camera she says: "I've got it! Larita — the Filton Divorce! I knew I'd seen her face before!" It's time for action, and Hitchcock cuts to a MS of Mom leaving, SL. Sis follows.

Cut to a MS in the study of Colonel Whittaker smoking a pipe, Larita reading on the divan. (I feel like we're in the board game "Clue," with Mr. Green in the kitchen with a rope.) In CU he gazes over at her, concern on his face. Cut to a CU of Larita, sad and pensive. He goes to her, sits, and places a hand on her hand.

Cut to a MS of sis and Mom, going through old magazines. Aha, found it. Mom straightens, proof in hand. Hitchcock milks the suspense leading up to the coming confrontation for all its worth. Cut to a long shot of Colonel Whittaker and Larita. The older sister enters from outside, stands behind them and asks, "Anything wrong?"

The moment of reckoning upon Larita, the younger sister runs into the study ahead of her mother and blurts out the truth directly into Larita's face in that childishly innocent and hurtful way youngsters have about them. Mrs. Whittaker has her best self-righteous sourpuss expression on. Leaning over Larita, she procures the damning piece of evidence. Melo-dramatically, Larita recoils in horror, jumping up and back. In ECU, straight into the camera, Mrs. Whittaker pronounces sentence. In a nearly exact precursor to Grace Kelly's starkly shot "trial" scene in *Dial M for Murder* twenty-eight years later, Larita is suddenly filmed in a mock mug-shot pose head on, light full upon her features and a blank gray wall behind her. We see alternate CU shots of Mrs. Whittaker ranting at us, no titles necessary, with Larita lifting her head with an air of defiance and dignity at us. It is all she has left. (Even this, we shall see, will soon be taken away.)

Cut to a CU of the Colonel, speechless as usual. (The fathers in all of Hitchcock's films are notoriously weak-willed.) Mrs. Whittaker says to the Colonel: "I knew this woman was concealing some vile secret!" Sympathet-ically, for we have just recently identified slightly with his concern for Larita, the Colonel's own light bulb goes on. We are next shown his only POV of the film, as the camera shoots Larita from *his* sitting position looking up along the left front side of her. Juxtaposed so soon against Mrs. Whittaker's accusatory stare, Larita now looks pathetic and so very sad — her true self — as seen through *his* eyes. After a brief internal debate, the Colonel comes to her defense, much as he defended John's decision to marry her earlier: "Larita's past life is no affair of ours." Good for you, Major. He may be ultimately ineffectual around the Missus, but his heart is in the right place.

Unfortunately, Larita, too, has been blinded by society's conventions, in a way that the Colonel has not. It is she herself who now proffers the damning photo to him, with the caption: "In the studio of Mr. Claude Robson, the brilliant young painter — Mrs. Aubrey Filton poses for her portrait." The Colonel mulls this one over as Larita walks away US. Cut to a CU of her standing in front of the mantle looking back at them all angry and hurt, near tears. She lights up a snurd.

Cut to an outdoors MS of John and Sarah. Sarah: "Something's happened, John — but whatever it is, you must stand by Larita!" John enters the study, camera behind his right shoulder again in this, at least the eighth angled shot of this room. He is handed the photo. Cut to an ECU of Larita watching John, alert. She has little hope for his support, and it shows on her knowing, expressive face. Cigarette goes to her mouth. Cut to a CU of John reading. As the truth begins to dawn on him, Hitchcock cuts back to the same ECU of Larita. She pulls the cigarette out of her mouth after a heavy intake of breath and smoke, and looks almost triumphant in prescient certainty of his response. Slowly, she lets her smoke out in a narrow and steady stream. Cut to a CU of John looking her way. Cut to his POV in MS, a look of sad relief mixed with an almost hopeless sense of longing lingering across her features. His accusatory how-could-you glare withers her heart, though, and he drops his head with tearful and pained anger. These are hard lessons for one as young and innocent (and naïve and rich) as he. For a long ten seconds we see him go from being crushed to lashing out at his older sister, then turning his head down again in shame.

Cut to a LS of all the characters, left to right: John, Sarah, the Colonel (centered), Mom, and Larita. Mom crosses to John to comfort him, a medium two-shot of her hand on his shoulder — both wearing mourning black — as she looks nastily over that shoulder towards Larita. Cut to a MS of Larita as she stumbles back into sitting on an arm of a high-backed chair in the corner by the mantle. She hurls her cigarette away, defiant to the end: "We married because we loved one another — no explanations were necessary on either side."

Cut to an ECU two-shot of Mom and John. Mom snaps: "Even if my son was content to receive no explanation, you owed one to me — to the family!" Another arbitrary convention exposed. John has lifted his head up now, mimicking his mother in both look and temperament. (Claude Rains' revelation at his own mother's feet in *Notorious* nineteen years later might easily spring to mind here.) He has become completely spineless and gutless by now. CU of Larita, that wry smile of hers creeping in again: "What happened before I met John affects no one but myself." One at a time, Noel Coward and Alfred Hitchcock are exposing the many flaws in the ironclad rules of so-called civil decorum.

Cut to Larita's POV now, a two-shot MCU of mother and son revealing *them* as the accused, a startling reversal of images from the earlier one of Larita. Mom seems to break the fourth wall by heading directly towards us, her image growing larger and more imposing with each step, until she finally veers just right of the camera. Title: "On the contrary, it will utterly disgrace us— it will make us the gossip of the entire countryside." The evil truth to society's hypocrisy is thus exposed — the terrible fear of gossip.

With steps and a doorway framing Mrs. Whittaker in MD profile, she confronts Larita with the dictum: "In our world we do not understand this code of easy virtue." CU of both women in confrontational profile, Larita facing SL, her accuser facing SR, exactly as in the trial at the beginning of the film. Larita retorts: "In your world you understand very little of anything, Mrs. Whittaker."

Relief arrives (even Hitchcock knew he was pushing our tolerance for preachiness to the breaking point by now) as the gardener enters the study, an ELS showing him carrying two absurd-looking lamps. Approaching Mrs. Whittaker, he asks which of the two he should use. Finally freed of her horrible secret, Larita laughingly chooses one for him with an authority that supersedes and embarrasses the other woman no end. Brilliant cut to the same scene shot from the outdoor patio in MLS, the gardener with his back to the camera and Larita's clever, laughing face seen between the frowning mother and the gardener. He turns and heads straight towards us led by the older sister, lamps in hand. They veer just right of the camera. The Colonel sends the younger sister outside, too, the four main protagonists left in the study. The room opens up in our mind as Hitchcock cuts to a reverse angle PAP, yet another view of this space, as it takes on the air of an outdoor setting and a stage, further relief and distancing imparted by the director.

The Colonel makes one last ditch attempt at an argument with his beloved sourpuss, then harrumphs and leaves. Larita shrugs it off. CU of Larita looking John's way reveals a palpable sense of relief and self-forgiveness on her part — she can finally stand tall in the truth that always wins out. None of Hitchcock's planted hats or shadows will block this lady's vision, and ours of her, again. With a daring and freed smile on her face, she now withers John's immature stare into the shamed boy he really is. Larita turns to go up the stairs: "Now that you have quite exhausted your venom, I shall go to my room." Mom, soured out but still a bit blanched, exclaims: "I hope you will have the decency to remain there until to-night's party is over." (Flash forward to a similar party scene in *Under Capricorn*.) CU of Larita mulling that one over, then laughing at the absurdness of it all, the sounds of more conventions popping in our ears.

Cut to another room, where the Colonel takes Larita by the arms: "It will all come right, Larita — if my boy still loves you." Larita tilts her head back as he speaks with her arms at her sides, eyes closed. She lets his words wash over her, unfazed. "But he doesn't — it's only his family that he loves!" Pushing the Colonel away, she ascends the stairs.

Cut to that evening's dinner party, the room more darkly lit and claustrophobically unpleasant than ever. Larita's empty chair starkly splits the space at the table between John and Sarah. Hitchcock shoots the whole scene like a morgue. John gets up, upset. "The only way to prevent an open scandal is for us to behave as if nothing unusual had happened," shrugs sourpuss. More unruly rules are dictated and reinforced by Mom, the keeper of convention.

Enter the musicians. Sarah decides to go upstairs to see Larita, but Mrs. Whittaker apprehends her on the lower landing. Shot in profile, Sarah stands one step above her as sourpuss exclaims: "Why should *you*, of all people, act as peacemaker between that woman and my son?" Kindly, Sarah responds: "Because I'm terribly sorry for both of them." Flash on Olivia de Havilland's character in *Gone with the Wind*. More guests are seen arriving as Mom turns and leaves SR. Sarah, shot sympathetically (not unlike one of those nuns in *The Sound of Music*), watches her go.

Upstairs in a two-shot CU, Larita entreats the maid to cut her gown in ever more revealing ways, undoubtedly intending a big surprise. Contrasted to the smarmy and rather cold introductions all around downstairs, we are suddenly privileged to an ECU of her plunging chest line, breast curve and exposed skin of her back, both arms visible. Titillation indeed.

Downstairs, a buxom and overweight guest exclaims, in the direction of Mrs. Whittaker, "I've been so looking forward to meeting your son's charming wife." In a scalding CU aside towards the camera, sourpuss spits: "Poor Larita is laid up with one of her severe headaches." (Another flash on *Under Capricorn*.) More Rubenesque guests arrive downstairs as Larita continues her preparations upstairs, smoking obstinately. Cut to a wonderful

LS taken from above head height of the guests milling below an empty, expectant staircase and banister, seen prominently in the upper half of the frame. This is shot from the same spot from where we first saw Mrs. Whittaker arrive onscreen a half hour ago, and hence is a set-up in our minds for Larita's approaching visual and metaphorical supplanting of the mother in this space.

CU of John slumping bummed out on a couch, older sister to his right. Shoving him, she makes her own sourpuss (but funny) face at the camera, mocking his expression. In a MS the musicians begin to play (violinist, oboist, pianist), and we see the guests begin dancing in the same earlier LS, stairway prominent US.

Larita's nearly ready upstairs and, boy, is she a knockout! All glittering in white and bedecked with a huge, feathered fan, bracelets and jewelry, she's showing a lot of skin. Cut to the dancing downstairs, then three old biddies jawing (oh, one of them is Mrs. Whittaker — I couldn't tell right away). "What a pity your daughter-in-law is missing this lovely party," says a biddy. (We will get to know quite a few of these kinds of women in *The Farmer's Wife*, two films hence.) CU of Mrs. Whittaker faking a laugh in profile right as she faces SR. Suddenly she turns her head towards USL with a rapid change of expression. That's our cue.

Cut to her POV, the first shot of its kind in the film that is nearing its end. We see Larita standing in MS at the top of the landing, left hand on the corner of the balustrade. She is radiant, and holds her huge fan in her right hand down by her side. Quick cut to a two-shot of a couple of guests — the prosecutor and his wife (Mr. and Mrs. Greene) — as they react with sharp intakes of breath. Cut to Larita's POV (the *exact same shot* as Mrs. Whittaker's first entrance) looking down on everyone as they look up at her. Cut to a CU of Larita looking at Mrs. Whittaker, then a quick reverse angle from sourpuss. Cat fight coming, folks.

High LS from above dancing guests shows Larita's descent to the first landing, then an ECU of her gazing Mom's way, expectant and defiant. Cut to Mrs. Whittaker fuming. Cut back to Larita, a slow smile playing upon her lips. "Gotcha," we can hear her say, though no title is necessary.

More walking downstairs, then a cut to a MS near the bottom where John is sitting, oblivious. Stopping, Larita tickles him with her fan, triumphant and smirking. John turns his head and, in what can only be interpreted as a shot that did not get edited out of the picture (a blooper!), he does a quick double-take guffaw completely out of character! It is quite funny and, in its own mistaken way, furthers the self-referential technique of this director.

Quickly back in character, John jumps up, astounded at Larita's audacity. We see Mom hurry over to them in a long shot taken from behind the left shoulder of a guest, granting us another wonderful sense of three-dimensionality to the room. Contributing to this rich feeling of depth and space, Larita's huge white fan dwarfs all comers, including Mom's rather limp one.

Cut to a CU profile confrontation, this time with Larita to the left, the power spot: "So your headache's better, my dear?" ECU of Larita, smilingly mocking: "Headache? I haven't had a headache." Mom visibly and amusingly deflates. Biddies gather round, gawking. John enters the frame SL. Cut to an ECU of Larita turning her head. Intimate two-shot leads us to expect something will happen now between them, but in the same manner with which John left Larita in her bedroom when they had a chance at reconciliation, Hitchcock refuses us any such act. Larita treats him similarly. *Touché.* She spies someone over John's shoulder and passes between him and the camera. Cut to a MS including Mom and biddies as she continues left past the camera.

Cut to a three-shot of Larita with the prosecutor (Greene) and his wife. He takes her hand. Cut to an ECU of just the two of them in profile, him kissing her hand. Larita quickly looks left, then right. Cut to an audacious reverse angle shot, an ECU of Larita *from behind* and a little above Greene's left shoulder (we can just see part of his head). Conspiratorially, she says: "I suppose it was you who set them spying into my past life? Surely you've harmed me enough already?" Cut to a reverse angle ECU over *her* left shoulder, just her hair visible. Greene: "I swear I've not said a word — it was bound to come out — you can't hide a thing like that." Back to his earlier shoulder shot, then cut to a MD angled shot from behind Greene's right side.

Mrs. Whittaker gets the musicians going again and Larita and Greene dance. She stops him and asks to step into another room, where they go to sit alone. She confesses: "I think marrying John was the most cowardly thing I ever did ... poor boy!" Good for the soul, Larita is finally on her way towards a healthier outlook on life and love, regardless of what will happen to her. Self-deprecatingly, she primps for Greene, exclaiming, "This is how his family always pictured me." They both laugh good-naturedly. Larita turns somber again. "It won't be difficult for John to get a divorce, will it — if I leave the suit undefended?" No titles follow as they continue conversing, Hitchcock letting that one hang in the air, too.

Cut upstairs to the maid packing Larita's things. Downstairs we see the dancing stop in a medium shot taken from a low angle looking obliquely up at the empty, looming staircase. John looks around. Greene goes to get Sarah, sending her out to the garden and Larita. "I'm going away to-night. John's family will be rid of me forever," Larita explains to her. Sarah protests, but sees that Larita is serious. CU shows Larita giving the lightest of permissive kisses to her, saying: "Sarah —*you* ought to have married John." Face to face, Larita hesitates— then turns abruptly and leaves. Quick blackout.

CU shot of a divorce bill: "Probate, Divorces and Admiralty Division: Undefended Divorce Causes, Whittaker v. Whittaker and Unknown." Dissolve to the same CU of the Justice's wigged head at the beginning of the film, rising up to stare/sneer at the camera. Same prosecutor in LS speaks, but this time no one's in the box.

Larita, all wrapped in black and wearing a black hat *not* covering her eyes, stands high above the proceedings looking down from the gallery, tears streaming down her face. No rabble this time, only one forlorn-looking gallery member leaning asleep against the banister. A reporter downstairs, bored, starts to snooze. Suddenly noticing Larita, he excuses himself as the prosecutor drones on and on. Running outside, he tells the other snoops, "...*the notorious Larita Filton!*" as the fourth estate prepares its ammo.

Larita exits the courthouse and then, in CU, accusingly decries straight into our eyes via title, "Shoot! There's nothing left to kill," while instinctively reaching for her throat.

Fade to black.

Six

The Ring

Produced late summer 1927, first screening September 30, 1927

Six of the eight film review compendiums critiqued *The Ring* with ratings ranging from a low of one star (HA) to a high of three stars (LM). Apparently there are quite a few versions out there of this film for, while three of the films reviewed run a short 73 minutes (HA, LM, MP), others report 82 (VH), 106 (VA), and 116 minutes respectively (HA), a 44-minute range!

Still, as wide apart as the ratings and lengths are, *Halliwell's* one star review found a way to praise the film by quoting from the *London Evening News*: "Succeeds in that very rare accomplishment of being the purest film art and a fine popular entertainment" (p. 704). *VideoHound* (two-and-a-half bones) said it was "interesting as a measure of the young director's developing authority" (p. 635), and London's *Time Out* gushed, "Arguably the finest of Hitchcock's silent films ... sees the young director completely confident in his control of the medium.... Impressive, too, is Hitchcock's keen eye for social detail, and his command of expressionist visual devices to suggest his characters' states of mind..." (p. 1014).

As this chapter will demonstrate, *Variety's* review most closely parallels my own perspective, and merits a complete reprinting:

> Hailed as the greatest British film yet produced, this picture merited unusual attention for many reasons. It was the first offer from Elstree after the studios were taken over and reorganized by British International Productions [*sic*; "Pictures"]. It was, at last, the performance of the long-deferred "promise" of Alfred Hitchcock.
>
> Carl Brisson is overshadowed by the acting of the heavy, Ian Hunter. He is a first-rate film actor with an engaging he-man personality and a strong flapper appeal.
>
> Gordon Harker, on the screen for the first time [well, second], nearly steals this one as a hard-boiled cynical trainer. His sense of screen com-

edy is acute and restrained at the same time and he makes his points with lips and eyes in a notable fashion.

Hitchcock gets more out of Lilian Hall-Davis than any Continental director and at times makes her reminiscent of Lya de Putti [1899–1931; Hungarian actress famous for her vamp roles in the early German cinema]. But the story gives her a rather unsympathetic and incredulous role and her sudden revulsion in favor of friend and husband is not too convincing [p. 721].

Bioscope (October 6, 1927), too, called it the "most magnificent British film ever made," outdoing even its own comments on *The Lodger* released earlier that year.

Over the credits we see an ELS down onto a brightly lit, freeze-framed boxing match, masses of onlookers visible around it in the partial darkness. As the credits reveal, this film is the first one written and directed by Hitchcock himself, although it was also cowritten by his soon-to-be wife Alma Reville.

The principals include "One Round" Jack Sander, who is played by our erstwhile, all too naïve and sympathetic hero, the Danish-born actor Carl Brisson (1893–1958). He will next appear in *The Manxman* as the even more naïve and sympathetic Pete Quilliam. The all-too-fickle Girl (sometimes referred to as Nelly) is played by Lilian Hall Davis (also spelled Lillian Hall-Davis; 1897–1933), who will also play the long suffering farmer's housekeeper Minta Dench in Hitchcock's next film, *The Farmer's Wife*. Ian Hunter (1900–1975), who had already played Archie in *Downhill* and the plaintiff's counsel prosecutor in *Easy Virtue*, here makes his third and final appearance in a Hitchcock film as the champion Bob Corby. The wonderfully facile Gordon Harker (1885–1967), as Jack's trainer, will next play the perfectly named Churdles Ash in *The Farmer's Wife* and Betty's father in the following *Champagne*. By now, Hitchcock's sixth directorial feature, it has become more than clear that the director enjoyed and repeatedly employed a large clutch of strong and dependable character actors, as Charles Barr correctly notes in his *English Hitchcock*: "One of the striking features of Hitchcock's early work is the continuity of casting. For each new film, he consistently retains at least one leading actor from the preceding film" (1999, p. 43).

The credits fade to black. Fade up on an ECU of a tom-tom beating a drum. Cut to a disorienting MS taken from below focused up at dozens of whirling bodies rapidly circling clockwise on a seat carousel, darkened figures swinging wide towards the corners of the frame as they foreground a bright sky. Quick fade out. Quick fade up on another disorienting shot, a right angle MS of numerous crescent-shaped fairground chair-swings rocking hypnotically left and right to different rhythms. Fade again to black.

Fade up on an ECU of a laughing/screaming woman's face (shades of *The Lodger* and *The 39 Steps*), ostensibly in one of these contraptions, a blurred background bobbing in and out of view. (The first time I watched this film on video I had just eaten an egg roll and was already wishing I hadn't.) Immediate dissolve to that woman's POV, the chairs' rails and fairground imagery whizzing by.

Fade out and in to a MCU of a barker in his booth promoting Fatty, a sideshow freak. Dissolve into an *extreme* ECU of the barker's mouth barking, each of his uneven lower teeth prominently displayed for our pleasure. Such in-our-face close-ups, as startling as the director's extremely extreme long shots are (among many others, one can think of Roddy's departure from his home in *Downhill*, Roger Thornhill's exit from the United Nations in *North by Northwest*, or the birds-eye view of Santa Rosa in *The Birds*), they force us to strain to recognize objects and people, and they are almost vulgar in not only their invasive proximity to a character's face and space but to *our* eyes, too. Such bald-faced audacity powerfully asserts Hitchcock's authority over a picture and his audience, at the same time as providing us with a startling, self-conscious awareness of his technique and our participatory viewership. In such a case as this barker's extreme ECU, we physically and mentally jump back in near revulsion.

Dissolve into an ECU from a slightly different angle of the same grotesque-looking mouth. Dissolve now to an ECU of a huge *painted* mouth on some kind of board, pipe-like "teeth" sticking out and up as they are being knocked "out." This is quickly recognized as a target in a gun booth, and may be the director's little joke at the expense of the barker: "Oh, how I'd like to knock this noisy guy's teeth out," we can almost hear ourselves say — or him ours! Quick fade to black.

Quick fade up on a MS of the painted mouth's *POV*, fairgoers' guns aimed right at us. With all of the preceding rapid cuts and ECU's, we can also feel as if that we are the barker being aimed at. Dissolve to a MCU of balls being gunned down off pilings. Quick dissolve to a low angle CU of a bell being struck by the hammer of a fairgoer. Cut to an unrecognizably dark shot (bad video print?). Cut to a LS of a black man as a clown in a top hat being tipped off a platform, then getting back up and resetting himself on a precarious perch. Cut to a MS of the crowd laughing at him, anxious to see him knocked down again. Cut to a CU of the clown, grinning. Cut to a MS of him falling again. Cut back to the crowd, thrilled and almost sadistic. Cut to a CU of a particularly ugly couple of semi-toothless bystanders grinning evilly. Cut to a CU of two boys pushing to the front of the crowd, preparing a couple of raw eggs to throw. Cut to a closer CU of the black man's face, swaying and grinning tauntingly. Cut to a CU of the boys, ready. Cut to a LS from above and behind the crowd of the clown being pelted with various items. With all of the close-ups forcing our identification with these inhumane thrill seekers, this quick LD shot suddenly makes us feel ashamed, as its distancing has placed *us* within the crowd.

Cut to a CU of the boys, letting fly. Cut to a CU of the clown, a direct hit in the face, sputtering egg. Cut to a LS of his POV, the crowd laughing at him/us. Cut to a CU of a cop in the front row, very ugly teeth protruding from his mouth, also laughing raucously. Quick cut to a LS of the clown's POV of the crowd. Cut back to the CU of the policeman still laughing, then sobering up and remembering his duty. Cut to the clown's LS POV again as the cop turns to chase the boys OSR, crowd derisively laughing at them now.

Finally — and we palpably feel some relief — Hitchcock cuts to a longer, seven-second change of tone, a MCU of two unidentified men centered onscreen. The shorter one — actor Harry Terry playing Ware, the traveling promoter — nods and directs the other's attention — Ian Hunter, playing Bob Corby — OSL. Cut to their gaze left, a MCU of the crowd with no one in particular standing out. Camera holds long enough (six seconds) for us to suppose they are looking at the profile of an attractive woman SL, but Hitchcock's framing of this part of the crowd does not highlight her more than anyone else. However, it's a fair bet that my 21st century eyes would not recognize the then famous actress Lilian Hall-Davis as quickly (if at all) as my 1927 brethren — if that woman were her. But, it turns out, she's not.

Cut back to the two-shot of the men, taller one (Corby) in thought still gazing SL, the shorter one (Ware) laughing at the clown. Withholding information from his audience to allow us to ponder upon the screen narratives and to be reeled in by his manipulative techniques has already become a major trademark of the director just three years into his films. Quick cut to a MLS from behind the crowd at shoulder level — once again, for no *apparent* reason. This shot, too, does not focus on any one person, but by now, because the screen has been so often charged with anticipation, quick changes, and vertiginous, audacious shots, we have been put on deliberate alert to search for whatever Hitchcock is up to — if not now, soon.

Quick cut to a CU of Corby's head and shoulders as he still stares at something OSL. Cut back to a MLS of the backs of the crowd members. Suddenly we see a ghostly-looking, superimposed female face in profile right come zooming in towards the camera! Cut to a CU of Corby's face looking down and speaking. Cut to a MS of the crowd with the two men now centered in the frame, moving OSL. Cut to a MS of the backs of the crowd somewhere else in the fairgrounds, the two men's backs now coming and moving past the left of the camera into view. Cut to a MS over the heads of the crowd of their *finally revealed* objects of attention (or so we think): a promoter (SR), a boxer (center), and a black trainer (SL), yapping on a riser. Cut to a MS of the trio from a 45-degree angle to their right as they stare OS and upwards left. Cut back to the same MS from behind and above the crowd's heads. Cut to a two-shot CU of Ware and Corby staring just to the left of the camera/us. Cut to a CU of a bored-looking, lovely shot of a woman chewing gum, ripe and ready. First title of the film appears over three minutes into the film: "The Girl ... Lilian Hall Davis."

Stop the presses! Rewind back to the first shot of these two men looking OSL. We have been deceived! (What else is new?) The MS of their POV of the crowd with an attractive girl SL was merely a decoy, a hidden plant. Close, and I mean close scrutiny of that MS reveals Lilian Hall Davis is *already* in that frame far away in the distant upper left corner, visible but nearly unrecognizable. In retrospect, we also realize that that tiny image of her correlates exactly with this attractive CU. Fast forward two shots ahead to the back of crowd shot that I'd remarked upon as perhaps proving important. What do you know, there she is in the middle distance and upper left corner of that frame, still hidden but now visibly closer in our view among all those bodies. Fast forward two more shots ahead. The superimposed face coming towards us begins at that image, and is hers! *Hitchcock has surreptitiously, subliminally and successfully transposed Corby's attentive focus on one person — not the trio of trainer, boxer, and barker, like we thought — through a disorienting crowd scene straight into our minds.*

Perpetuating this extraordinary deceit, the director had us believe these two men were more interested in the boxer's entourage, until Hitchcock *wanted us* to become aware of this lovely girl, who turns out to be a major protagonist in the picture. The 1927 British audience knew quite well who Lilian Hall Davis was, as she had already appeared in nearly 30 films, and I suspect that Hitchcock no doubt wanted our first view of her to be as surprising as possible. The tingling tension between being manipulated and being self-consciously aware of that manipulation is always quite singular with this director.

Fast forward to the earlier 45-degree angle right MS of the crowd. This second time around we can clearly see the two men pushing their way through the bodies from the back. Disorienting, dizzying, and difficult to distinguish individuals, one easily can recall similar crowd scenes in Hannay's escape through one in *The 39 Steps*, the umbrella scene (and our earlier introduction to the scientist) in *Foreign Correspondent*, as well as the ballet audience running from the house fire in *Torn Curtain*, among others.

Cut back to a CU of the Girl staring OSL at something. We can almost feel the camera as a character now standing neutrally off to one side, inauspicious yet primed for movement. Cut to not quite her POV, a CU of Corby's head and shoulders focused back just right of camera. Hitchcock withholds some of his trademark direct camera-to-us facings early on in this film, I believe, in order to parallel the natural pace of his characters' burgeoning relationships — not quite straight on, not quite developed yet.

Cut to a LS from above and behind the crowd — we feel this as a brief respite and release — of the barker taunting a particular audience member to fight the boxer. Cut to a MS of that person from above and to his right as he's pressed by his buddies to take up the challenge. Boys from the earlier clown scene are visible in the lower right corner of the screen.

Cut to a MLS over the heads of the crowd at the Girl behind her booth — she's the ticket taker — a wholly new angle. She isn't even given a name in this film (although some books credit her as "Nelly"), so Hitchcock wants us to suppose that she represents all girls, much as the lodger could have been anyone, even us. We suddenly see a young man exit a tent flap behind and to her right who begins flirting with her, taken from the same 45-degree angle used earlier. She opens a piece of gum and pops it in his smiling mouth with a familiar flair.

Cut to an ELS of the same scene, the images of the girl and boy extremely small in the upper left corner of frame, the boxer's entourage in the upper right, and the crowd below them. Cut back to a MS of the now convinced young audience member, challenged to fight. Cut to a MS of a couple of crowd members buying a ticket from the bored looking Girl as she stares out from within her booth with that air of "What's-new-out-there-in-the-world, Show-me" attitude, as her "boyfriend" stares ignorantly at her.

Cut back to a lovingly rendered CU of the Girl, who shyly but lasciviously peeks out from beneath hooded eyes towards Corby in the crowd. She makes eye contact. Cut to a CU (not quite as close as the earlier one, from the chest up) of Corby, contact acknowledged, a sly, hopeful smile creeping in on his features as he catches his breath. Cut to a new and startling 45-degree angle from behind the crowd, a MS over their heads with the crowd's foregrounded bodies covering the bottom half of the frame. The girl and boy are seen in USL and the barker USR as he gestures for the challenger to come up.

Why, there's Gordon Harker, the wonderful Hitchcockian character actor who we will get to know very well in the next film, *The Farmer's Wife*, and again in *Champagne*. When did he arrive onscreen? Rewind. Oh, when the two men bought their tickets and entered the tent. Harker had then walked out of the tent picking his nose. As with our first close view of Hall Davis, Hitchcock loved to introduce his characters on the sly with our attentions focused elsewhere — in this case, on the Girl, to where our identification had been deliberately shifted. Cut to a MS of the platform, Harker as the boxer's trainer SL, the boxer C, and the barker R. Title: "'One-round' Jack … Carl Brisson"— our "hero." Cut back to the same shot, Harker with a stogey in mouth as he picks up a huge clapboard with the words "One Round Jack" on it upside down. It's a funny shot.

Cut to a LS of the crowd from the front, milling about. Cut to the earlier three-shot again, barker patting Jack on his back, Harker playing with his snurd. Cut to a CU looking down on an uncertain couple in front debating with themselves whether they want to see him fight. Cut back to the three-shot, Harker now picking his teeth with a pinky. Cut to the two-shot, woman looking pretty dubious. Cut to a MLS from head height *within* the crowd of the earlier young sucker already being helped out of the tent, woozy. Cut to a CU of him wiping blood off his nose and swaying a bit. Cut to a two-shot of the original dubious couple, man recoiling behind his woman (men so often remain milque-toasts in Hitchcock's oeuvre).

Cut to a new angle MS at head height and taken from 90-degrees left of the first victim, showing him being helped along through the crowd. It's hard to see him the way it's filmed, and this is no doubt deliberate — he's already being forgotten, Hitchcock wants us to think. The director's crowd scenes continue to be disorienting and troubling, visual stumbling blocks to information, and we must work hard to stay with the characters he wishes us to identify with, for he knows that our efforts towards that goal will only intensify our identifications. Put another way, such deliberately encouraged efforts ensure that all of our attention is focused on his machinations/manipulations.

Cut to a three-shot CU of an imposing Jack flanked by his seconds. We now realize that 'One-Round' Jack is the "boy" who had been out flirting with the Girl immediately prior to the couple entering the tent earlier. And if we're to believe in the real-time seeming flow of the action on the screen, that earlier bout must have happened incredibly fast — say, about the length of time one round might have taken! *The Ring* was Carl Brisson's introduction to British film audiences (he had made one film in his native Denmark), and so the 1927 British audience might not have noticed who he was— like us— until Hitchcock showed them a title saying so.

Cut to a MS of the crowd truly amazed and completely taken in by Jack's skills. Cut back to a three-shot, barker pounding home the marvelous scam. Brisson and Harker couldn't look more bored, the latter having finally found the piece of corn in his teeth (or whatever he was searching for) and holding it up to look over. Cut to a CU of the Girl, also used to the scam, turning to eyeball the tall man who will take her away from all of this (she hopes). Finally, our sense of filmic convention is fully engaged as we subliminally understand and accept the romantic triangular struggles about to begin. (Perhaps we flash on the similar triangle of Joe, Daisy, and the lodger from *The Lodger.*) Cut to a CU of Corby's head and shoulders taken from just to his left this time, about fifteen degrees to the left of his earlier CU.

Change of expectation or, perhaps, deferral. CU of the Girl has her nodding towards the tent, then miming fisticuffs. She is using her sex appeal to try to draw Corby in, we sadly note. Cut to the same CU of Corby shaking his head "No, thanks" and smiling. Cut to a LS of the crowd from the front. Oh, there he is, shaking his head. With each successive film, we see that Hitchcock is learning

The Ring, 1927: Jack's curmudgeonly trainer (played by the inestimable character actor Gordon Harker) and the Showman barker (played by Harry Terry) defiantly promote "One Round" Jack Sander (played by Carl Brisson) to any and all takers.

better and better when he feels he needs to stay in a CU and when he is certain our attention is fully focused so he can jump back to long shots. These early silent films are wonderful lessons at searching for and seeing everything in his frames.

Cut to a new angle, a ninety-degree left MS of the Girl in profile right looking OSR, Harker, Brisson and barker above and to her left behind her. Why does Hitchcock suddenly cut to such a unique perspective and distance? Just for a new view, right? Wrong. It's another set-up (of us). As the Girl stares in medium shot OSR, we're startled to see Corby suddenly enter the frame from OSR and tip his hat. Rewind. Nothing in the previous shot even remotely suggested that Corby would be making a move in her direction. In fact, the last time we saw him he was almost lost in a LS sea of faces in the crowd. Wait. Think a second. OK, the crowd scene was a static set-up to lull us into not being ready for the Girl's profile scene. Therefore, with Corby's sudden entry into her MS frame, Hitchcock knew that it would create a greater impact than if we were tipped off, not set up!

Cut to a similar angle CU, this time perhaps 10-degrees from the right of them in a two-shot profile, Corby flirting and the Girl chewing gum and trying to tease him into the tent again. He shakes his head "No" again and then they both turn to react to something OSR. Cut to their POV, a MCU at their eye level looking up from waist height at the three men on the platform above them. The barker is still boisterously barking and all three men's heads are cut off at the top of the frame. This may be my print of the film, or Hitchcock's intention — it's hard to say. Cut back to a CU of Corby and the Girl. He nods back over his shoulder, then we see a title appear: "A friend of yours?" Corby asks about Jack. Cut back to the two-shot, the Girl thinking. Title comes up before we see her speak: "A *very* great friend." This is a highly ambiguous comment and typical of the director visually, but now with dialogue.

Cut to a MCU of the barker importuning another would-be sucker in the crowd, a tall sailor shot from above the crowd's heads and behind them. Due to the camera's close positioning to him, the barker looks like he's barking down at *us*, his face at the upper edge of the frame. Cut to an autonomous camera angle MCU of the sailor, dubious. A strongish man behind him pushes forward and the sailor realized he might miss his chance, so he hurriedly volunteers. Cut back to the MCU of the barker barking. Cut to his POV, a CU now of the sailor — a handsome lad — being sucked in. Cut to a MS of the barker from behind and above the backs of the crowd's heads as he ducks under a railing into the sailor's (and our) line of sight. Cut to a MS of the sailor in the crowd.

Suddenly, a matronly woman wearing dead foxes (Larita from *Easy*

Virtue twenty years on?) around her neck hustles her elderly husband to the fore volunteering him. Cut to a LS of the crowd from behind filling up two-thirds of the screen, Jack moving to the left of the stage US. Cut to a two-shot MCU of Jack looking OSL, the barker patting him on the back. Cut to a CU from the mid-torso up of Jack smiling and then looking troubled, still focused OSL. Cut to a MCU of his POV from above the back of Corby's head and hat, the Girl chatting away with him. Cut back to a CU of Jack. He looks to be in his early twenties and the tall man in his mid-thirties, so it's easy to imagine him feeling threatened by this seemingly more sophisticated and wiser older man — another Hitchcockian play on conventions. We see Jack in a MCU call out to her. Cut back to his same MCU POV as Corby turns around, both looking his way and smiling, lost in conversation.

Cut to *their* POV in MCU, Jack challenging Corby to fisticuffs. Cut to Jack's POV, a surprising medium shot — not the same earlier MCU of his view, which we were expecting — but one that now includes onlookers and his trainer SR. It feels like a long shot in comparison to the CU's we've just seen, and the startling jump to such a MS once again demonstrates not only Hitchcock's supreme confidence and control of the medium but his willingness to reveal — and encouragement in us to acknowledge — his technical audacity. What's particularly intriguing about Hitchcock films from an objective perspective is that we have to constantly adjust *our* viewing skills if we are to fully appreciate — or even see — all of the director's extraordinary montages.

Cut back to their MCU POV of Jack engaging the crowd to his left now and pointing Corby out to them. Cut back to his earlier POV MS, which now gives us the illusion of being *closer* than the earlier one because our attention is more involved. Hitchcock has just applied the Kuleshov experiment with people (the same expression of an actor's face juxtaposed with different scenes) to a screen image (two same-sized compositions):

> *This is actually the purest expression of a cinematic idea. Pudovkin dealt with this, as you know. In one of his books on the art of montage, he describes an experiment by his teacher, Kuleshov. You see a close-up of the Russian actor Ivan Mosjoukine. This is immediately followed by a shot of a dead baby. Back to Mosjoukine again and you read compassion on his face. Then you take away the dead baby and you show a plate of soup, and now, when you go back to Mosjoukine, he looks hungry. Yet, in both cases, they used the same shot of the actor; his face was exactly the same.*
>
>   *In the same way, let's take a close-up of [James] Stewart looking out of the window at a little dog that's being lowered in a basket. Back to Stewart, who has a kindly smile. But if in the place of the little dog you show a half-naked girl exercising in front of her open window, and you go back to a*

smiling Stewart again, this time he's seen as a dirty old man! [AH, in FT, 1985, pp. 214, 216]

The crowd is gaining in force and numbers now, for fairground gypsies know only too well how to control its masses. Cut back to a MCU of Jack, taunting and triumphant in his element. Cut to an ECU of a right profile of the Girl, fuming for a moment and breathing heavily, her eyes moving from Jack to Corby and back. This shot is highly charged as we're privy to just her thoughts. Conventional wisdom makes us reach out in our hearts to support her defiance over such chauvinistic bravura on the part of Corby, but then we see her change her tune (against our manipulated wishes) and smile evilly, relishing the coming confrontation. Our sympathy towards her falters a bit — also as intended.

Cut to a two-shot CU of the Girl and Corby as she proffers an open hand towards Jack as an invitation. Cut (release) to a fresh MLS from above and behind the crowd, Corby L, trainer C, Jack above R — an artistically staged, symmetrically arranged composition. Cut back to the two-shot CU of both the Girl and Corby smiling. She says: "He doesn't think he can stay a round, Jack!" That gets Corby's goat, coming from her, and his face darkens a moment. Taking a coin out of his pocket, he smiles, then plunges in. Cut to a slightly closer MLS of the two of them from behind the crowd. Jack is out of the picture just OSR. Corby gestures to his promoter Ware to join him as they lead the entire crowd into the tent.

Cut to a 90-degree left MCU of the girl quickly selling tickets, masses of bodies entering the tent. Cut to an ECU of the tickets themselves spinning off a spool in fast motion, which dissolves into the spool seen half empty. Cut to a 45-degree right MCU of the last stragglers getting their tickets. Girl turns to an open flap of the tent behind her. Cut to her POV, the tent flaps in CU framing an ELS of the ring in the distance, small figures punching at each other just visible behind the dark heads of the crowd. Cut to the *ring's* POV, a CU of *the Girl*, framed by the tent flaps, staring directly at us. Cut to a LS from inside the tent of the deeply shadowed dark backs of the audience covering four-fifths of the screen, a smoke-filled top fifth revealing the barely visible fighters. Cut to a MLS of about one-half the ring and the fighters visible, the crowd all around them.

Cut to a CU of a hand ringing a bell. Cut back to the MLS of the ring, Jack sitting down in a far left corner. Oh, that was a preliminary bout with other fighters, we realize, not our boys'— another directorial fake-out. Harker is seen foreground right gesturing to the earlier sailor and then taking his coat. Hitchcock always gives us a wealth of details. The sailor enters the ring and sits down in a corner LSR. Cut to a MS of Corby sitting in the audience, he and everyone else in the dark. He looks about doubtfully as Ware smokes a cigar to his right. Cut to a CU from behind and to the left of the trainer from outside the ring, the sailor clumsily rising to his feet behind him with his boxing gloves awkwardly raised. He shuffles OSL as we see Harker open the sailor's coat just before the sailor stumbles backwards into the frame again, knocked back with just one blow offscreen that we didn't need to see. (It's a clever shot.) Pulling his gloves off, Harker helps him back on with his coat. Cut to a CU of the same scene, the sailor having difficulty walking. Harker steers him out of the ring by pushing him OSL. Cut to a ninety-degree right CU of Harker SR looking bored, sailor in the background staggering back into his chair.

Cut to the ring's POV again, a CU of the sailor shaking his jaw and the crowd first laughing at him, then solemn. Cut to a CU of a row of would-be fighters, 90-degrees left, peering around. Cut to their POV, a CU of the exit sign. Cut back to their worried expressions. Cut to a MS of Jack sitting comfortably in his corner, the referee calling for the "next" victim. Cut to a CU frontal shot of the middle-aged husband of the fox-wearing wife thinking it all over while gazing directly into our eyes. He opens his own eyes wide as Hitchcock cuts to a CU of a mean-looking Jack staring back at us. Hitchcock then superimposes first one, then two, then three, four and five ghostly faces around Jack's face, all mean-looking pugs staring back at us/the husband. Cut to a 45-degree left CU of the by now thoroughly frightened man. Cut to a MS of the row of "fighters," man's wife suddenly by his side urging him on, ripping his hat off, and gesturing him into the ring. Hitchcockian details are all so sharply etched in these shots, and they come fast and furious.

Cut to a MLS from behind and above the crowd — a now popular angle — as the man steps into the ring and trips. Everyone laughs at him and the referee gives him a mock three-count. Cut back to a MS of the line of "wanna-be's," our hapless sailor centered in the frame. Back to the referee's mock count. Cut to a CU frontal shot of the sailor, still in real pain and holding his jaw, as the crowd laughs uproariously at this new victim in the ring. Hitchcock is really tweaking *our* complicity now over everyone's tendency to laugh sadistically at other people's misfortunes, particularly *this* now forgotten "clown" in the ring. It's a powerfully effective montage.

Cut to a disorienting new angle 90-degree right shot from behind the crowd, a MLS with the referee R and Harker with his back to us L. The middle-aged man staggers up and heads out of ring L as quickly as he can, never even bothering to fight, he's so embarrassed and scared. Cut to a

MS of the line of front row would-be fighters. Last man in line has had it, too, and he gets up and hurries out of the tent OSL.

Cut back to a CU of the referee: "Next gent, please," waving at the crowd to cease and desist. He points OSL. Cut to his POV, a MS of Corby centered in the crowd. He gets up, also fed up (for other reasons), and steps over the rope into the ring. Cut to a MLS as he strides towards Harker's corner L. As he turns around, Hitchcock cuts to a MCU of him now facing the camera and peering past it. Cut to an extraordinary shot from his POV, an ELS of the dark figures of the crowd in the foreground and the Girl watching through the tent flaps far away in the UR corner of the screen. Quick cut to a CU of her looking back at us, curious and hopeful.

Cut to a two-shot of Corby L and trainer C. Always concerned with filling the screen with bits of interest, Hitchcock populates his backgrounds and foregrounds with people and objects— here we see a crowd of enthralled onlookers pressing in outside the ring around Corby and the trainer. In the same shot we see Corby meticulously fold his overcoat up, much to the bemused if still relatively unfazed curmudgeon Harker, then hand him his hat. Corby dons his fighting gloves with an apparently skillful eye. Harker trucks off US with his back to camera. Sudden cut to a full-faced CU of Harker, a private, startled expression dancing upon his features, as he looks out just past the left of the camera, transfixed and talking to himself.

Next cut is all the more confusing because, rather than providing us with a satisfying disclosure of Harker's POV, we are shown a MCU of a bored and reclining Jack in his corner (deferring our gratification), unwittingly waiting for the next comer. Hitchcock is now educating us as viewers to carry more than one thought or narrative line in our heads at once. Finally looking into the opposite corner, he spies Corby and smiles. Cut to a medium two-shot of Corby and Harker in the other corner. Harker is now carefully hanging Corby's coat up, unlike the previous comers. Obviously he has recognized something different in this fighter, and the attentive viewer, even if not knowing why, has been partly taken into Hitchcock's confidence. This is a very satisfying moment for us, knowing (or, at least, hoping) what we think will happen at the expense of Harker and Jack. Almost reading our minds, Corby glances backwards and smiles a knowing smile at us!

Cut to an ECU of the tattered-looking "Round 1" sign being slid into a post. Quick cut to a CU of a bell being rung. Cut to a 90-degree right two-shot MCU as Corby heads OSL, Harker SR. Once more we're fooled, for Harker immediately grabs the coat and takes it off the hanger, old habits dying hard, in preparation for suiting up Corby. Quick cut to a CU of the back of Harker's head (from *inside* the ring) as he turns around, his knowing smile turning instantly into a surprised expression. Cut to his POV, a medium two-shot of Jack and Corby exchanging blows, Corby more than holding his own.* Cut to a reaction shot from that same 90-degree right angle, a profile left shot of Harker with his mouth hanging limp. He begins to viscerally react to the fight, and we want Hitchcock to cut back to that fight, but he holds off our desires by staying on Harker a tension-filled six seconds. Our identification with the trainer's palpable reactions to the proceedings, *all imagined in our mind's eye*, is transformed into our own impatience with Hitchcock! It's a wonderful feeling.

The next montage is another example of cinema at its finest, as the director demonstrates his exceptional technical skill at presenting rapid-fire changes of perspective and points of view.

Hitchcock finally cuts back to a two-shot MCU, other trainers in the background, as the boxers clutch in a wrestling hold. Cut to a two-shot, 90-degree left CU from behind Jack, Corby's face grimacing and working hard. He quickly glances directly at us. Cut to a full-frontal CU of the Girl staring wide-eyed back at us again. Cut to the same two-shot CU, a wild, winning look in Corby's eyes as he begins to get the upper hand. Cut to a quick one-second, full-frontal CU of the Girl as she turns to call OSL past her tent-framed face. Brilliantly, Hitchcock cuts to a one-second shot of a 90-degree right angle CU of the Girl from *outside the tent* as she gestures towards OSR. The director then quickly cuts to a two-second LS of the barker turning to look from behind the crowd. Another quick cut to a three-second LS of the Girl from *in front of the barker*, then a cut to a CU of him walking past and away from the camera towards her with his back to us. This last shot is awe-inspiring because, in watching him walk away in motion already as he comes from behind and just to the side of the camera/us, we almost feel as if the girl was gesturing towards *us in a crowd of which we are a part*. In other words, it feels as if the barker was being called to come towards the girl out of *our* audience, with us as Hitchcock's crowd on the screen! It's an extraordinary sleight of cinematic identification transference.

Cut to a three-second, two-shot profile CU of the girl telling the barker about the fight inside the tent. He mouths, "What?" Cut to an ECU of the worn "Round 1" sign being replaced with a spanking new "Round 2" card. Wonderfully pleasurable pressure is propelling us along in this section of the film. Cut back to the two-shot of the Girl and the barker, both flustered. He rushes into the tent as the Girl goes back to her peek-a-boo flap. Cut to a LS from inside the tent of the flap as the barker walks

---

*According to Hitchcock, Brisson was actually a trained boxer, while Hunter really got socked a number of times. See SGI, 1995, pp. 41–42.

from behind R of the camera towards the ring. Cut to a full-frontal CU of the barker cheering his man on, stupefied. He looks around L. Cut to his MS POV of some empty seats. Cut to a disorienting CU of his back as he moves away from the camera and out through the tent flap in the background. Cut to the outside again, a two-shot CU as he reaches the Girl and urges her to sell more tickets. Cut to a MLS of him barking at the crowd from behind and above them: "One-round Jack's met his man at last! Roll up and see the fight of your lives!" Cut to a MD reaction shot of the crowd, not particularly fired up, just staring at the camera (another joke at the barker's expense?), both the carousel and swings of the fairground swaying in the background in ELS. Cut back to the barker going after them harder. Reaction shot again. Now some of them are laughing, while others still just stare. It's becoming a bit unnerving, actually. "Why don't they react as we do?" we wonder.

Cut to a 90-degree right angle MS of the Girl selling tickets to a now convinced crowd as it moves into the tent. Maybe Hitchcock was trying to tell us how difficult it is to initiate control over the masses, but once sparked, they move of one mind. Cut to an ECU of tickets being unwound at super speed on the spool. Cut to a longish, six-second shot CU of the Girl turning back to look into the flap. We watch the back of someone's head straining to see the fight through the crowd as *we palpably strain to look with her*. We know from earlier shots that her view is smoke-laden and distant, yet Hitchcock toys with our sense of anxiousness over the proceedings by painfully extending this shot at our expense. *In many ways, there is no better and more unique feeling of pleasure with an artwork than having one's sensibilities* willingly *being manipulated at the same time* knowing *one is being manipulated at the same time being shown very clearly* how *one is being manipulated*. This is the education of an audience in viewing film, I think, that Hitchcock truly believes in.

> Hitchcock's lifelong concern for manipulating audiences is well documented, and part of what makes him such a characteristically "modern" filmmaker is his awareness of how this manipulation is accomplished [inside] a film via cinematic structure and style…. [W]e must also add a recognition of Hitchcock's sincere desire to educate his audience…. [I]t is the filmmaker's responsibility to cultivate audiences capable of noticing and appreciating subtleties [SG1, 1995, pp. xvi–xvii].

Cut to a maddeningly interminable twenty seconds of the Girl's view, only the backs of heads and smoke visible. Twenty seconds! The audacity! We have not seen a shot last longer than *six seconds* throughout the entire film up until this point! Hitchcock unmercifully puts off any possibility of fulfillment in our minds for as long as possible and … we love

it! All heads are straining now to see the fight, including ours. Finally —
finally— Hitchcock cuts to a *MLS* (a CU is not necessary, because we're so
caught up in the film by now) of the referee counting someone out, but
the crowd and the smoke still hide two-thirds of the action in the ring. If
we look carefully we can just make out a "Round 4" card visible in the
background. Someone *mercifully* sits down in the foreground of the frame,
that same person we always wait for to sit down in any theater we may be
in during the applause because we cannot see past him.

Finally —*finally*— Hitchcock gives us a glimpse of the fight, still in a
MLS, though, and it's Corby who is still standing. Immediate cut to a 90-
degree R MS of Jack's seconds helping drag Jack off the floor. Still in MS,
Corby heads back towards the camera, where a stunned Harker helps him
off with his gloves. Corby waits to have Harker help him on with his coat
but the trainer ignores him, moving towards Jack's corner. Corby humorously slides the coat hanger into the back of Harker's pants and puts on
his own coat. Cut to a MCU of the back of Harker still moving towards
Jack's corner. Cut to a MS of the barker bull-shitting the crowd as he digs
into his wallet and own pocket to find Corby's prize money. Cut to a two-
shot CU of Corby receiving his reward and heading OSL, the barker
humorously bowing phonily towards the camera, thanking us for coming.

Cut to a CU of Harker's back leaning over Jack. He feels the coat
hanger in the back of his pants and flings it angrily (humorously, for us)
away. Moving aside, we see Jack, stupefied. He stares OSL. Cut to a MCU
left profile of his POV, Corby sitting in the crowd and laughing over his
earnings with his cigar-chomping buddy. Corby leans forward and looks
back past Ware SL. Cut to his POV, a CU of the disheartened Girl, head
downturned. Even though she helped set this fight up, our sympathy suddenly goes out to her.

Cut to a disorienting MLS of Corby's head peering around the cigar
and Ware SL, Jack USR still very much shaken. Corby gets up and heads
towards the camera as Ware heads towards Jack. Cut to a MS as Ware
enters the frame and taps Jack with a cane. We are expecting to see a confrontation between Corby and the Girl, so Hitchcock shows us this instead.
Cut to a full-frontal CU of Ware talking to us. Cut back to a M shot of
Jack and his trainers, angry. Cut to a CU of Ware turning away and heading US, stopping twice to glance back at Jack and the camera.

Cut to a three-shot MCU outside the tent, left to right: Girl, Corby
and Ware, chatting it up. We're dying for a title by now and Hitchcock
knows it. What have they been saying to each other? Cut to a three-shot
CU, L to R, Ware, Corby and Girl, with the Girl admonishing them both.
Finally, via title, Ware says: "We heard he was good and now we know!"

Breaking with convention as it suits his purposes, Hitchcock uses titles only at the sparest of times, not when *we* think they're necessary. Both the Girl and us realize now that Corby and Ware have scammed Jack, not the other way around, and the Girl berates them further: "We were hoping to get married, and now you've probably lost him his job!" All is never as it appears and now, while we thoroughly enjoyed seeing the cocksure Jack get his comeuppance, Hitchcock takes the wind out of our sails a bit for, having identified somewhat all along with the Girl (as convention has it, the "Charming Girl Heroine"), we feel for her even more.

Ware writes something on the back of a card. Cut to a CU: "Don't fix any other job until I have seen you tonight." A hand flips the card over: "James Ware" in big letters above "Bob Corby," in smaller ones. Cut to an extremely flattering ECU of the Girl reacting to this news as she looks at Corby and mouths, "That's you?" Beneath our consciousness we realize that Hitchcock did not allow our newly forming sympathies for the Girl and Jack to last very long, for we suddenly gain some insight into this now fickle, fair-weather girl. She is being seduced by Corby's power and prestige and to hell with her upcoming marriage, we will soon find out. Cut to a CU of Corby nodding "Yes." Cut to a three-shot MCU as Corby and Ware head OSL, Girl all attentive and flirty now. As with our wanting to believe in Jill's complete goodness at the beginning of *The Pleasure Garden*, Hitchcock will not allow the Girl or us to feel anything absolute — positive or negative — about any of his characters, including ourselves.

Cut to the Girl's POV, a MS of their backs departing into the crowd. Corby stops to turn around a moment. Cut to a CU of the Girl, lust rising. Cut back to Corby and Ware getting swallowed up by the crowd, a long ten-second shot. Dissolve into the same shot at night for a full twelve seconds, masses of bodies in motion. Dissolve to the same shot even later that night, just three seconds long, everybody having gone home. Cut to a LS of people taking apart tents.

Cut to the inside corner of the tent with a MS of Jack foregrounded R dabbing at a shiner in the mirror, the Girl, Harker and barker in far background L at a table. Cut to a CU of Jack's POV, a reflection of himself in the mirror with the Girl coming towards him in the far left background. A burning candle is artfully positioned between himself and the mirror. Both the real and reflected images in the same frame have a kind of formally symmetrical unity to them, in that they literally mirror each other. Before cutting, we see the Girl arrive on his R (our L) in the reflection. Cut to a two-shot CU, not in the reflection this time, of the Girl on L, Jack on R. Because the previous shot had her to his actual R, this shot should show her actually on his L, but it doesn't. Hence, the artificial construct of this shot should be disorienting but it's not, because it looks just like the earlier mirror image! It's a very clever construction, this brief montage. Frankly, in this case I think Hitchcock set up these two shots against each other to see how closely we're paying attention; just a little game of his, while still part of his education of our viewing skills. It's also a further directorial experiment done with mirrors that began in *Downhill* with Archie and Julia's smoking scene.

At any rate, she asks to see his eye, our sympathies returning to these two lovebirds as Hitchcock cuts to a CU of her gentle attentions. "Ah, so she *does* love him," we think, as our identification with her continues to seesaw. He shrugs his shiner off as unimportant, smiling, but she pushes him back down in the chair to take a closer look. Cut to an almost exact same CU, this time taken at his sitting eye level. She makes a hot compress and lovingly washes his cut out for him. Cut to a closer two-shot of just his head SR and her upper torso and head SL as she washes his entire face, a loving intimacy passing between them and across the screen into our hearts. As she strokes his hair, he tries to kiss her moving hand; he looks serenely playful, she serious. It's a deeply touching moment, another in a long series of occasionally poignant, loving shots that Spoto rarely acknowledged and Brill wrote a whole book about. It recalls Mrs. Edgar's loving comments to her daughter Marnie at the end of that film ("I've always loved you, Marnie. You're the only thing I've ever loved"), Devlin and Alicia's intimate kisses in close-up in *Notorious*, or the first shot we see of Hattie, just her hands, lovingly encircling Flusky's neck during her barefoot entrance at the dinner party in *Under Capricorn*. These and many other tender scenes reflect a truly sensitive, life-affirming attitude in our director.

Back to the film: Cut to a quick, two-second, LD two-shot of Jack's POV past her R shoulder, Corby and Ware entering the tent SL, their dark coats melding into the deeply shadowed background of the tent. Cut back to the two-shot CU of the lovers as Jack just stares OSR. Girl turns, continuing to wash his face without seeing what he sees. Then she starts to smile. Cut to an extraordinary 90-degree R MD two-shot of them SR, the mirror centered in the foreground of the frame. Corby and Ware enter SL, symmetrically balancing the frame, as the Girl fixes up her skirt. Cut to a CU of her bringing a hand to her face, acting surprised and pulling out Ware's card. Apparently she had forgotten to mention this to Jack — a harbinger of her self-centered, greedy attitude towards life that, we will shortly find out, she will never overcome. Our sympathies unconsciously begin to swing away from her again.

In direct contrast to our pivoting loyalties, Hitchcock now holds

on a lovingly rendered, fourteen-second two-shot CU of the Girl — the
director's CU's of women right from the beginning of his career were
almost always extremely flattering, and given extra lighting for just that
effect — as she uses the card to give Jack the introductions. She mouths,
"This is Ware" and "this" (she gasps a little here, still in awe) "is Corby."
Cut back to a medium four-shot as she nervously finishes. Cut to a com-
positionally fascinating three-and-a-half shot from behind Corby's R
shoulder at the Girl's eye level (she is us/the camera now), Jack's face
looking at Corby, Ware's bowler hat just visible over Corby's shoulder.
The Girl hands Jack the card. Cut to a CU of Jack's face looking down. Cut
to a CU of the card. He turns it over to read its back. Cut to a CU of
Jack looking up, asking a question. No title. Another good example of
Hitchcock withholding information to encourage his audience to suppose
what might be said. This directorial decision, as with so many others
already discussed, keeps us *in the action*, and is a strategy Hitchcock will
similarly use later in the sound films by withholding dialogue during his
particularly long silent passages, or by using deceptive, misleading dialogue.

Cut back to the earlier MD four-shot, Ware now visible and explaining something. Jack suddenly turns to look US. Cut to their POV, Harker
telling a joke to three fairground workers in MCU. Cut back to the four-
shot, Jack nodding in their direction and Ware agreeing. Ware grabs the
earlier candle to re-light his cigar, and Jack moves OSL as the Girl looks
thoughtful. Lots to speculate on without titles in this short scene, but in
retrospect, even though we may have wanted titles to follow the action,
they are not necessary, really.

Cut to a CU of Jack's back moving away from the camera, his head
above the frame. Cut to a right-angle two-shot CU of the Girl L and Corby
R, Girl watching him look OSR at Jack's receding figure. He turns back to
meet her eyes (note the similarity to his turning back to gaze at her in the
earlier fairground scene, after he won the fight), moves a little closer, and
they seriously flirt for a twenty-five second count, all alone.

Whammo: a brilliant cut to a MS of the three fairground workers
staring accusingly right at the camera. Hitchcock's earlier cut to our view
of them, so innocuous at the time, now proves itself to be another clever
plant to set up this shot. It is wonderfully effective, because we as audience members had just become completely implicated in our enjoyment
of this privileged, voyeuristic scene of the two illicit lovers playing with
each other, and now, we literally feel the embarrassment of being found
out by others spying on them (us). This sudden, two-second shot — so
hard upon the lingering twenty-five second one we were permitted to

indulge in — gives us the fleeting feeling of being a little ashamed with our-selves— quite deliberately, I believe.

Cut back to the two-shot of the couple as they stare OSL in the direc-tion Ware and Jack had gone. This shot confirms that the previous one was meant for just for us and the two-shot we watched could not have been the fairground workers' view. We had been caught by Hitchcock's camera as voyeurs, and the three workers had stood in for that camera!

Corby nods behind himself OSR for the two of them to find a more private spot (perhaps from us?). Disorienting, audacious and boldly cre-ative, Hitchcock now cuts to a slightly out-of-focus two-shot from behind the Girl, her back filling fully half of the screen and just a part of Corby's dark form visible at the edge of SL. The previous shot had them looking OSL, so we now assume (wrongly, we will shortly find out) that they are still staring that way, this shot taken from 90-degrees R of its predecessor (we have been subliminally "trained" to expect this kind of 90-degree R shot over the last twenty minutes of the movie, if the reader will recall). As they make their way away from the camera and into focus in a LS, we see that they are actually exiting in the direction *Jack* had taken off towards earlier. The Girl's peek-a-boo tent flap, a guidepost for our view, is visi-ble SL. Therefore, Hitchcock's cut was from 90-degrees *left*, not right, in relation to the previous shot, and the girl and Corby had *turned* 180-degrees around between shots (or Hitchcock had repositioned them).

Hitchcock's joy at filmmaking always seems to be his pleasure alone first and foremost as he seeks always-new solutions— at our expense and for our benefit — to the camera challenges and the presentation of numer-ous character perspectives in his films. His montages and frame compo-sitions are so dense and intricately constructed that we feel compelled to go back again and again to see how he did it. Which is how it should be, shouldn't it, because aren't the best gifts we give away always the ones we most want for ourselves?

> [W]e must also recognize ... another of Hitchcock's key motives...: his irrepressible delight in his work. Unlike the classic magician, Hitchcock, the modern magician, always shows his wand.... [His films embody a] meticulous attention to special effects, camera angles, lighting, and set design, and also his underlying assumption that cinematic art is unimag-inable without cinematic craft. And one senses that the audience's plea-sure is intimately related to that of the filmmaker... [SG1, 1995, p. xviii].

And, in Hitchcock's own words:

> *For those who want it I don't think films should be looked at once. I think they go by too fast. But the critics sit in there at their 10:30 A.M. sitting, and*

they see a film through once and that seems to be sufficient. But I don't really think it is. Most films should be seen through more than once [AH, 1963; in SG2, 2003, p. 50].

Cut to a medium two-shot from outside the tent as they emerge, the Girl chilly and rubbing her arms. Cut to their LS POV as they look out, a very dark shot (remember, it's nighttime now, and it looks like Hitchcock actually shot this scene at night) of what looks like a trailer with a light on (Jack and Jill's home?). Cut to a dark two-shot CU, Corby thinking something over, the Girl and he then deciding to head off (where?). Cut to a medium two-shot as they move OSL. Cut to a LD dark shot of the trailer as we barely make them out moving towards it from behind them. Ah, the limitations of video and DVD created 75 years on.

Cut to a medium shot as they arrive alongside what looks like a heavy-set woman sitting and smoking on the trailer's step. She gets up and moves into the trailer. Cut to a MS inside the trailer as we see the woman cross R to L. Cut to a CU, still quite dark, of the back of the woman looking out a window. Cut to a 90-degree right angle MCU of her brightly lit face staring out at us. Cut to her POV, a two-shot CU of Corby and the Girl in the dark. He speaks as he pulls something out of a pocket: "A present for you from the money I won." He opens it as she happily mouths "For me?" Cut to a CU of his brightly lit hands holding an exotic, serpent-headed bracelet. Because of his coat's black sleeves and the nighttime, his hands, the bracelet and its box emit a disembodied, charged quality across the screen (it's reminiscent of the self-conscious spotlight shot on Jill's handbag from *The Pleasure Garden*). Cut back to the two-shot, the Girl enthralled with her present.

Startling cut to a slightly better lit, over-the-right-shoulder, one-second CU of the woman inside the trailer, turning around quickly with anger on her face. Before we can even attempt a guess at why she's so upset — it doesn't really matter *what* she's angry over because just the simple but sudden one-second CU of this stranger after the languorous two-shot CU's of the Girl and Corby is enough to jar our sensibilities — Hitchcock cuts to her POV, an ECU of a boiling and no doubt noisy teakettle bubbling over. Wonderfully manipulative cut to a release/withhold 90-degree right MS of the inside of the trailer as she moves to turn the stove off. It's a release because the shot looks utterly tranquil — quite in contrast to her apparent anger — and it's a withhold because we are not viewing Corby and the Girl anymore, either through this woman's eyes or through an AC shot that Hitchcock could afford us. Hence, the director is now forcing us to imagine what *might* be happening between the couple outside in much the same way that he withholds his titles, leaving us to guess. Once again, we in the film audience are turning out to be his most important characters, as he controls our sentiments at least as well as he does his screen actors. (The woman's angry face could even be our angry face, too, over this narrative disruption.)

More sustained release/withholds are presented as our now deferred gratifications begin to build up as tensions and expectations. Cut to a medium high shot of Ware and Jack pacing about in the dark somewhere else, talking shop. "Oh, that was where Ware was, with Jack!" we realize. No wonder Jack took off. Another bit of information belatedly shared.

Cut back to the M shot in the trailer, the woman finished with her teapot and now able to go back to the window. Cut to a CU of her face peering out of a different one. Cut to her POV, a CU of Ware and Jack — on the other side of the trailer, apparently — in profile facing each other, blackness all around them except some light reflected off both men's faces and Jack's light-colored sweater. So, the first shot of Ware and Jack was not just an informative one reminding us of their whereabouts, but also a set up for this woman to see them, too.

Ware speaks: "...and if you win this trial fight you can be Bob's sparring partner." Finally, we are given an important enough detail to warrant a title, and partially satisfy any of our reasonable guesses about earlier conversations. It is all that is necessary. Here, Hitchcock had sustained our interest in this montage by awarding us an occasional but rarely complete confirmation of our expectations. Also, rather than just showing the couples Jack/Ware and Corby/Girl separately, Hitchcock has created and increased tension out of nothing except having them spied on (and us spying on all five) by this unknown woman surreptitiously mediating between both couples in her trailer. It's really quite a remarkable, and efficient, arrangement.

Cut back to the two-shot of Jack and Ware in profile, Jack smiling and going to shake on it. Cut to a CU of them shaking hands, Jack adding his other hand for emphasis. *Brilliant dissolve into a CU parallel shot* of Corby's hand sliding the serpent-headed bracelet onto the Girl's wrist and beginning to move it up her arm, the upper part of which is OSL. The shot is artfully stunning in its simplicity and singularity. These two "hand-related" shots are powerfully felt by us for another reason: they represent the film's only dissolve of its kind, the content of which involves a business transaction connected to a sexually seductive allusion. Hitchcock will pursue the use of hand imagery with a vengeance throughout his fiftieth film *Torn Curtain*, in much the same way that he will fixate on feet and legs in both *Strangers on a Train* and *Marnie* (see my book "Hitchcock's Worst Films (And Why They're So Good!)" for a detailed description of those scenes in first film).

Cut to a MCU of the Girl pensively caressing the bracelet, now up around her bicep. Cut to a two-shot CU from their torsos up of Corby leaning in, the Girl brooding their situation over. Cut to a ten-second dark ECU (this whole scene is noirish in its intensity) of the Girl looking out at us, a Mona Lisa smile — should I, or shouldn't I — turning brighter as she turns towards Corby. Cut to a long, sixteen-second two-shot CU as she spontaneously gives him a quick but intimate kiss on the lips, then immediately pulls back with that breathless combination of shyness and excitement all of us have over doing something forbidden. Corby is now leaning in dangerously close to her, his face all but invisible in the dark beneath his ever-present, wide-brimmed hat (shades of *Easy Virtue*). He roughly pulls her close in a deep embrace, her right hand opening out against him in half-hearted but overwhelmed protest. Cut to a closer CU, only their heads partly visible in the dark, what little light available reflecting off of the Girl's arm around his neck, the bracelet brightly ringing her bicep. Cut to a quick two-second ECU of Corby's hat and collar, the Girl's thumb just visible in the lower left corner of the screen. Cut to a MCU as they finish the clinch, a gorgeously shot twenty seconds of rich afterglow as the Girl pulls away just enough to realize what she has done. She is breathing heavily. Somewhat aghast for a moment, she brings a hand to her mouth in awe as she stares directly into our eyes, thinking of Jack. Then she looks to Corby for the next move. He's ecstatic.

He looks OSL a second. Cut to his POV, a LS of Jack and Ware, Jack looking around the tent for his Jill. Cut to a medium two-shot as Corby and the Girl straighten themselves up and then head OSL. Cut to a LD two-shot from 90-degrees left as they walk towards the camera in the near darkness, the Girl's left hand covering the bracelet up around her right bicep. Cut to a LS reverse angle of Jack and Ware as the couple's backs move away from the camera towards them, their figures obliterating Jack's image — yet another extraordinary shot that could have been treated simply but isn't. The whole film, in spite of the romantic triangular entanglements multiplying in our minds, is turning out to be an extended and extraordinary experiment of varying audience manipulations and sympathies.

Cut to a medium four-shot of the two couples. Cut to a MCU three-shot as Jack embraces the Girl with his good news, Corby US splitting them. Cut to an ECU of the girl's hand still covering her brightly lit bracelet as she unobtrusively slides it down her arm and hides it at her wrist. Cut to an almost pitch black four-shot, then a CU of Corby, still mostly in darkness, his eyes down-turned towards the Girl's surreptitious actions. Cut to his POV, a CU of the girl's hands hiding the brightly lit bracelet from

Jack. Cut back to a CU of Corby, who suddenly smiles. Cut to a CU, including her hands on her bracelet, of the well-lit girl as Corby's disembodied hand reaches from OSR to congratulate her (yet another stunning, artfully composed shot). She smiles, looks down at the proffered handshake, and then calls his bluff by mouthing, "Thanks." Cut to a CU profile of Jack watching, smiling to himself and thinking she didn't shake Corby's hand because it was too intimate an act. Hitchcock has fully involved us in this *ménage*.

Cut to a dark M three-shot as Corby tips his hat instead and moves OSL. Jack holds the Girl's arms briefly and follows Corby OSL. Quick cut to a CU of the Girl as she stares at us, then fondles her bracelet while looking OSL. Cut to her POV, a LS of the trailer front door facing us. Cut back to a CU of the Girl suddenly smiling and running OSL. Cut to a LS as she runs from SR to L and up into the trailer. Cut to a cross-section MS inside of the trailer as the Girl messes up a deck of soothsayer cards. Aha, so *that's* who that heavy-set woman in the trailer was—a gypsy fortuneteller! Cut to a two-shot CU of these same movements.

Cut to a full-frontal CU of the gypsy woman smoking a pipe and leering OSR at the Girl. Cut back to a two-shot CU as the Girl shuffles the deck again, then hands them back. Cut to a CU of the Girl looking down from under intense brows, transfixed. Cut to a CU of the cards being laid out in a circle, some in the center. Cut to an ECU of the King of Diamonds being turned over and placed in the center. Cut back to a CU of the gypsy woman tapping a finger on the King for emphasis. Cut to a CU of her sneering: "…a tall rich man!" Cut to her turning her head to look further OSR. Cut to her POV, a CU of a dark, closed window curtain, the same window from which she had eavesdropped on the Girl and Corby. Cut back to the gypsy in CU facing the Girl. Cut to a full-frontal CU of the Girl staring at us with her bright open expression and mouthing, "Really? Tell me more, more." Cut to an ECU of a finger tapping on the King of Hearts. Cut to a MCU of the Girl as she unconsciously clutches her bracelet and turns to look OSR.

Cut to a one-second shot of a CU of dark shoes walking upstairs towards the camera. This is yet another stunning shot in its audacity and singularity. (We will see a similar and longer-lasting CU shot of shoes in *The Farmer's Wife*, an entire theft scene via legs in *Champagne*, and an entire study of legs-as-characters in *Marnie*—another book worth writing?). Cut back to a CU of the Girl, thoughtful. She looks OSL. Cut to her POV, a MS of a small mirror on the wall and a LS reflection of Jack in it. Two typically creative and unique ways the director uses to introduce a character.

Cut to a CU of Jack standing in the doorway. Cut to his POV, a MLS of the Girl sitting on the edge of the gypsy's table looking back at us. Cut to a CU of the gypsy, leering and heavy-lidded. Cut to a first-of-its-kind (in this film) *panning* CU of her gaze as it travels searchingly from the Girl's face down her chest and across her arms to settle on the hidden bracelet. *The choice of using a relatively slow panning shot in CU after all the previous quick cuts gives this shot a kind of lascivious, violational quality.* Cut to a CU of the gypsy secretly smiling to herself. Cut to a three-shot MCU as Jack enters the frame from SR to kiss the Girl on her forehead, the gypsy looking on while the Girl continues to hide her gift. Cut to a two-shot CU of Jack holding the Girl from behind. Cut to a CU of his hand picking up the King of Diamonds. Cut to a two-shot CU as he speaks: "That's me. Diamonds—I'm going to make real money now." Hitchcock is able to get as much tension as possible out of his films precisely because he provides his audience with complicit knowledge about various characters at various times. Because we know and Jack doesn't of Corby and the Girl's secret—even the gypsy now knows—tremendous suspense is generated onscreen through *our reflected projections*. (Need it be said that we think Jack is merely the Jack of Fools or the Joker at this point, and not the King of Diamonds?)

Cut to a two-shot CU, Jack smiling from over the Girl's shoulder, she darting a quick glance towards the gypsy on his comment. She mouths towards Jack an abrupt "Why?" Cut to an ECU of the back of Ware's card in his hand with the note on it. Cut to a two-shot CU with the Girl eyeing the gypsy OSL, this time with Jack watching, a dawning awareness appearing on his face of something between them. Cut to a CU of the gypsy staring up at the two of them, then shaking her head "No." Cut to an ECU of the King of Hearts. Cut to a CU of Jack and the Girl smiling, both of them and us understanding different things about what and whom that card symbolically represents. Cut to a CU of the gypsy, a dark shadow falling over her. Cut to a second ECU of another ravishing yet voyeuristic pan for both the gypsy and us from the Girl's head down and across her chest to the covered bracelet, Jack's hand on the girl's arm just above it—this shot feels even more penetrating than the earlier ones. Cut back to a dark look of foreboding crossing the gypsy's face. Cut back to the ECU of the pan, the gypsy's POV, continuing down from the covered bracelet to the Girl's hand in which she holds the King of Diamonds. She gently rubs it with her thumb as Hitchcock fades to black.

Fade up on a long shot of the countryside, a pastoral scene of the trailer SR in a clearing, Jack kneeling and shaving at a pond's edge SL. It is such a typical LS by Hitchcock that one must strain to make him out.

The Girl walks from the trailer door towards Jack, now out of sight OSL. Cut to a two-second, CU profile of the Girl pausing and looking OSL (apparently still at Jack). Cut to a reverse angle M two-shot, the Girl in the foreground now walking away from the camera towards Jack in the background, both of their backs facing us. She kneels to pick up a small stone. As she throws it into the pond from close behind him, Hitchcock cuts to a CU of its rippling effect upon Jack's reflection in the water. As the ripples ebb, a remarkably clear two-shot appears of the happy couple in reflection, smiling at each other. They kiss.

Immediate cut to a one-second ECU of the bracelet slipping off her arm, followed by another quick, one-second cut of a CU of it splashing into the water. Cut back to a two-second CU of their reflection, now marred by a more disturbing ripple. Hitchcock's control over seemingly arbitrary, innocuous events and details, juxtaposed as they are with each other and laden with different meanings, is masterly.

Cut to a twelve-second two-shot CU of the couple kneeling SR —*not* in reflection this time — as Jack rolls up his sleeve to retrieve the object, a worried look flashing on the Girl's face. After looking it over he asks her what it is. She downplays its significance by lying: "He bought the bangle because he didn't like taking the money he won." He chews on that awhile as she digs the hole a little deeper: "…So it was really you who gave it to me." Knowing what a naive sap he is, she isn't surprised that he falls for this flimsy excuse (the actor Carl Brisson will shortly play an even more naïve fool in *The Manxman*), but is surprised when he gets serious and takes her hand — the other one, her left — and tenderly slides the bracelet around her ring finger, saying "then I gave it to you for this…." Cut to a CU of her hand and his with the bracelet treated like a large ring — it's an absurd and almost vulgar image, for some reason. Cut back to a two-shot CU as she caresses it in the same way she always has since Corby gave it to her, so that this caress feels like a doubly disloyal and deceptive act for both her and us. Cut to a closer two-shot CU as they move closer together. Cut to an ECU of both faces coming together for a warm kiss. Another uneasy feeling wells up in us, for she and we know she is a two-timer. (The 1920's audience might have felt this much more strongly than our jaded 21st century audiences.) Cut back to a MCU of the end of the kiss, a sense of betrayal still hovering over her lips.

A comment on a comparison of the two kisses, the one with Corby and the other one here. The former was much more lustful, eliciting deep breaths, while the Girl kissing Jack seems more appropriate and sincere, in spite of the sense of cheating we feel. These differences subtly register in our thoughts.

He speaks: "If I win the trial fight, we'll get married the day after."

Cut to a CU of the Girl facing OSR nodding a thankful "Yes," then staring halfway between SR and the camera with a faraway look in her eye.
Her problems *seem* temporarily over. Cut to an ECU as she slides the
bracelet back over her right arm, sealing her lie to both of them.

Cut to a temporal title description: "The day of Jack's fight." Cut to
a MS of the troubled looking Girl back at the fairgrounds outside the tent
selling tickets to customers. Trainer Harker emerges from the tent picking at an ear and asks: "Heard 'ow Jack's got on yet?" Harker hangs around
the Girl still picking at the ear with a pinky. The Girl sighs deeply and
responds: "He said he'd send me a wire." Cut back to a medium two-shot.
Harker now picks his nose, wipes it on his shirt, and heads back into the
tent. Cut to a CU of the Girl profile R, worried and looking around for
news. Cut to one of Hitchcock's beautifully charged ECU's of the girl, eyes
widening as her imagination takes off. As she starts to breathe hard, we
see a superimposition over her features of Jack being wiped down (like she
had done for him earlier, actually) in a corner of a ring, dissolving into a
M two-shot of Jack and another fighter punching away, dissolving into a
CU of the other fighter going down, dissolving into the arm of the referee
counting him out. Hitchcock is showing her *willing* Jack to win. The superimposition fades out as we continue staring at the Girl, her chest rising and
falling with emotion. Cut to a MCU of her in profile R, lost in her hopes.

Cut to a MS of what looks like a young messenger entering a crowd,
his back to the camera. Cut to a CU of the girl spotting him, reacting. Cut
back to the crowd and the boy's back. Cut to a full frontal of a young boy's
face scanning the crowd (he is the messenger, but once again Hitchcock
introduces a character in a unique way, withholding showing us his face
until now). We're not sure if he's looking for someone or at the ride before
him, another typical directorial ambiguity thrown in. Cut back to the Girl
calling out to him. Cut to a MLS of the boy moving OSR through the
crowd. Cut to a MLS as he approaches the Girl on the *far left of the screen*,
crowd to the right, tent flap center. So, once again, after several singularly
angled shots, we realize that while the Girl had established eye contact with
the messenger, Hitchcock did not show us that POV but rather an AC shot
of the boy's back taken from 90-degrees L of the Girl's position. This,
therefore, would have been the *boy's* earlier position POV prior to his
arrival onscreen! Hitchcock's uniquely personal, self-referential style of
directing and creating montages refuses to follow conventional camera
movements with simplistic shortcuts—for example, of the boy and Girl
simply finding each other from a neutral camera angle. What this particular sequence has done is two-fold: it gives us a greater respect and awareness of the three-dimensional space of this fairground—a singular piece

of Hitchcockian thoughtfulness—and it allows us to more clearly experience the actual difficulty that a messenger might have looking for someone in a crowd. One may recall Hitchcock's own comments on the difficulty of really killing someone, perfectly embodied in the gruesome murder of Gromek in *Torn Curtain*; or, in a lighter vein, but no less problematic, the challenges of moving through crowds, as in Sarah and Michael's struggles during the ballet scene in the same film.

Cut to a CU of the Girl as the boy moves OSR, his task—and Hitchcock's for him—completed. She impatiently tears open the wire. Cut to a CU of it: "Have won. Shall see you at church tomorrow morning as arranged. Jack." Fade to black. Fade up on a long shot of the empty fairground shot from twenty feet or more high above. Fade to black.

Fade up on a long shot of the inside of a church from the back as the guests arrive. It's time to burst religion's bubble. Siamese twins hobble down the aisle arguing and pointing towards opposite pews—shades of *Saboteur*! Cut to a MLS as a freakishly tall man and a midget enter the screen side by side from behind left of the camera. They decide to sit in a pew SL. The twins are seen still arguing but then decide to sit in a pew SR, as we note the giant on SL completely blocking an average-height man's sights behind him. Cut to a MS of a priest entering from OSR and reacting with horror as he looks around at everything OSL and OSR. Perhaps he's really commenting on *our* sensibilities as he stares out at the movie theater audience.

Cut to an extraordinary reverse angle LS of the Girl on the arm of an over-dressed man (he turns out to be the barker) as they walk directly towards the camera after just entering the church. Their presence pierces its way through the previous LD objective shots until they arrive before us in CU. Because this shot from the *front* of the church is immediately juxtaposed with the previous humorous scene from behind, we get an eerie feeling foreboding as the Girl peers around, nervousness and uncertainty visible beneath those hooded eyes of hers. In contrast, with his oversized suit, corsage, moustache, and goofy grin, the barker stares happily about, the designated best man in this sideshow.

The next shot is stunning: *Without a cut* from this CU, the camera *dollies* slowly backwards as the couple begins to half-step it down the aisle—it looks like a staged walk so it seems like they're covering more ground, marching to the Wedding March. But the extraordinary thing is that the camera keeps them in a CU, so as they come forward towards the receding camera (shades of Roddy and Tim's approach toward their headmaster in *Downhill*), the pew members coming into view on both sides of the frame look like they're *moving backwards*. The shot is really an early *horizontal* experiment with vertigo that culminated in the now famous *vertical* shot (a zoom forward while tracking backwards) looking down the winding stairs in *Vertigo*. This is the first appearance of a dolly shot in this film, too (unlike, say, its frequent use in *Downhill*), and so its use here in the church is both startling and self-referential. The whole scene takes an indulgent and satisfying twenty-four seconds.

Cut to a reverse angle LS of the priest taken from the altar moving up the aisle to meet them, then escorting them to the front row R. Cut to a CU as they sit, best man and others excitedly looking about. Cut to a CU of the priest looking severe, staid, and aghast at this freak show in *his* church — Hitchcock's comment on the hypocrisy of religion, certainly. Cut back to a medium two-shot of the Girl sitting calmly next to the goofy looking barker, everyone else chattering up a storm. Cut back to the priest, snooty chin held high above the proceedings. Cut to a LS from the back of the church as two figures hurriedly walk away from the camera to the front row on the other side. Their movements are so quick that, while we can (and do) assume it is Jack and Harker (the next shot shows Harker's face, but only the other figure's back), Hitchcock challenges us to distinguish who is who in the shot, particularly in contrast to the extra care and time given to the Girl's entrance. In fact, its juxtaposition feels both jarring and disorienting, which is also no doubt deliberate.

Cut to a CU of Harker's profile left from behind him as he talks across the aisle to someone OSL. Cut to a medium two-shot, profiles of another priest and the first one, the second complaining about the noisy and strange wedding guests and the first brushing him off. They both head back OSR from where the original hypocrite came on. Cut to a medium shot of the hypocrite entering the church proper from the rectory and crossing the frame's foreground to exit OSL, followed by the high priest. Cut to a CU of the stern priest in LS clapping his hands together for attention. Half the congregation rises while the other half — the naïve fairground folk — remain seated and begin clapping, too, thinking they're supposed to. The priest, furious, mimes what he really requires— sitting to rising — disdain and horror written all over his face. Cut to a MS of the left side of the congregation (from the priest's perspective), Harker in the foreground, the long aisle and outdoors discernable in the background SR. Harker goes to sit again but gets up hurriedly, mistaken. Ostensibly a comment on these fairground folks' inability to follow directions, Hitchcock is really critiquing the absurdity of the rituals of organized religion.

Cut to a MS from behind the congregation as they all face the altar. The hypocrite priest gestures the wedding couple and their seconds to come forward. Harker mistakenly takes his place beside Jack — we still *assume* this is Jack, even though Hitchcock has yet to show us his face in the scene. It looks like him from behind, but ... we can't be sure. (If we had a thought about it on first viewing, we might wonder why we have been withheld this information, too. As with all of Hitchcock's pre-planned shots, we will shortly find out.) The Girl moves Harker brusquely aside and replaces him with herself. The priest exchanges the best man and Harker in what has become a humorous slapstick gag — presaging the cake problems in *Waltzes from Vienna* (see my *Hitchcock's Worst Films* book for a description of that scene). Hitchcock is mocking all arbitrary customs by now. Cut to a three-shot CU of the Girl and the back of a man (he *must* be Jack, yes?), the priest centered in the frame facing the camera behind them.

Cut to a LS of Corby and Ware entering at the back of the church, then sitting SR. Cut back to the three-shot CU of the marriage couple and high priest. Cut to a CU of the priest reciting the marriage oath. Cut to an ECU of his cupped hands with a calligraphic title saying, "*Wilt thou have this Man to thy wedded husband...?*" superimposed over his clasped hands. Cut to a CU of the Girl staring ahead, attentive and adorable. Cut to a CU of the priest, continuing: "'...for better or for worse....'"

Cut back to the Girl, eyes down-turned, and then she slowly turns her head right to look OSL. Cut to her POV, a startling CU of Jack in profile left. The shot stuns us because it's our first look at him in the entire scene! Collectively breathing a sigh of relief, because we knew this person had to be Jack (even seeing Corby just enter US), we still couldn't be sure because of the way Hitchcock had filmed the entire sequence (and the way he's kept us off balance the whole film). In other words, by withholding Jack's features until now — the moment of their vows— I believe the director is saying a number of things to us: (1) "See! Even when you're sure of something, I can make you doubt it. You cannot always trust your own eyes in my films (or in real life)"; (2) Hitchcock allows us to see Jack at precisely the same time that the Girl first does in this scene, helping us to identify better with her as she considers the priest's words carefully; (3) Such withholding also subliminally prepares us for her next fickle change of heart.

This POV CU of Jack is also powerful because Hitchcock starts it in profile L and then has him turn slowly to look at the camera (Girl) with a never-before-seen *neutral* expression on his face. It is inscrutable as the Girl (and us) looks at him as if for the first time. Cut to his POV, a CU of her looking right into our eyes, gulping her heart down. She slowly turns to face SR and, because of Hitchcock's withholding of Jack's identity and the multiple POV's and camera angles, we are better able to *feel* their mutual trepidations over marriage.

Cut to a medium three-shot, the backs of the couple split again by the priest intoning towards them: "'…'till death do us part….'" Notice the quotes within quotes— shortly, these vows will be sorely tested.

Cut to a CU of Corby stifling a yawn — Hitchcock at his most cynical. Cut to a medium four-shot of the marriage party staring stupidly out at us, immobile — a not too particularly handsome group, and shot as Anybodies. Cut to a CU of Harker, a sneeze fighting to come out, his wonderfully expressive features working furiously to suppress it. He raises a gloved hand to his nose, middle finger with a hole in it entering his right nostril. Self-consciously exchanging that one with his index finger, this one fully gloved, he uses that finger to pick it, then sighs impatiently. "No nose picking in church," we can hear Hitchcock intone, "at least with an ungloved finger!" Cut back to the priest, droning on. "Who needs or wants title cards now?" we can hear Hitchcock mock. However, the director *will* put us through this slow and dull ritual, make no mistake about it — and it's the reason many people including myself left the church when we were old enough, believe me.

Cut back to Harker staring OSL, bored out of his gourd and daydreaming (about nosepicking?). Cut to the best man calling to him OSL. Cut to a two-shot CU of the couple looking OSL, too. Cut to Harker staring up OSL, still daydreaming. Cut back to the best man chastising him. Harker, turning back, looks OSR. The best man gestures to his own finger and mouths "Ring. Ring." Wakey wakey, Gordon. Harker, annoyed, thinks the barker is commenting on picking his nose, and he raises his middle finger questioningly, the one with the hole in it. (We in America know what a raised middle finger means, so it takes on a humorous significance to many of us.) Harker then turns his head away, mumbling to himself. Best man persists, his query shot across a couple all the while not shown but stuck between this banter. Harker turns back, still clueless. Back to the best man, patient, spelling it out, making an oval circle with his hand. Harker, finally cognizant, smiles and mouths, "Why didn't you say so in the first place?" Looking OSL again, he rummages about in his coat.

Cut to his POV, a CU of three seconds staring back at him — the same three men who stared at Corby and the girl in the tent. (Our Greek chorus?) One of them, centered, is the black clown. They break into huge grins right in our face. Cut back to a CU of Harker who still can't find the ring (another convention and cliché played for laughs), and he drops to the ground out of camera range. Cut to the best man aghast, mouth open, still in profile L staring OSL. Furious, he slams his fingers down on top of his top hat, crushing it. Cut to a three-shot CU of the men laughing. Cut to their POV, a high-angle CU of Harker kneeling down and frowning back over his shoulder at us. Cut to a frontal, high angle CU of the top of his head as he looks around on the floor. Quick cut to an ECU of a strange looking, disorienting shot of a ring in a field of white (a braided rug), a dark shoe and calf next to it SL. Cut to a quick CU of Harker, coat button popping open. Cut to a CU of Harker staring at us open-mouthed and droopy, the perfect stooge. Quick cut to a CU of a hand grabbing at something — the button, or is it the ring? — on the white carpet. Cut back to the same curious CU shot of the top of Harker's head, still rummaging about.

Standing up, Hitchcock cuts to a CU of him reaching his closed hand near SR where the vicar's hand is outstretched. Cut to a reverse angle ECU of the button now in the vicar's hand. Cut to a CU of the priest, hand open with the button in it, a dry, bemused expression on his face as he looks OSR. Cut to Harker breathing heavily and milking the scene for all it's worth. Realizing his mistake, he reaches with his same hand toward the priest's, and we see the ring magically replaces the button in his hand. Because we only saw him actually grab *something* off the floor, this switch comes as a surprise (what else is new?). In retrospect, we realize Hitchcock even takes care to fiddle with such an innocuous shot as a lost ring in order to regale us with Harker's inanities. Cut back to Harker, mock exhaustion and heavy breathing on his features—a final exasperated "Whew" given extra camera time by a director who really allowed this wonderful character actor full play. He will have even more of a field day in the next film, *The Farmer's Wife*.

> *I found Gordon Harker on the stage [as] I was looking for a Cockney "second" for Carl Brisson in* The Ring, *and I happened one night to drop into Wyndham's Theater to see Edgar Wallace's* The Ringer. *Harker was playing a Cockney part, and I saw in him the very man I needed.... He is a brilliant character actor, and perhaps you'll remember that I gave him the role of a Devon Farmhand in* The Farmer's Wife. *He made a very good job of it* [AH, "My Screen Memories," 1936; in SG1, 1995, p. 13].

Cut to a full-frontal CU of the priest, brightly lit, placing the ring on an open bible and presenting it to us while looking at us, too. Cut back finally to a two-shot CU of our protagonists again. Jack, with his naïve, trusting smile, is on SL, and the Girl, with her mixed happy/sad face, is SR. Jack reaches for the ring just within camera range at the bottom of the screen. Cut to an ECU of an artistically staged shot of Jack's large, shadowed left hand facing palm up towards SR as he holds the Girl's smallish left white hand palm down, dwarfed but brilliantly lit in his hand. His right hand slowly places the ring on her left ring finger.

Just as we begin to wonder why Hitchcock might be drawing out this ritual for us on the screen, the ring reaches its destination and Corby's bracelet slides down from OSU onto her wrist. Hitchcock can create suspense out of any thing, person or place. From OSL and above Jack's hand comes another hand with a cuff on it to push back the bracelet. Whose hand is this? Corby's ethereal presence sneaking into the marriage party via a disembodied arm? We'll never know. Dissolve to blackness with what appears to be rice dropping into space. Hitchcock will shortly create a prolonged scene with rice in *The Farmer's Wife*; here, he need only show a quick two seconds of it to get the point across.

The dissolve continues into a CU of a horseshoe on a brick wall, another sign of connubial bliss, but it immediately falls off the wall and conks an old woman on the head—the gypsy fortune teller, it turns out, nibbling on a sandwich—who happens to be sitting under it. Another emblem undermined with humor at someone's expense.

Cut to a long shot of the wedding guests at an outdoor table all turning to laugh in our direction. Somehow, they've seen this unlikely event (Hitchcock can always make more of a scene simply by changing the camera angle), so suddenly, our laughter at this old woman is directed back at us by these guests, subliminally implicating us with the pathetic victim of their scorn. Cut to their POV, a medium shot of the woman searching for the horseshoe, still a little stunned. Cut to a CU of the Girl and Jack, left to right, also laughing at us—shades of our guilty pleasures at the expense of the clown and sailor at the fair earlier. The Girl and Jack are now implicated as well, for Hitchcock remains focused on their cruel laughs for an extra second or two. Cut to a CU of the gypsy woman, horseshoe in hand, her face aglow with animosity.

Cut to a CU of Corby—a surprising shot considering the circumstances—first staring OSL, then towards the woman, a more tempered expression on his face than all the other guests. Cut back to a CU of the fortune teller, who gets a twisted smile going on her mouth, yet is still looking somewhat inscrutable and worked up. She starts towards the right of the camera, almost walking past it and us. Cut to a three-shot MCU from the wedding couple's POV, Corby and Ware SR, the woman entering the center of the frame, horseshoe still in hand. Corby and Ware are in black and the woman is sharply etched in her multi-patterned gypsy outfit. Cut back to the wedding couple wearing light colors and still laughing. Hitchcock has made them seem ridiculous by now as he forces them to keep laughing at her expense while holding his camera unmercifully on them.

Cut back to the three-shot as the fortune teller moves between Corby and Ware and slowly places the horseshoe on the table. She leans in to Corby and whispers, all seriousness: "Better luck next time." Cut to an

ECU of Corby registering the comment, his eyes agleaming. Cut to a new 45-degree right angle M shot of Corby with the gypsy leering over him as she gets a last laugh in. Then turning, she walks USR. Cut to a 135-degree left M shot of the dinner table, Corby and his group now framed SL and the wedding couple SR. Lots of eating and drinking business ensue (Hitchcock loved to shoot food table montages throughout his career). In a LS Harker, at the head of the table, gets up to propose a quick toast, but is ignored. Cut to a CU of Harker then stuffing himself and pouring beer down his throat while his mouth is still crammed with food.

Cut to a CU of Corby, who extracts the wishbone from his chicken. Looking about for someone to pull it apart with, he proffers it to me (the camera). Cut to a two-shot of the Girl and Jack as Jack urges her to pull it with Corby. Cut to an artfully composed right angle CU of their hands holding the wishbone centered above the table. Quick cut to an ECU of Jack, suddenly looking wiser and a bit sad as he looks on. Quick cut to the wishbone breaking as Corby wins the larger piece. Quick cut back to Jack, who is secretly smiling to himself. Cut to a full-front CU of the Girl, disappointed, conceding me the victory.

Cut to a CU of Harker still stuffing himself. Cut to an ECU profile R (!) of Harker and his filled beer glass. Hitchcock stays on this shot for a full twelve seconds as he rapidly guzzles the whole thing down. Cut to a CU from front left, a new angle of Harker, and for the first and last time in his four films with Hitchcock his face breaks into a radiant, satisfied, youthful, and glorious smile that erupts off the screen — one of the director's most gorgeous shots. Looking around at the guests, he seems for a moment like the happiest man alive.

As quickly as his beaming came it leaves as he spots something OSR, bringing his frown back. Cut to his POV, a MS of Corby standing, backs of heads in front of him (as if *he* were the barker in this scene, not Harker), about to make a little speech. Cut to a CU of Corby, also a little drunk, from the couple's POV. Title: "I think the prize at the booth should have been this charming bride," he says, with barely concealed irony.

Cut to Harker guzzling more beer. Cut back to Corby in CU: "...anyway, now he's my sparring partner. I shall take my revenge." CU shows him miming mock fisticuffs. Cut to a two-shot CU of the Girl and Jack as Jack stands up and, a little more seriously, says "I shall always be ready to fight for my wife against any man." But he's just joking, too, the next shot reveals— although the rest of the film will show him working years to get the opportunity to fight Corby again *for her*. Cut to a CU of Harker getting really drunk, and he suddenly looks aghast. Cut to his POV, a blurry MS of Corby and Jack mock fighting over the table. Cut to a CU of Harker pointing at us and stammering out something as he begins to take off his coat, drunkenly thinking it's a real fight. Cut back to his POV as the fighters' images ooze down towards the bottom of the screen more and more out of focus, then fade out.

Hitchcock seems to have lost interest in the rest of the film from a technical and experimental perspective, for it suddenly takes a sharp turn into a straight-ahead narrative after the wedding meal. (The film feels about 30 minutes too long, actually.) Jack may be married on paper but he soon loses his wife to Corby. More accurately, the Girl falls hard for the limelight of the champion's world, not Jack's humble life. Spending most of his time working up to a rematch and immaturely believing that winning will win back the Girl, that's exactly what happens when he finally knocks Corby out. She comes back to his corner. "Does he *really* win her?" Hitchcock asks, or better, "Can anyone really win anyone else's heart by fighting someone for it?" Foolishly learning nothing, Jack accepts her return as the film ends on a typically ambiguous note.

As Spoto rightly states, the director began to increasingly rely on a number of "purely cinematic devices (blurred images, distorted montages)" (1983, p. 112) in this film, especially when Jack temporarily gets knocked down in the final fight. This montage, with sixteen stunning shots in the space of twenty-five seconds, prefigures the justly famous shower scene in *Psycho* by thirty-three years, and truly gives us a sense of what it might look like from Jack's perspective as he temporarily falls to the ground.

> When I produced The Ring, with Carl Brisson and Ian Hunter, the high-spot of the picture was the last round of a boxing match. Brisson had to win.
> Brisson was a trained boxer. He was, actually, a boxer before he was an actor. Hunter was only an amateur. It was, incidentally, his [Brisson's] first — and very successful — film.
> On the day we were shooting this last round — the previous rounds had been photographed before with trick photography to speed up the effect by "undercranking" (turning the camera more slowly) — I ranged four cameras round the set and told them to go all out [AH, "Life Among the Stars," 1937; in SG1, 1995, p. 41].

That they did. As Corby charges towards the camera from a MS to an in-our-face ECU, we see the following shots surrealistically dissolve one into the other: Pow, right in the kisser comes a Corby haymaker at the camera; a variety of lights rapidly blink on and off four times, fuzzy images of the crowd barely visible between the flashes; now focused in MCU on a standing Corby, the camera tilts down and to the right of the boxer at an

ever-slower pace, mimicking Jack's vision of what he might see as he falls
to the ground, stunned by a near knock-out; double parallel lines of the
ring's ropes crisscross each other on the four diagonals of the screen, the
out-of-focus crowd still visible in the background; quadruple sets of six
brightly lit light bulbs are superimposed in the now shuddering frame,
then slowly come into focus; and finally, saved by the bell, we see a gong
being gonged.

And, while Jack quickly recovers and then does win the match and
the Girl — the film's last shot shows her fawning over him in his corner of
the ring — her love and loyalty remain, in our minds, dubious at best. An
extraordinary film.

Seven

The Farmer's Wife

First screening March 1928

Hitchcock's *The Farmer's Wife* is the first of two film versions (the other was in 1941) adapted from the play of the same name written by the British Victorian novelist and playwright Eden Phillpots (1862–1960). I have seen his last name also spelled with one and two "l's" and "t's." Six of the eight film-review compendiums used in this book critiqued the movie with ratings ranging from two-and-a-half stars (or bones) (LM, VH) to three stars (MP, BB), reflecting an above average to good assessment, and their generally positive comments are right on, I think:

"Alfred Hitchcock toyed with slapstick comedy, [and the film includes some] unusual point-of-view shots [that] feature characters talking to other people by looking directly into the camera" (MP, p. 363). "Interesting early Hitchcock best known for its beautiful photography" (BB, p. 340). "Enjoyable rustic comedy..." (LM, p. 438). "Charming comedy of rural manners [with] a great deal of subtle slapstick and witty caricature, especially in a marvelously sustained sequence at a tea-party" (TO, p. 390). *Bioscope* (March 8, 1928): "Hitchcock has succeeded in conveying the Devonshire atmosphere [and] he has many happy inspirations ... which greatly strengthen the theme of the story."

The available film versions vary in length from 67 (TO, HA) to 93 (BB) to 97 minutes (VH, LM, MP). On the LaserLight DVD 1999 version that I viewed of Hitchcock's film, by the Delta Entertainment Corporation, the "newly recorded music score" of unknown origin sounds mostly like Chopin, and supplements rather than overpowers the visuals quite well, whoever wrote/compiled it.

Jameson Thomas (1888–1939) plays the rather dimwitted farmer Samuel Sweetland. Lilian Hall Davis, fresh off her role as the fickle fairweather Girl in *The Ring,* switches roles completely here and plays the long-suffering Araminta (Minta) Dench, his housekeeper. In a true tour de force, our old friend Gordon Harker, also fresh off his curmudgeonly role as 'One Round' Jack's trainer in *The Ring,* here outdoes himself in curmudgeonliness as the aptly named Churdles Ash, Farmer Sweetland's handyman. Maud Gill, who had the same role in the long running London show, plays the uptight spinster Thirza Tapper. Louie Pounds plays Widow Louisa Windeatt, she of quite fierce independence from men. Olga Slade (d. 1949) plays the hysterical (not merely funny, but truly overwrought) Mary Hearn, Postmistress. Ruth Maitland (1880–1961) plays the barkeep Mercy Bassett, who seems amenable to Sweetland's advances.... These last four are the farmer's so-called love interests. Antonia Brough (c. 1900–1937) plays Susan, Thirza Tapper's stupid and silly maid, and Gibb McLaughlin (1884–1960) plays Henry Coaker, the endlessly annoying elder gabfest.

Charles Barr rightly notes that *The Farmer's Wife* is "easily his most satisfying film since *The Lodger,* technically as inventive as *The Ring* but at the other extreme from that film's aridity"(1999, p. 52). I couldn't agree more. Maurice Yacowar devotes as many lauditory pages to it as he does to *The Lodger* (thirteen), Hitchcock's popular masterpiece of the time, and even Raymond Durgnat called it a "pleasure to watch" (1974, p. 82). Similarly, I found it to be the richest, most rewarding and impeccably constructed film of the entire series of silent pictures. It is the one film that I could not stop recounting and analyzing — hence, of all the chapters in this book, *The Farmer's Wife* is a complete account of every shot in the film.

Opening scene: a LS of a pastoral countryside (Hitchcock filmed on location in Devon), some tree leaves in the foreground providing both scale and depth as a piano tinkles along on the soundtrack. Cut to a sign pointing SL stating "Applegarth Farm" this way. Camera obliges, panning slowly left and following the arrow to rest on an ELS of the farm in the distance at the end of a tree-lined country road. Segue dissolve to a long shot of a man approaching the farm (possibly weary, based on his deliberate walk, but seen too far away to tell for sure), removing his hat before entering the farmhouse. His shoulders look slumped. Dissolve into a MS of the same scene as the man enters the house through two vertical posts framing an entryway, the camera set up behind the man and a little to his left.

Dissolve to a MS of a man (at this point we're not certain if it's the same man or a different one, because we never saw the earlier man's face) gazing out SR from what looks to be an upper floor, cast iron-framed window. This will turn out to be our erstwhile "hero," farmer Samuel Sweetland. Dissolve into a CU of the same man looking slowly to his right (OSL), then back to his left. It is impossible to infer any emotion or thought on his part at this point; he seems to just be looking.

Cut to a LS of his view (we assume), domestic animals strolling about the front yard area. Cut to a LS of a shepherd herding cows within a fenced-in area, the lovely Devon countryside visible in the distance. Quick cut to a horse in profile right at his stall, eating. Cut to a MS of two spaniels sitting in the yard side by side foregrounding a gaggle of geese strolling SL in the background. One dog gets up, heads DS and off, and the other follows. Their movements take a leisurely five seconds of screen time. Cut to a MS of the dogs crossing the yard, sniffing about (four more seconds). Cut to another MS of the dogs entering the house through the same posts (three seconds); quick MCU of them scurrying through an inside door (two-and-a-half seconds); quick MS of them crossing an interior room in the house; quick cut (a feeling of increased speed is being transferred to us with all this cutting, as each shot lasts a shorter and shorter time) to a two-second shot from behind the dogs scurrying up a staircase; quick cut to the dogs coming towards the camera shot from the top of the staircase (one second); and finally, a quick cut to an ECU of first one dog's head, then the other's coming to a slow, faithful rest upon the last step (seven seconds!), heads side by side looking at the camera "Oh, aren't they cute!" we say in unison. And they are, too, with their hangdog expressions and roving, what-me-worry eyes.

Cut to a unique reverse angle CU from *behind* the dogs and level with their heads as we see a man's shoes slowly walk towards them for a leisurely nine seconds (flash on Jack's entrance to the gypsy woman's trailer in *The Ring*). Cut to an eleven-second, achingly slow MDS of an extremely weary, heavy shouldered older man descending the staircase, dogs rushing ahead. During the last two seconds of the shot the man has moved OSR, part of the staircase still visible. He crosses to a coat rack (same camera angle, but in a MS now) and defeatedly grabs a hat, plunks it on his head, and heads out the front door. If we did not know who this person was (Gordon Harker, playing Churdles Ash, the farmer's handyman), we could easily assume it's farmer Sweetland himself, having just come downstairs after looking out the upstairs window. And, I think, Hitchcock may have wanted us to be uncertain as to whom he was in order to place some tension in our minds as soon as possible in this, as in all of his, films. Remember, we've met Harker already in the previous film, but Jameson Thomas is making his first and only appearance in a Hitchcock feature, so it's quite consistent of the director to place some uncertainty about these characters in our minds prior to their identifiable introduction in the film.

Cut to a MDS of his exit taken from the outside, and we finally do realize that it's the same man who first entered the house — by his walk and by the similar, if reversed, filming. Cut to a MS of Sweetland now, still upstairs (completely confirming that they are two different people) and looking out a window. Now, after two minutes of our wondering in the back of our minds if they were the same man or not, we know they are not. Cut to his POV looking down at Ash. CU of Ash as he turns, an exaggerated frown tinged with depression on his face, peering up at Sweetland from beneath his pulled-down hat. Harker was perhaps Hitchcock's finest character actor (out of seemingly hundreds) and a man of innumerable and mobile facial expressions. Cut to a MS of Samuel shaking his head now from side to side for some unknown reason — more consternation deliberately implanted in our minds. If Hitchcock gave us the time to think about it, we'd consciously wonder why he's shaking his head and why Churdles is looking so forlorn, but all these clues do at this point in the film is accumulate just beneath the surface of our minds. Cut back to a CU of Churdles lowering his head beneath his hat and looking more depressed than ever, if possible. He turns left to move off. Cut back to the same MS of Sweetland at the window, then turning R and moving back into the room.

Cut to a MS of Sweetland from within the darkened room. He turns to his right to face SR, hesitant and watching something, and then takes a tentative step forward in that direction as the camera pans ever so imperceptibly to keep him centered in the frame. Hitchcock then cuts to a MS of what he sees. What *we* see is a surprise, because there had been no inkling up until now that there might have been anyone else in the room, let alone the whole house. Four women appear before us SL, two sitting, one standing, and the fourth lying in a bed rocking her head from side to side, apparently ill. There was an empty spot on the wall where a picture was missing above the lodger's head in the film of that name, and that spot has now been replaced with a portrait above this woman's head. Cut to a side view — what I have called a proscenium arch perspective (PAP), a neutral, stage-like view of the proceedings (it is also both a privileged shot for us and of Hitchcock's autonomous camera (AC) presenting an objective yet assertive perspective) — of Sweetland now SL approaching the three women centered behind the bed, the sick woman SR in the foreground.

Cut to a CU of the three women, same privileged PAP, the central figure significantly older and in black than the other two in white, with the clasped hands of the woman in the bed visible. If we know our actors we immediately recognize Lilian Hall-Davis, the fickle and fair-weather Girl from the last film, as the closest woman to the bed. In this film she plays farmer Sweetland's soon-to-be long-suffering housekeeper Araminta (Minta) Dench. Slowly but suddenly the sick woman's left hand falls limply to the side, towards the camera, while everyone remains impassive. Cut back to the earlier MS PAP side view tableau for several seconds, nobody moving. Then Hitchcock makes a swift and stunning cut to a *CU* of Sweetland facing SR and shot from just below him up towards his face. We see him slowly turn his head around to the left and away from the camera. For us this is a powerfully charged, private insight into this man's emotional pain, for the director has his actor hide his expression from the camera's eye, forcing us to imagine his feelings instead of seeing them on his features.

Cut to a MS of all five people in the room, the man's head still turned away, as the closest standing woman — our heroine, Minta — bends down and helps the prone woman to a sitting position, cradling her. Apparently she's not dead yet (nod to Monty Python). CU of just the two of them, Minta's face lovingly rendered with the dying woman's unseen face turned towards the housekeeper. Apparently she's whispering something, for we suddenly see the first title of the film five minutes in: "…and don't forget to air your Master's pants, Minta." This is an extremely suggestive and odd sort of statement for someone breathing their last breath, and this title, it turns out, is also a strong portent, for Minta will eventually become the real farmer's wife of the picture, in law if not already in common law. She will also certainly have her chance to do more than air the Master's pants, in a typical Hitchcockian double entendre.

Cut to the privileged, for-our-eyes-only CU of the two of them again, Minta nodding she won't as the woman finally expires. Shadow of a hand pulling the curtains closed appears above the bed on the wall to Minta's right as she clutches her own bosom with her right hand — a symbolic motion that will reappear several times in the film. Fade to black at the end of this lovingly rendered, twenty-five second shot.

Fade up on the camera slowly panning left to right now in CU's of five alternating scenes dissolving into the other, each lasting about ten seconds. Shots one, three and five show Minta indeed airing out the master's pants, placing wet long johns in front of a fireplace (the middle shot shows the maid without an apron on, implying passage of time), while shots two and four reveal the same drying method only placed outdoors on some bushes. Camera, never stopping, continues to pan L to R for all five shots, even during the dissolves, which also connotes time passing. Fade to black.

Fade up on a spanking clean made-up bed, a MS from the footboards, as a vest, tie and shirt are progressively placed on it from disembodied arms OSL. Cut to a MS PAP, Minta straightening everything up. Enter Sweetland, still in black, but now he has long mutton chops for sideburns. Cut to a two-shot CU of them bustling about and active, Samuel rapidly dictating orders. This CU, we shall see, is Hitchcock's first suggestive plant for the most hopeful and longest lasting relationship in the entire film, but it will take the whole of the film to get them and us to that point. Sweetland sends Minta out of the room.

Next shot reinforces their predestined yet subliminal connection, as we observe in MCU and then in a quick CU Minta descending the stairs in a flattering follow pan R to L, the camera staying on her from behind as she enters the kitchen and recedes into the middle distance of the screen. This privileged, ten-second pan powerfully increases our identification with her. In fact, the camera's subliminal power is even greater because, when Hitchcock cuts to the CU of her coming down the stairs, it's taken from that same looking-up-from-down-under angle that privileged Sweetland's turned-away head at his wife's deathbed. Only these two characters will merit such unique perspectives in the film.

Cut to a MS from behind Minta coordinating the kitchen help, then a cut to a MS from outside the door as she moves towards the camera, deep in thought. She then turns right and heads OSL. The camera has been closely keeping her centered in the frame via pans and dollies all this time. Opening a door, she heads directly up some stairs toward the camera, which is now stationed above this back-of-house staircase. This shot further "opens up" the house three-dimensionally in our mind. Camera cuts to a reverse angle MS of Minta from behind now climbing the remaining stairs. In a room, we see her hurry L to R to help a woman fix her wedding garments. With this shot and with the information Hitchcock has shared, we are meant to immediately assume that Sweetland is to be remarried to someone else. What else could we think? Of course, this will turn out to be another of Hitchcock's deliberately intended false assumptions he loved to implant in our minds.

Cut during this realization to an ECU of the widower upstairs in his room from that same unique up-under shot, fighting to get his tie tied (shades of a similar scene with the Buntings in *The Lodger*), contortedly screaming for help. Hitchcock is quickly puncturing our budding romantic hopes between the maid and the farmer with these two quick shots.

Minta hurries down the back stairway to return and help Sweetland via a MS of her retreating back, and then we see the real bride-to-be get ever more frantic in her upstairs room. Two handmaidens are no help whatsoever. Crossing L to R in the dining room in MS, Minta stops and looks OSR. Cut to a MS of old Churdles Ash (a wonderfully onomatopoetic name), the handyman, entering the front doorway (Minta's POV). He takes off a dilapidated hat, plops it down on a rack, and begins to wipe his brow with a mangy handkerchief. Noticing Minta, he stops. Cut to his POV, a MCU of her telling him he should not be in the house, now of all times. Dumbfounded and muttering to himself, he grabs his hat, slams it on his head, does his best frown, turns, and exasperatedly huffs back outside — a funny bit.

Cut to a privileged ECU of Minta from her right as the camera hurriedly yet flowingly pans to keep up with her as she ascends the first stairway back up to her master's wing. Her movements and the camera's swift accompaniment with her have a unique, palpably loving feel about them. Quick, almost seamless cut to a MS of her back as she enters his bedroom, camera at landing height. It stays on her directly from behind as she crosses the threshold of his door, framing her clearly within its rectangle, her apron making a white "X" crisscrossing her back (and prefiguring the crisscross patterns that run rampant throughout *Strangers on a Train* twenty three years later).

Cut to a two-shot CU in profile of Sweetland huffing and puffing over his collar and clothes, Minta acting helpful. The whole scene so far is an absurd spoof on wedding preparations, a perfect opportunity for Hitchcock to burst yet another convention of society (all the beforehand goings-on to the actual wedding scenes we saw in the earlier *The Ring*). Sweetland waves Minta out again, nothing accomplished except that Hitchcock has given us another unbroken view of these two together for a generous twenty-three seconds.

By now, Hall Davis as Minta has put on what seems like miles of running all over the house, the only person, apparently, capable of getting *anything* done in this household. Cut to a new medium shot from behind Minta as she leaves the room. Then, shot from just *outside* the bedroom door, we see her head down the stairs, also in MD. It's a stunning cut because it's such a fresh angle and, hence, a strong intimation of change. Camera holds immobile at first as Minta recedes from it, then pans with her in a MS as she descends the stairs, seen at one point through the banister. At the bottom we see her bark exacting orders into the kitchen as she heads SL. We catch a glimpse of even more of the dining room as she passes through that room, enlarging our concept of the floor plan even more as the camera continues to shoot her from above on the landing looking down through the railing. Still shot from behind, we see her cross to the front door and open it. All of these rear shots suggest a speed of movement so quick the camera can barely keep up, which lends a wonderful sense of breathlessness to this charming and funny montage. A powerful autonomy is being associated with this extraordinary woman for, if the camera cannot even keep up with her, what other things might she be capable of in the film? Good question.

From a MCU of Minta at the door Hitchcock cuts to a LS looking at the house from the outside, which makes us take a moment to get our bearings. We are only given two seconds of the shot, too, Hitchcock forcing us to work hard if we're to keep up with him. On the far left of the screen we can barely make out a figure, but with the next cut, a two-shot CU, it turns out to be Churdles in a humorous *tête-à-tête* with Minta over his consistent incompetence, this time at tying bows onto the side of the horse-drawn carriage. Based on our assumptions about all the goings-on about the house, the title we read of his comments reflects another typical directorial red herring: "He'll be the next to wed now his daughter's marryin'." This is only the second title in almost ten minutes of film, and stuns us into uncertainty. Without giving us a moment to think, Hitchcock immediately follows this proclamation with Minta chiming in: "Why not? There's something magical in the married state ... it have a beautiful side, Churdles Ash."

Aha, we finally realize something! It's not Sweetland getting married, but his *daughter*! That makes much more sense than such a quick marriage after his first wife had died, which we have been wrongly assuming was happening all this time. More deliberate deception successfully perpetrated on us by the director, for we didn't even know Sweetland *had* a daughter until now!

Hurrying back inside — Minta apparently sees to everything, unlike Hattie's unfortunate inability, mocked so ironically in *Under Capricorn* twenty-one years later — we view her entering the house from a LS PAP, ostensibly Churdles' POV. The same is true for the next scene from within, also a LS PAP, but this time with a milk pitcher in the foreground and a clearer view of the dining room table. Hitchcock's generosity of vision, detail and his breaking of the imaginary fourth wall of the movie screen are only equaled by the effectiveness of his presentations.

Staying with a long shot throughout this entire scene — a challengingly long twenty-six seconds, compared to all the earlier quick shots — Minta goes to the kitchen with a maid. The kitchen door is now seen USL, further disorienting us. Suddenly the wedding party comes onscreen from the daughter's door DSL as the bride adjusts her outfit and her two incompetent maids of honor flutter nearby. Minta rushes upstairs partway to call for Sweetland, who hurries down putting on his coat. The sense of breathlessness onscreen continues to rush things along for us.

Cut to a CU of Minta hurrying the bridesmaids out the door, then turning left while adjusting a loose lock of her own hair. What she sees: POV CU of Sweetland on R, hands on daughter's arms, gazing lovingly at her and planting a kiss on her cheek. Father then lowers his head, possibly out of sadness in memory of his own wife's death. Cut to Minta, *full frontal CU*, staring directly at us sympathetically, then turning her head right and down briefly herself, a lump in her throat as she feels the farmer's emotions exactly—for him and for herself.

Quickly collecting herself and swallowing—this whole scene lasts a leisurely, even poignant sixteen seconds—Minta snaps them both out of their embrace and urges them to leave. Cut to her POV as they both brighten up and smile—one of Sweetland's few throughout the film. Cut to a MS of her bustling them outdoors to a MS of the waiting carriage, which takes off SL, Churdles seen walking toward the house behind the carriage, Minta to its left. Quick cut to the retreating carriage, a lovely MS *mise en scène* with a stone carriage house foreground right, the path before the carriage center screen, and the beautiful countryside in the distance SL.

Churdles follows Minta through the post archway of the entrance in a MCU shot. Cut inside to the dining room, the camera panning in MCU as Churdles continues to follow Minta into the kitchen. First-of-its-kind MLS of the kitchen from a side view PAP, kitchen door now to the right as they cross SL. More previously withheld details of this room must be noticed quickly, or the video/DVD rewound and paused—otherwise they will be missed due to the brevity of this three-second shot: a blazing hearth and stove, some chairs, a stone floor, various kitchen items. The details are still coming fast and furious in this film.

The next scene is all Churdles, a comic tour de force, as the camera stays with him through a long subjective feature of this wonderful character actor in action. Clearly, the mobile expressions on this man's face appealed to Hitchcock, who apparently relished giving him a chance to shine after seeing what he could do in *The Ring* the year before. Hitchcock would continue to almost arbitrarily pick at least one character per film and compel his audience to identify with him or her, regardless of its effect on the plot. (Lila Kedrova's Countess Luchinska in *Torn Curtain* and Jessie Royce Landis's comic turns in *To Catch a Thief* and *North by Northwest*, as Jessie Stevens and Clara Thornhill respectively, are just three that come to mind.) The next nearly four minutes belong to Harker and Harker alone, who does, in fact, touch on some important emotional narrative along the way.

The focus of the camera picks him up beginning on his entrance into the house behind Minta, centering him as the camera shoots from behind, but it takes us a minute to realize that he has now been given that role because we have been previously identifying so closely with both Sweetland and Minta. In fact, even as Hitchcock had already begun to bring more attention to Churdles by including him in Minta's frame more often, retrospect reveals to us that we'd stuck with Minta until we became consciously aware of Hitchcock's focus change! In other words, our identifications with both of these characters were functioning on conscious and subliminal levels simultaneously!

For example, prior to their entrance into the house, the camera had panned with both of them in a MS. Upon entering it stuck with both again. But, once in the kitchen, a stationary PAP shot of the activities, Hitchcock cuts to an immediate MCU of Churdles, thus beginning the camera's relentless centering of our attentions on him.

Spotting something OSL, the camera pans and dollies with Ash, still in a privileged MCU, as he walks in that direction and leans forward to reach for it, his hand going out of the frame as one of the kitchen servants crosses in front of him and our view R to L. Cut to a frame-centered CU of him admiring a bottle he now holds, still facing SL. Minta crosses behind him to appear upscreen, admonishing him. She retrieves the bottle and places it back OSL, chiding and waving him OSR. With an ever dour, hang-dog expression transfixed on his face, Churdles shuffles SR to retrieve a cup, the camera staying on him in a CU pan but slightly backing up to keep his image the same size.

Harker is quite funny and funny looking in this scene, so he is a pleasant, even welcome diversion from the rather harried narrative up to this point. Grumbling and shuffling back SL, the camera not cutting during its panning CU, the hand with the cup in it reaches onces again OSL as a maid pumps him some water in the background. Cut to a closer CU, almost extreme, as he disdainfully glares at the liquorless liquid, his face contorting squeamishly. He hears something OSR and turns to grumble several invectives in that direction, the camera staying immobile. Attempting to ingest the vile potion, he finally decides against drinking it and flings the water OSL in helpless impotence to both the water's power and the unseen space, perhaps also magically powerful, of OSL.

Cut to a MS PAP, slightly angled left towards Churdles. He exaggeratedly duck walks upscreen towards a bend in the corner of the kitchen just to the left of the hearth. Cut to a closer MS as he pats down the seat of a bench chair there and sits, becalmed for the moment, his scrunched up hat pressed low over his eyes. Our eyes start to rest with his as Hitchcock holds on this shot a full four seconds, but we're jarred awake with him as Minta enters SR and heads towards the fireplace. Cut to a CU of Churdles SL, his face in the corner of the frame and the bright light of the upper left corner of the hearth SR shining full upon his face — yet another artfully composed and evocative shot by this highly experimental director. Churdles rubs his nose eccentrically with his left thumb pressed against a fist, a signature gesture of his, and poisedly smacks his lips, then gesticulates importantly with the same fist and thumb pointing upwards as a title card lustfully and editorially proclaims: "Beer-drinking don't do 'alf the 'arm of love-making." Feeling certifiably vindicated, he harrumphs a self-satisfied smirk.

Quick cut to a highly charged shot from Churdles' POV, a first-of-its-kind, lovingly rendered CU of our heroine with the hearth light full upon her face, its two quick seconds literally blinding us with its beauty. The shock of seeing Churdles' POV of the lovely Minta and his short-lived, brightly lit perspective cause this image's energy to jump off the screen into our minds. We see her smilingly respond to his comment, but Hitchcock then cuts immediately to a CU of Churdles from her POV, also directly at the camera, his left fist and thumb almost three-dimensionally fore-grounded in front of our faces. Grace Kelly's hand straining towards me in *Dial M for Murder* during the attempted murder on her life, filmed in 3-D but never seen as such, immediately comes to mind. The across-the-screen quality of the ECU of Janet Leigh's near-death hand reaching for the shower curtain in *Psycho*, and help that will not come, also rushes in on the consciousness.

An audacious title reflects Churdles' next brazen comment: "If I were the Government [capitalization here simultaneously highlights and paro-dies its authority], I'd give the drunkards a rest and look after the lovers." A progressively reactive thought indeed — also a portentous accusation, we shall find out later. Cut to a MS profile of a fully lit Minta waving away Churdles' comment, him deep in shadow now, as she moves toward the camera and OSR. "I've seed the Master [translation: Government] 'ave his eye on a woman or two of late," calls out Churdles, still animated and shot in that MD view as if he is on his throne by the hearth. "To see an old man in love be worse than seeing him with whooping cough!" Philpotts' words fall liltingly off this rascal's tongue.

The tension in our minds with this scene, one supposes, should have been released with Minta's leaving. In fact, by next holding on a CU of Churdles for a full five seconds, we might expect to see (in any normal film) a fade out on him at the end of such a long, static shot, with back to back to back titles coming at us. Not so, with Hitchcock. Going against expectations every time, especially when he is manipulating us full force, the director gives Churdles not only an abundance of screen time here but an overabundance. Hitchcock is testing our patience through tolerance, then frustration, and finally, satisfaction.

Sixteen more seconds roll by, half with Minta back at the hearth hang-ing some chops to cook. CU of Churdles leaning back on his throne. His features are so expressive we can almost smell the chops cooking with him.

Cut to a CU of the meat turning on its rope. Surprise — now we get the fade out ... on the chops!

But, surprise again, Hitchcock fades in on a CU of the chops again, still turning, but now they're nearly cooked. A full twenty seconds fills up the screen before another cut occurs. The first five seconds are the CU on the chops, the next four the same CU with a spoon ladeling gravy over them connected to a hand OSL. Minta's? No, it's Churdles'! Of course, he was OSL in relation to the meat before the fade out. How could we have thought otherwise? Churdles is distastefully performing and complaining about yet one more duty. Quick cut to a CU of Minta drying a glass, lost in her thoughts (love?). A series of twelve amusing rapid-fire alternating cuts shows Minta and Churdles in a cat-and-mouse peek-a-boo game of hers trying to catch him dipping some bread into the gravy and pigging out, all in MD shots. The final cut on Minta is a CU, still trying to catch him, but these alternating shots subliminally signal a change of focus in the film from Churdles back to Minta.

We see her turn and listen to something OSL. Cut to a distant shot of a church bell tolling. Cut back to a CU of Minta, excited. She speaks, but the camera cuts to her POV of Churdles bitching: "Holy Matrimony [authorial capitals again] be a proper steam roller for flattening the hope out of a man and the joy out of a woman." Even such a sour commentary cannot dampen the thrill Minta holds for the affair. Surprise cut to a MCU of Minta's back as she walks hurriedly toward the kitchen window, another angle of the room we've yet to see that further expands our 3-D sense of this space. But she hastens past the window not towards it as we thought, and we see her enter Churdles' frame over by the hearth. Déjà vu and disorientation set in as we realize we have seen this shot before, just not from quite such a sharp angle behind Minta. In retrospect, and two more reviewings, we realize that the MCU of her back *disguised* her spatial position in the room until, during her movement towards Churdles, the camera backed away from her a bit and tracked right to arrive at that earlier MS — another fascinating technical act by this ever experimenting director.

Poking him, Minta tells Churdles to go outdoors. He gets up, passes in front of her, and shuffles toward the door OSR, the camera panning to follow his back in a MS. Reverse angle of his POV, the earlier MD outdoor shot of the carriage receding, but this time the carriage in MD with the bride and groom is coming towards the camera in the bright outdoors from the left. Strongly charged CU of Churdles staring OSL, gesturing behind him and calling for Minta to come quick. Cut to a MS of Minta at the hearth stirring the gravy, then looking at the camera (and hence, towards the *front door's* POV, from whence Churdles calls). She reacts to his call and stops her chores to come. Cut to a MS from *behind* Churdles—the *door's* reverse angle POV—facing out onto the courtyard, another first-of-its-kind, briefly disorienting shot as he moves to meet the carriage entering the frame from OSR! Hitchcock's interesting angles continue to multiply. Cut to a MD shot of Minta in profile hurrying across the dining room L to R. With Churdles unseen OSL, Minta hurries to the carriage in the same medium shot from behind to help the newlyweds out of the carriage. Minta steps between both husband and wife, gets a hearty handshake from him and leads the wife towards the camera and the outside door ahead of the groom.

MD profile shot inside again, Minta still standing between the two. She grabs the groom and places him SL, bride's right, and stands back approvingly. Long pause. Minta grabs the farmer's hat and goes quickly OSR. The film looks speeded up here, in almost slapstick fashion, as we see her cross quickly behind the couple and disappear through the kitchen door. In a MCU the couple stands uncomfortably still as if waiting for Minta to do something else. Nothing happens. Naturally. Cut to another long, uncomfortable CU of the couple, ten seconds worth, rather out of sorts with the whole proceedings. "What do we do now," they seem to say. So do we. Finally, the bride proffers her ringed hand to the groom and he shyly, almost reluctantly, kisses her, Hitchcock's wry little comment confirming Churdles' earlier thoughts on marriage.

Cut to a MS of the outdoors as the wedding guests arrive in two carriages SL to R. Cut to a MS from inside the dining room looking outside through the doorway, an interesting angle and somewhat disorienting, as the guests disembark and cross the threshold of the camera almost into our living room. The camera is much further back than we think at first, and as the guests walk towards us/the camera/the door their bodies nearly fill the frame—hence the feeling that they're almost on top of us.

LS PAP of the guests entering the dining room. MS of the dinner table in the foreground, guests milling about. Slightly more distant MS of the same table and guests from a totally new vantage point obliquely left of the camera, the outside door now centered in the background. These three shots together provide us with an excellent sense of this room's size and proportions.

Hitchcock's love of crowd scenes is now indulged in for, during the next thirty-five seconds of real time and in LS, we watch all the guests clumsily find their places at the table. Finally all seated, we realize Churdles has entered the frame, too. CU of him reaching to take his hat off and putting it on a peg by the door, but he discovers all the pegs are already covered by all the guests' garments. Straight out of the caricature school of music halls and vaudeville, he removes a bunch of hats from his peg and plunks his own down on it with a "So there!" type expression, then turns to take his place at the table, an absurd, mock furious smile upon his face.

Cut to yet another — the fourth — perspective of the proceedings, this time a MCU of the table shot from head height with the guests framing the screen on both sides. At this close position, with everyone laughing almost on top of us, it's as vulgar as it is funny — Hitchcock's curious ability to simultaneously bring together opposing and seemingly incongruous qualities into one unique shot. As it's always done with his signature mix of self-reflexiveness, audacity and sure-handedness, attentive viewers frequently experience a singularly complex sense of rich and satisfying generosity on this director's part.

In the same MCU we see Sweetland rise to say grace in the background of the screen, centered at the head of the table. With the camera at such a low angle, his arising appears magisterial. Cut to a two-second CU of the farmer saying grace, revealing his somewhat suspicious, surreptitious looks around the table. Audacious cut to a disorienting MCU shot of all the guests now standing, heads bowed, until we realize the shot is a reverse angle of the farmer's POV taken from his head height.

Back-to-back dissolves — simultaneous fade out and in to another scene, (another first) of the same angle shot, but now everyone is seated — the camera is a bit above everyone as they pig out. Another camera dissolve to the same shot as an elderly gentleman is seen center screen standing and recounting a story. Cut to a CU of him, who turns out to be the groom's father, Henry Coaker. Cut to his POV CU as he pokes his daughter-in-law playfully with his cane. She laughs uproariously in our face, to him and the camera, with the groom smiling behind her R shoulder. Cut to a reverse angle CU as she turns to look over that shoulder right into the camera. Her smile immediately melts. Cut to a MCU of her POV, her father sulkily sitting alone at the end of the table. He turns his head towards her/us, deep lines etching his crestfallen face. Cut back to a gorgeously lit CU of the bride, so full of life but unhappy for him, too. Cut back to a MCU of the farmer, who musters up a weary but genuine smile of approval, as if to say, "Go ahead, everyone. Have fun!" The bride, relieved, smiles back, and the camera, paralleling the release in tension, simultaneously cuts back to a MS of the proceedings, the bride still lovingly lit but framed now by her husband and the guests. A short and simple scene, perhaps, but another sublime example of the director's total grasp of pure cinematic expression.

In the background we see Minta enter the scene and lean down between the bride and groom at the table. Cut to a closer MS from a neutral camera position across the table and to their left. The three of them (they're all of the same young and beautiful age) debate the lateness of the hour (I suppose) and eye the groom's father. Cut to Coaker in CU licking his lips lasciviously and glancing slyly to the left proclaiming: "...and there be many here who have oft been wishful of a partner...." In a film that uses them sparingly, this is the first title in over three minutes.

> *I made a silent film,* The Farmer's Wife, *a play that was all dialogue, but we tried to avoid using titles and, wherever possible, to use the pictorial expression instead. I suppose the only [silent] film made without any titles at all was* The Last Laugh *[1924, by F. W. Murnau], with Emil Jannings* [AH, in FT, 1985, p. 31].

Cut back to a CU of the old man as his eyes swing back to the farmer. Cut to a full-frontal POV CU of him smiling at us in acknowledgment. Slowly turning pensive, he bows his head and turns slightly left, looking down and OSL. Cut to his POV, a CU of an empty rocking chair by the hearth. Camera pans across the fireplace L to R to settle on another rocker facing its twin, both empty bookends of a relationship that no longer exists. Startling cut to a CU of the farmer from *the hearth's* POV, Hitchcock anthropomorphizing the farmer's memories through the camera's eye back onto himself — a potently voyeuristic violation of this man's private thoughts. He comes out of his reverie and turns his head back, now right, to his guests. Cut to a CU of the old man finishing his sentence, further reinforcing the singleness of the farmer's thoughts in his own imagined dreams: "...and the need of a strong man to lean against."

Cut to a CU of a blushing young female guest, a horrid and huge fake flower centered above her face on an equally ugly hat. She is caricatured to be a giggly, visual mockery of such a woman needing a strong man to lean against, and will turn out to be Thirza Tapper, the third of Sweetland's four failed wooings. Quick cut back to Coaker rambling on as he looks around the table. Cut to a CU of the camera panning with his POV and stopping on a different caricature of a young woman already looking old-maidenly, the never marrying type, gulping guiltily. This is the widow Louisa Windeatt. Cut back to the old man looking further down the line. Cut to a quick camera pan to the next woman, mock butch and overweight, a bland looking, phony flapper type laughing him off. This is Mary Hearn, the Postmistress. Surprise cut to a CU of her POV of the old man as he waves her down. With his heavy lower lip and hovering presence, now brightly lit from below from her POV, he looks surprisingly like a thinner but easily recognizable stand-in for Hitchcock himself, chiding his children!

Cut to a MS of all three ladies side-by-side, suddenly becalmed and thoughtful. Cut to the old man now looking like honest Abe, a MCU AC shot at eye level of him in profile right, talking more to himself than anyone else. Cut to his POV (although he's not looking anywhere in particular), so the camera is actually showing its autonomy by focusing on the transfixed guests, Sweetland centered in the background profile left. No heads move, and the shot, lasting only three seconds, acts as a kind of surrealistic tableau pause in the action. Cut back to a MS of the old man raving on. Hitchcock is completely foregoing the use of title cards here, and one misses them not in the slightest.

Pops suddenly slams down his cane, and *that* wakes them all up from their idyll. Quick cut to a medium shot of the guests from his POV showing them to be all boisterous again, as if nothing had changed, further eliciting a Twilight Zone kind of feeling.

The hour is late and, once again, Minta plays the ever-efficient escort, this time for two ladies heading out the door. Camera pans with her from across the table left to door right, then back to foreground R of the table to its head and Sweetland. Cut to an intimate whisper from Minta into her master's ear, similar to the MCU shot of the private thoughts of the farmer to the camera earlier, but this shot is taken from behind his right shoulder. He rises to announce the evening's end. After Hitchcock's distinct camera shifts, it always takes us a delicious extra second or two to reorient ourselves.

Nearly thirty seconds go by now in a funny bookend exodus to the guests' entrance, Churdles ignoring everyone and continuing to pig out (*à la* a similar shot in the previous *The Ring*), but we only need to see him from the back this time, oblivious as always to the proceedings. More crowd humor fills the next twenty-five seconds as the camera pans with old man Coaker badgering a hapless guest who is vainly seeking refuge away from him all throughout the dining room. Shot tightly in MCU, with the old man literally in his face, we get a strong sense of claustrophobia ourselves, particularly when the camera's eye, while following the two of them, crosses in ECU behind a lady's huge hat as she faces another guest, nearly blacking out the screen in our faces! Hitchcock's tight MCU allows us to actually begin to feel the tight pressing in of the bodies in the milling party crowd, all a little drunk as they push and bang up against one another. This is the beauty of director's manipulative skill on us— he is able to elicit visceral feelings deep within us with his ever-stimulating screen work.

Finally finding a group large enough to escape into, the harangued guest eludes his torturer. The old geeser is only momentarily setback, however, and immediately finds another unwilling victim. It matters not who will listen, Hitchcock seems to say, only that he can talk.

Cut to a MS of a sympathetic looking Churdles, as ignored by the crowd as he ignores them. He collects his hat, a look of derision all over his face towards these people. In retrospect, this quick, five-second shot explains why he is the man he is. Elaborate cut to a MS of a guest importuning Sweetland: "Now don't forget, *dear Mr. Sweetland* [handwritten script here, for emphasis], you are coming to my little affair next Thursday...." They both nod approvingly. "...and may Mr. Ash [Churdles] stand at the door and announce the guests?... I have a livery he can put on."

Once again, a seemingly innocuous shot — Churdles getting up from the table — turns out to be a deliberate portent of something coming, for Hitchcock cuts to—you guessed it—a CU of Churdles powerfully shot waving a desperate "No" at the camera. The next shot, Churdles' POV of the back of the guest who had invited Sweetland, reveals that the previous shot was Sweetland's *imaginary* POV of Churdles, not the man himself, the camera standing in for him. Scratching his chin a moment, Sweetland catches up to the prescient camera with a quick glance towards it now — his *real* POV of Churdles. Cut back to Ash, even more agitated. In a marvelous reverse angle MD three-shot (the farmer, guest, and Churdles L to R, foreground to background), shot from over Sweetland's right shoulder, the farmer agrees now with a knowing, mock sadistic nod. We can't see his face, only the agreeable guest's and Ash's ham-bone, crestfallen look. As the two chat on, Churdles snaps his fingers in a "curses" gesture and stuffs his disheveled hat upon his disheartened head. Cut to a CU as the ever magically appearing Minta hurries him out the door, not without a final indignant thrust at the camera by the hapless servant.

Before we can even register his leaving, and with confident expediency, Hitchcock closes the door on Churdles and pans tightly in on Minta moving among the guests. With rapid fire efficiency Minta dispatches Ash, gives doggie bags to all the guests, bustles half of them out the door, hurries over to the upstairs door, calls up for the bridesmaids to come down, orders Sweetland to move the rest of the guests out, and ushers the bridesmaids towards the outside door herself — all in thirty seconds of real time. Reinforcing the pace in our minds— make no mistake, Hitchcock has our responses well in hand — the director brilliantly pans with Minta in a centered CU throughout this whole scene, and if we watch carefully, we can see and feel the challenged cameraman doggedly dolly along with her, rapidly zooming forward and back and panning side to side to keep her image rock steady in the middle of the screen. It's really quite a breathtaking montage, and very effective.

Cut to a PAP of the bride (L) and father, then a CU of Minta (L) and the groom in conversation US. Minta's feelings are strongly revealed again as she adoringly looks back towards father and daughter, right at the camera. We know by now — or we should, if we haven't figured it out yet — just how much she loves the farmer; but Sweetland stares back unawares. Cut to a perfect mirror image POV of Minta's, farmer on the left, daughter on R, so we can easily imagine Minta "standing in" for the daughter. Dad plants a kiss on his daughter's cheek, and how all the generous camera angles, private subjective shots, and various POV's pay off for us emotionally across the screen, for we have identified so much with Minta that we almost feel *his kiss on our cheek*!

Quick cut to a neutral PAP of goodbyes and well-wishes all around, Minta hurrying the newlyweds out the door with her commanding yet unobtrusive, indispensable authority. Cut to a MS of all of their backs leaving the house and the camera, and we surprisingly see it's still daylight outside. More goodbyes and felicitations, until another of the director's freshly charged over-the-shoulder shots in a MCU from behind

The Farmer's Wife, 1928: Farmer Samuel Sweetland (played by Jameson Thomas) in a bittersweet moment as he wishes his daughter Sibley (played by Mollie Ellis) all the happiness he has lost since the death of his wife.

Sweetland, his POV watching the newlyweds showered with rice and Minta crying with grief for herself. This is seen but still not understood by the farmer, his face hidden from our view. The frame is carefully constructed here: Minta in the extreme bottom left corner kissing the bride good luck and crying, her face visible; the daughter, hat hiding most of her face, bending down to kiss Minta; the groom vacantly staring off in profile from behind his new wife, the smallest (most insignificant) figure yet dead-center in the screen; and the father's back and head filling the foreground, immobile. And who is that sitting in the carriage's driver's seat, an imperious, terse, surly, comic expression on his face — why, it's our old friend Churdles, who I would never have noticed had I not stopped the film, that's how dense this *mise en scène* is.

The rice raining down on the participants looks like bursting fireworks. Minta vanishes OS down L and Sweetland takes her place, standing in for *her* now in goodbyes. More bursts of blinding rice. The carriage takes off OSR and the camera stays on a MCU of the farmer in right profile gazing after it, alone. Quick cut to his POV, a long shot of the receding carriage. Cut to the carriage's anthropomorphized POV of the farmer, all his guests still behind him, as he waves back past the camera to its left. They all turn to go back inside.

Farmer turns back for one last look, and Hitchcock cuts to a deeply touching CU of the forlorn man covered with rice as he waves his hand. The camera holds on this lonely farmer for a relatively long eight seconds, allowing us to share in his mixed emotions. He has now truly lost both the women in his life. Four more seconds show us his back from that privileged up-under shot, slowly walking inside, his dark overcoat contrasting sharply with the brightly lit guests beyond the door.

Cut to a MCU of him standing on the davenport and becoming aware of something OSL. His head turns and Minta magically appears at his side again, whispering something. He nods his approval and enters the fray once again, in MLS USR, his guests below left. A very fast, two-second, fresh cut (even though we're getting used to them, each new angle is so quick and different that we are never quite ready for them, and so we must go through that pleasurable reorientation each and every time) to an AC view (no one's in particular, or so we think) of the farmer facing the camera, slightly down screen and to the right, as the guests one by one march out. The door is to the farmer's right now, our left.

As the next guest approaches, an even more startling two-second ECU of Sweetland's face fills the screen. He lifts his head to stare directly at us, eyes wide open. Immediate cut to his POV, another ECU of the blithering young vapid head Thirza Tapper giggling hysterically at us/him, her frighteningly outlandish hat vulgarly displayed on her head. We're treated to two ECU seconds of this horror. Quick two-second cut back to her POV, an ECU of the farmer staring right into our eyes. Still feeling assaulted by this image before him, he manages to bow a gracious farewell. After our private sharing of his grief moments earlier, these powerful alternating ECU's are very disturbing, and we don't quite know why we're so troubled by it. Hitchcock really has us in his grip now.

Cut back to a neutral release shot PAP, the next guest approaching — this time a man. Thinking we're free from further confrontations, we forget there are two other biddies to come. Sure enough, Sweetland turns his head L back into our eyes, another ECU of his invaded face. The widow Louisa Windeatt is next. We get three seconds of Sweetland's ECU this time — one extra second than the previous one with Thirza — and three seconds of Louisa's. They each nod into the camera in CU. Louisa looks as if she may be missing a couple of teeth, Hitchcock's black humor razor sharp. Cut to a PAP as she passes in front of him and out the door left. Three more guests pass, and we hope (subliminally, subliminally) that he and we will escape the third ... but no such luck.

Hitchcock milks it for all it's worth, though, this time showing her arrive in the same profile shot and holding on the two of them just long enough to allow us to think he might let her pass without comment. But the director cuts to an ECU of the farmer facing the camera (perhaps just a little off to the right), a now ever so slightly strained smile clinging to his lips. We get *four* full seconds of each of them this time plus a longer PAP profile shot, too. The ECU cut to the final, middle-aged hopeful, Postmistress Mary Hearn, is an excruciating combination of desperation, humor, and pathetic human frailty on display. She finally passes on out the door and the camera cuts to one final, long, four-second frontal CU of the farmer, a POV from the last girl's facing position as he looks over his shoulder at her receding figure (out of frame, but his line of sight is out the door)— a touching denouement to brief but painfully charged close encounters of the worst kind. In spite of Sweetland's obvious aversion to the thought of marriage with any of these creatures, Hitchcock forces us to consider along with him what such unions might be like, implicating us in Sweetland's distaste for them as well as setting us up to be harshly embarrassed along with him when they all shortly reject his advances! It's quite an effective montage and sets us up for much of the later action.

Cut to an exterior MS of the farmer following the last of the guests outside, bidding his final farewells. Twelve seconds of handshakes segues into a full twenty-six seconds of the stationary camera on Sweetland, lost in thought. Hitchcock's confidence and grasp of the medium's power is sure as our identification, completed through the previous montage, allows us to comfortably gaze at this man doing nothing but think. He peruses his grounds and home and us as the camera shoots him from a medium distance, rapt and appreciatory. Because we are now so strongly identifying with him, the conventional CU at this time is wholly unnecessary. A genuine sense of release and relief fill our hearts along with Sweetland — he surely has a sweet land to survey. Turning, he enters his home. Cut to the pensive farmer in MS from the inside of the house, hands deep in pockets, a maid occasionally just within sight in the frame scurrying about, table already cleaned up in foreground.

Cut to a frontal CU, his brow now furrowed. Turning his head right, he stares at something OSL. Cut to his POV, a MDS of a closed door leading upstairs to the bedroom, a dark shadow cast upon it and two brightly lit paintings to its right — one of Hitchcock's carefully constructed, highly charged "still lifes." Cut back to a CU of the farmer, the whites of his eyes strongly radiating with thought. Lowering them briefly, he then raises them again and turns his head further R. Cut to his POV, a MCU of Minta exiting the kitchen door and wiping her hands on her apron, busy. A quick glance at the camera/farmer, she immediately zips OSR for more chores. Cut to a MS (another self-conscious, classic director's statement) PAP of Minta clambering up the stairs in the background, Sweetland's profile left in the foreground. With us still strongly identifying with him, we see Minta as imagined through his mind's eye in real time, and we can almost *feel* his thoughts at work.

Powerful cut to a MD shot from a bit further L, twenty-one seconds worth, as Sweetland meanders over to the mantle and turns to stand with his back to it in profile right. He is now directly foregrounding the stairway, and we can clearly see the upper landing above and to our right. Minta comes back out of the upstairs bedroom door holding a coat and marches down the stairs, momentarily obliterated from sight behind Sweetland's head, then emerges from behind him as if coming out of his head. She stands before him SR in profile left and presents him his jacket. Brusquely he directs her to leave it on the table, and she goes.

Cut to another long shot, twenty-four seconds worth of a full frontal CU of Sweetland, frustrated in thought and trying to work out something in his mind. Gazing downward, he looks at the coat he is wearing still covered with graffiti and rice and angrily begins brushing it off. Collecting some in his hand, a revelation slowly steals across his features, and he turns to look L. Highly dramatic cut to a powerfully privileged, five-second ECU head shot of Sweetland *from behind* as he turns round L to look upward at something OSR, reminiscent of a similar shot of the lodger in *The Lodger* also at a mantle. For the first time in the film Sweetland is shown in bright light, happy and even triumphant, and it is quite a lovely shot. Cut to a CU of his POV, his wedding portrait high on the wall behind him.

Cut back to a MCU of a tension-less farmer now in twisted left profile, still looking over his shoulder and half smiling. His eyes just barely begin to drop diagonally left as the camera pans to his POV quickly, moving in synch past the fuzzily shot mantle and coming to rest on an empty but now inviting rocker by the hearth (the Kuleshov experiment may flash into the reader's minds). Cut to a CU (from that chair's POV, but it takes us a moment to realize this) of the farmer blinking his eyes and letting his thoughts and feelings sink in. He steps backward and the camera cuts to an ECU of him moving to sit in a rocker (if we're quick, we realize it's the *other* one on the other side of the mantle that he sits in), transfixed. Cut to his POV, an ECU three-second shot of the first empty rocker staring back at him, expectant. Hitchcock's care with our identifications is so strong that even objects become anthropomorphized in our mind (another book waiting to be written, *Hitchcock's Inanimate Objects as Subjects*).

Cut to a generous thirty-two second ECU of the farmer's face deep in thought, the hearth's fire intermittently flashing bright upon the right side of his face, sparking his thinking. Quick cut back to the patiently waiting chair. Cut back to an ECU of the farmer's face beginning to see the dawning of a light. Leaning closer to the camera, he gets up, completely obliterating our sight momentarily (only his wedding corsage can be recognized for an instant, that's how close he is to the camera's lens). Cut to a long thirty-six second MS of Sweetland pacing back and forth before the hearth, the camera panning with him as he tries to figure out how to ask Minta for her hand, we surmise. Cut to a two-second CU over his right shoulder as he stares into a small mirror on the mantle, preening. Cut to his POV, a ten-second mirror shot in ECU of his egotistical smoothing down of moustache and sideburns. At one point he arches an eyebrow in both a serious and absurdly funny parody of middle-aged vanity. Cut back to a CU of his continued smoothing, more determinedly now.

Cut to a MLS of Minta in the kitchen, profile right (we assume it's his POV, with her back to his gaze OSR, so he must be looking into the kitchen from an oblique angle). As she turns to bring clean glasses out on a tray, Hitchcock cuts to the farmer, startled. The pressure is on now as he attempts to feign an air of nonchalance. Cut to his POV as the camera pans with Minta from above her and slightly looking down in MCU L to R. She crosses the dining room to put the glasses away. Cut back to a full frontal CU of Sweetland, his back against the mantle, harrumphing Minta's name out to come over for a minute. Cut to his POV, a MS as Minta turns to look his/our way. She walks directly towards him/us just to the left of the camera. Cut to a MCU profile left of Sweetland as Minta enters the frame in profile R, smiling.

Turning our way and obviously uncomfortable in asking, his title flashes: "I must take time by the forelock, Minta, else I'll be a lonely man soon." This comment effectively distances himself from any sense of equality or even awareness of her potential as a mate, even if he is hopefully thinking about her in that way, and it reflects his unconscious sense of class separation. It truly will take him the rest of the film to work through his blind prejudices. Cut to her POV, a CU of him rambling on: "twas my late dear Tibby's last wish that in the fulness of time I would take another ... but she didn't name no names." Bullshit avoidance. Cut back to Minta's POV, a CU of Sweetland surreptitiously peeking her/our way beneath his shy brows, the whites of his eyes all aglow in fearful expectation.

Cut to a ten-second, lovingly lit shot, a MCU of Minta in half-turned profile R (his POV) silently thinking this over, a delicate Mona Lisa smile upon her lips. She turns to face the camera directly and answers with no title in the affirmative. Cut back to her POV CU of Sweetland going on, eyes rolling (he can't bring himself to ask her directly), wimp that he is: "There's a female or two be floating around my mind like the smell of a Sunday dinner." Cut back to the gorgeous CU of Minta for seven seconds, openly and innocently egging him on. Cut to an ECU of her POV shot from below and up at him this time — that same privileged view of him we've come to know — his arching eyebrows framing a failed suppression of a grin. "Get pencil and paper, Minta, and us'll run over the possibles and impossibles!" The tense yet funny interplay between these two is thrilling. Quick cut back to her POV, then his (three times gorgeous), as she nods in assent and turns her back on him/us to get the paper across the room, then returns and sits at the dinner table.

Cut to an extraordinary MLS of Minta farscreen L sitting facing us and Sweetland turning to sit in the rocker with his back to the camera, a lot of space between them. Cut to Minta's POV, a CU of Sweetland in the rocker beginning his list. As he imagines the three women from his daughter's wedding party one by one, they materialize in his mind's eye and on the screen across from him in the other rocker. Middle-aged biddy Louisa Windeatt (even though we've yet to see any of these would-be ladies' names on a title) fades in to sit in the other chair, happily chirping away. Cut to an ECU of Sweetland, doing all he can not to laugh out loud over such an image. Turning to the camera he loudly proclaims her name to us— no title is necessary — and Minta.

Cut to a CU of Minta hurt by such a suggestion. Taking a moment, she determines she's "too old" (we read her lips, so no title is necessary again) and says so. Cut to a CU of Sweetland, mock surprise, both of them enjoying this little bantering game they've set up: "You know her back view's not a day over thirty!" Quick cut to a CU of Minta: "But you have to live with her front view." Well said, as Hitchcock keeps the camera in attractive CU's of both of them. Quick cut to a triumphant Minta — she's got him on that point. Cut to Sweetland, mock arguing. Well, put her name down anyway. Sighing in false exasperation, the camera cuts to an ECU of Minta's hand writing "Louisa Windeatt" on the paper.

Thoughtfully, Minta proffers, "How about Thirza Tapper?" Great, goony onomatopoetic names, the kind W. C. Fields would memorialize in his later comedies. Cut to Sweetland thoughtful, and then a fade in on Thirza (the young/old maid) blathering on in the rocker, prissy as a polyp. Sweetland gestures OK, put her name down. More mock exasperation by Minta. Cut to her writing Thirza's name. Last drumble bum fades in and out and farmer calls out her name, "What about Mary Hearn?" Minta gestures with wide, circular arms, implying "too fat, you don't want her." Title: "I don't mind they pillowy women ... So long as they be pillowy in the right places." Minta's got a good retort for that, too: "A woman that's a pillow at thirty be often a feather bed at forty!" Put her name down anyway.

Cut to a CU of the list being lengthened. With a hopeful sense of finality Minta rips the page off the pad, the list complete. Cut to Sweetland getting up to stand as we lip-read on his face, "Wait a minute, we're not done yet." Standing above the camera Sweetland points an emphatic finger at us and says: "Just put down Mercy Bassett of the Royal Oak for luck." Cut to his POV (camera looking down) of Minta, consternation written all over her face. Cut back to Sweetland, insistent. Back to Minta, miming: "Oh well, OK, if we must." The whole scene keeps building in that classic Hitchcockian light comedic humor of his British films.

Hurrying the last name down, Minta rises triumphant, not allowing Sweetland one more name on the list, and she rushes it over to him in MCU with her back to the camera. She hands it to him and we see them side by side, backs to the roaring hearth. They make a handsome couple indeed. Taking the paper in hand, Sweetland phonily surveys it. Cut to an ECU of the list, then a CU of the couple. "'Tis almost indecent to see 'em all on one bit of paper" he gleefully chirps over his shoulder towards Minta. Cut to a MDS (contrary to our desires by now, which are thoroughly engaged) of the couple chuckling.

In the same shot, Sweetland sits down in one rocker and Minta naturally takes her seat in the other. Their images frame the blazing hearth between them as we also see two candlesticks, two vases, two cups, two plates, two guns, two recessed hollows, and one teapot above them on the mantle, completing this lovely, symmetrical shot of pastoral tranquility. By withholding and stepping back from a clinch at this point, which the director makes sure we know will occur by the end of the picture, Hitchcock rewards us more fully by showing them happily if unconsciously conjoined in silence through this two-of-everything shot. The screen fades to black.

Fade up on a CU of hands polishing shoes, dissolving into a CU of hair being combed, dissolving into an exaggeratedly absurd ECU of a moustache being brushed, dissolving into a CU of a long-sleeved shirt being adjusted, dissolving into an ECU of a fresh flower being placed in a lapel. Hitchcock even shows us the minutiae of Minta's hand in ECU placing a pin in the orchid behind the lapel—five brief shots of livery preparations prior to the marriage hunt. All-suffering Minta continues her dogged and faithful efforts by retrieving her master's top hat in final preparation for his connubial callings.

Cut to a MS of the outside door shot from the inside as Churdles opens it and enters, horse and carriage visible and ready behind him. His POV of his master looking over his shoulder, with a glaring and defiant Minta staring back, is exchanged with her. CU POV of him, surly and knowing. Their eye contact exposes their mutual disdain — and our agreeable feelings of communion with them — over Sweetland's wasted follies. Through their quickly exchanged looks—another wonderful example of pure Hitchcockian cinema — we learn about and are privy to much more information than any title of dialogue could provide.

> *In many of the films being made, there is very little cinema: they are mostly what I call "photographs of people talking." When we tell a story in cinema, we should resort to dialogue only when it's impossible to do otherwise. I always try first to tell a story in the cinematic way, through a succession of shots and bits of film in between.... Whichever way you choose to stage the action, your main concern is to hold the audience's fullest attention.... [O]ne might say that the screen rectangle must be charged with emotion* [AH in FT, 1985, p. 61].

Cut back to a two-shot CU of Minta and Sweetland as she inhales deeply, momentarily straightening her own proud back and exhaling in compliant servitude. Churdles rolls his eyes and shakes a knowing head in constantly baffled acceptance over the stupid rich. In a way, Churdles Ash is Hitchcock's Greek Chorus in the film. Cut to a MS of Minta and the farmer in PAP profile, she giving him one final once over. Cut to a CU of the same profile shot, Minta always to our left of him, Sweetland's hand raised: "There's no need to wish me luck — Louisa Windeatt will come like a lamb to the slaughter." All three actors — Hall-Davis, Thomas, and Harker — play this absurd farce for all its worth.

Mustering all of her unwilling support, Minta attempts a smile, then defeatedly glances back at a CU of the empty rocker — hers, rightfully — which has also transfixed Sweetland's gaze momentarily. Cut to a MS of the two of them staring over DSL. Breaking out of their trance, they bid each other adieu and the camera pans quickly left with Sweetland as he strides for the door. Cut to a three-second medium exterior shot as he bows his head coming out, looking momentarily headless in the doorway's shadow. Reverse angle MS cut to his receding back where he slaps Churdles firmly on his as he holds the horse steady for mounting. Off he rides US as Churdles heads DS silently shaking his head.

Cut to an ELS of a dark, wooded hill cutting a diagonal swath from USL to DSR, dark and billowy tree-lined forests massive in the background, and a dwarfed path with rider winding its way from CS to L. It's an extraordinarily beautiful, twenty-five second, static camera shot of the English countryside, and is an especially powerful scene juxtaposed as it is immediately after all of those interior CU shots of people. Quick cut to a MS of the brightly lit Sweetland riding SL to SR, then hesitating. Cut to his POV, a reverse angle MLS of another rider on the path ahead of him moving up the hill from DSC to further away US. All three of these scenes, actually, confuse us through their quick confluence of angles, reverse angles, unique directions, different distances, and lightings. For a moment we think this third shot is just another one of Sweetland, until the surprise title confirms our guess: "The widow herself!"

Cut back to Sweetland urging his steed on. Cut to yet another extraordinary fourth angle of the great outdoors, a LS of Sweetland's horse catching up to the other's, R to L this time, as they climb the sloping hill DSR to USL. Cut to a fifth fresh shot of the scene, this time from behind Sweetland as he pulls alongside Louisa, both horses' asses now seen receding into the woods for another twenty five seconds of real time. With the camera still immobile, the horses walk from MD to ELD upscreen and out of sight. Cut to an almost equally long twenty-three second similar shot of the horses in somewhat closer MD as they cross the stationary camera's path R to L on this lazy day's meeting. The entire outdoor montage is rendered with a leisurely, pastoral grace (compare this montage to the extremely rushed pace of the wedding preparations), and it was no wonder that the Hitchcock's soon bought a home in the area — the director had been paid to do the site visits!

Cut to a M profile shot, Sweetland on our L helping hefty down from her horse, then walking her SR to a CU of him opening her home's door for her. She enters, but he pauses outside to breathe the clean air and gaze about. Spying two helpers (his POV is a MD shot as they look back at us), he makes their acquaintance, trying on the man of the house for a moment. Cut to their POV (everyone and many things have a POV in Hitchcock's films, especially this one, no matter how seemingly trivial they might appear at first) in MCU as he smiles at us, then enters the house behind him. Cut to a PAP of the interior as they stand about, Sweetland on L as Louisa prepares drinks. Cut to a CU of Sweetland's POV, Louisa pouring tea, shot to look older and uglier than ever and dressed in mournful black. As she turns her head to the R we realize we've been fooled again: "What brings you up my hill, Sweetland?" The previous shot was not Sweetland's POV but ours, Hitchcock's autonomous camera view asserting itself! Cut to her POV (or is it, really? Yes, it turns out — this time), a CU of Sweetland with the pressure on again.

Acting deep in thought but really stumblingly searching for words, he finds a few and, gazing sheepishly into the camera in CU — one lone plate hangs on the wall behind him to our right, recalling and contrasting with his own mantle of matching plates— he says: "I came over like the foxes you're so fond of ... to pick up a fat hen!" The double entendres even at this early date could not have been lost on Hitchcock's 1928 audience.

Cut to his POV, a CU of his "hen" in profile R as her head turns right to look hopefully, then doubtfully dubious into the camera. The china on the table behind her fills the background with one large and lonely plate leaning against the wall, further expanding our subliminal awareness of this room's space and placement of symbolic objects. Cut back to a two-shot profile (Sweetland always on L — Minta's position) as Louisa sits CS lifting a glass to her mouth. Cut to a CU of Sweetland patting her on the back (a new angle, a bit right): "Wait till you hear me ... and then there'll be something to drink to." Ever more doubtful, Louisa watches as Sweetland goes to cross behind her, but just before he passes to her right on SR Hitchcock cuts to his initial entrance shot, Sweetland US, which keeps him in our view to her left and in SL. What the director has done is prevent the farmer from crossing her imaginary screen plane, a clever, purely visual deterrent that keeps Sweetland from entering Louisa's space! (Such camera motifs are subliminal cinema at its finest, and bring to mind the subtleties of similar camera shots that have escaped most critics' eyes in two of Hitchcock's so-called minor films, *Waltzes from Vienna* and *Topaz*.) Cutting to his POV, Louisa looks back over her right shoulder at the two of us, more doubtful than ever. Cut to her POV, a CU of Sweet-land with his hand on his chest, all puffed up like a peacock. To the cam-era: "I be marryin' again, Louisa." By now we're beginning to tire of this man's fill of himself, and Hitchcock gladly deflates all stuffed shirts in his films through his relentless ability to dress down these would-be emper-ors.

Cut to Sweetland's POV as Louisa takes a deep breath and, without title, says, "Is that so?" All smiles, she raises her glass and toasts him. Cut to a MS as Sweetland, about as dumb as could be, crosses to explain him-self. He rambles on and on, and Louisa finally erupts: "Then the fat hen you want ... is it for the wedding breakfast?" Cut to a MS as Sweetland reaches behind her for a chair and pulls it alongside her (to our — you guessed it — left). Cut to a two-shot CU, both in profile, him conspirato-rial.

Before the title we know what his next mistake will be for, after he gestures to her, she tries to get up, embarrassed. He gently presses her back into her chair: "You're the first to know your good luck, my dear ----," he pompously presumes. Cut back to the same tense CU, him ram-bling on and Louisa getting a bit of dander up. "What impunity," we reg-ister on her face. Sweetland stumbles on: "-- -- -- and I am a man that a little child can lead but a regiment of soldiers couldn't drive." The dou-ble entendres are much more serious now and somewhat taxing for an audience of the 21st century, if not the 1920's. "Do you understand me," his face asks. "I sure do," hers replies. Cut to a charged over-her-left-shoulder CU of Sweetland (the first of its kind in a long while), his face flushed with excitement, just the barest profile of hers exposed. "*Yes* be a very short word," he says. No be even shorter, we expect. Cut to a charged over-his-right-shoulder CU of her shaking her head from side to side intel-ligently and empathetically. "But there's a shorter...." Cut back to her face in CU, still shaking. Cut to a profile CU release, Sweetland astounded, hurt and incredulous. She speaks: "I am not the sort of woman for you — I am far too independent."

Sweetland and us are pulled up short. Suddenly the film has become a treatise on the impertinence of men and the autonomy and strength of women! Wonderful! Who could judge Hitchcock as a first-class misogy-nist after such a retort and assertion as Louisa's? Not to be put off that eas-ily, though, Sweetland blunders on shamelessly, a sexist at heart: "You'll only feel the velvet glove and never know I was breaking you in." She laughs in his face, but without malice, a true gentlewoman. (Remember, we really know nothing about her, only what she looked like to Sweetland through Hitchcock's camera at the party.)

Cut to a MCU of Louisa, having already stood up as she brushes him off in no uncertain terms. Cut to an ECU of her POV of Sweetland completely incredulous now, glaring at the camera. "How dare you reject me," he sputters. Alternate shots of face-to-face POV's recall the wedding party goodbyes. Cut to a powerfully shot CU of Louisa, her lips thin from suppressed anger. Back to Sweetland, still blathering. Back to Louisa, controlled. Decisively, she extends her hand towards the camera in a blurred ECU. Immediate cut to a MCU profile of her open palm, a curt and rigid offer of luck to him. A little boy who isn't getting his way, Sweetland cannot take her hand, and Louisa slowly withdraws it, a knowing look upon her face. Grabbing his riding crop, he emptily threats: "Don't think that I shall come up your darned hill again!" Louisa silently smiles acknowledgment. She then bursts out laughing again as he wags his finger at her and scowls: "And you haven't treated me in a very ladylike spirit over this job [Job? Yes, I suppose that's all it was to him] ...you ain't nice-minded." *Au contraire!* Cut to his POV, a CU of Louisa still free-spiritedly laughing at the camera. Cut to her POV, the little boy's pride squashed. Opening the door, he turns back for one last impotent parry, aimed at her but really said to himself: "And it's no use changing your mind ... you've brought your doom on yourself." The film has now faced the issue of whether and how Farmer Sweetland might grow up.

Quick cut to more bawdy laughter directly in our faces. Cut to Sweetland, leaving. Cut to Louisa calling out after him. Turning back, he thinks he's heard her tell him she was only kidding, and his face lights up, childlike. She reaches behind her and grabs her glass again, toasting him and still laughing. Crushed completely, he's had it and storms out the door.

Cut to the outside, Sweetland in CU slamming his top hat o'er his head, furious. Turning, he spies the workers. They smile. Angrily, he importunes them to keep working and to go get his horse. Dumbfounded, they cooperate. Cut to a MD shot through a scraggly bare tree of Sweetland climbing onto his horse and waving the workers away SL. He gallops OSR as the workers follow L to R offscreen. Cut to a LS of Sweetland galloping out of the main entrance L to R, Louisa's lovely farmhouse and the beautiful Devon countryside in the background. Cut to the workers in a closer LS walking towards the house entrance as they querulously watch him leave. Cut to an ELS of their POV of Sweetland's horse receding into the pastoral countryside down the road. Fade to black.

Fade up on a MD shot of the pissed-off farmer galloping back to his house towards the camera, scaring the heck out a gaggle of geese in his way. Jumping off, the camera cuts to a M shot of his retreating figure storming into the house, his horse following through the posts with its rump prominently displayed. Cut to a ML shot from the interior, Sweet-land striding angrily SR to L with the camera panning and keeping him close to SL but not out of the frame, sustaining the tension. Cut to an amusing CU of the horse's head peering around the inside of the door, looking bemused. *Cut to the horse's POV*, a MS of the farmer's shadowed back retreating into the kitchen in a never-before-seen angle. Naturally — it's the first and only POV of the horse!

Cut to a MCU shot of the camera still panning on the farmer in profile left and now centered with a riding crop in hand. He and the camera stop to view Minta's back as she works in the kitchen. Cut to a CU of the fuming farmer from in front of him, a disorienting view as all these shots last no more than three seconds each. First he glares in Minta's direction (his L, OSR), then glares right. Cut to his POV, a MCU of Churdles snoring peacefully in his favorite corner. From this angle, the room takes on yet an extra tense dimension due to these frequent cuts *and* the farmer's anger. Cut back to a CU of the farmer reacting to someone he can now take his anger out on. He blurredly moves SL.

Cut to a MCU PAP of a startled Churdles amusingly and violently being roused from his dreamland, Sweetland's riding crop waving dangerously close. Churdles takes off SL and Sweetland turns back towards Minta OSR. Calling out to her, the camera cuts to his POV in MD as Minta turns to look back over her R shoulder, querulous. Cut to her POV, a MCU of Sweetland in profile L wagging his crop and belaboring her/us. Hitchcock's combination of rapid fire POV's here — the house, the yard, the horse, the farmer, the PAP, Churdles, Minta — as well as all the angles and body positionings (Minta and Sweetland, twisted looking over their shoulders, are the most highly charged) — lend tremendous power to these scenes. Cut to a title: "Don't let that fox-hunting old baggage, Louisa Windeatt, come into this house no more."

Cut back to the farmer's POV, a MS quick two-seconds (which adds to the shock) of Minta freaking out. She may never have seen her master this angry before and drops the china she is holding to the floor, which breaks. Cut to a CU of the farmer, Minta's POV, livid and screaming at her/us and pointing to the floor. Cut to his POV, a CU of Minta flustered and all apologetic. Quick two-second cut to her POV, a CU of him. The cuts are so fast now that we can't quite tell if Sweetland's not a little ashamed of himself for berating her. He turns his head quickly to face OSL. Cut to his POV, a CU of Churdles looking back in from the kitchen's outside door, then hurriedly leaving. Cut back to Minta's POV CU of the farmer facing the camera, a look of stifled fury amusingly playing across his face, as he pulls the "hopefuls" list out of his pocket and angrily crosses out Louisa's name. Fade to black.

Fade up on an ECU of the crossed-out name of "Louisa Windeatt" framed by the camera with darkness above and below. Camera pans down the list (or the paper slides up) to rest on the similarly lit name of "Thirza Tapper." Cut to an ECU of a handwritten letter invitation: "I'm pleased to see you. Don't forget the party commences at *four o'clock* punctual. Yours Sincerely, Thirza Tapper." Fade to black.

Fade up on a long shot of yet another beautiful country estate surrounded by trees nestled into a corner of a hillside. It almost looks like a landscape painting. Dissolve into a CU of the house from another angle, smoke lazily wafting out of a chimney SL. Fade to black.

Fade up on a CU of shuttered windows somewhere on the house. Dissolve to the interior, a MS of an empty table with all of its place settings in the dining room. Dissolve to a CU of hands cutting bread and preparing a meal in a kitchen. Cut to a NBS *camera dolly back* to a MS of this new kitchen, Minta doing the cutting (center frame), Churdles struggling with his livery wear, and a maid SR fighting with her outfit. Title: "It was very kind of you to come and help us, Minta ... and you too, Mr. Ash." Cut back to the same scene but via a PAP, Churdles churlishly frowning. Very slow dissolve, also NBS, of an ECU of Thirza in profile R washing her face with soap, another of Hitchcock's strangely fascinating juxtapositions to a shot of revealed intimacy, voyeurism, innocence and vulgarity. Reacting to something offscreen, she turns to face OSL. Cut to a very extreme ECU of a ringing bell. This shot allows us to almost hear the sound of its tolling, for Hitchcock uses the very extreme ECU even more sparingly than the ECU for powerful effect — it's literally *in our face.*

Cut to a different angle of a MS of Minta, Churdles and the maid, now L to R in the kitchen, also responding to the bell but looking OSR. They all turn their heads away from the PAP camera shot, then backwards towards the mantle. Cut to an ECU of a clock on the mantle showing 3:25 pm. Someone is 35 minutes too early. Who it could be! Cut back to the threesome, maid getting frantic. Cut to a third angle of the same group in MS, Minta pointing the large knife in her hand and barking orders. Camera pans with the maid R as she throws her apron on and goes out the kitchen door, camera keeping her center screen. Cut to a powerful shot from immediately behind the maid's back and head, an ECU all in shadow — the *kitchen doorway's* POV — splitting the screen with windows L and R, the outside door directly ahead of the maid. This extraordinary five-second shot is all in dark shadow as she hurries to the front door away from the camera. Cut to a slight right angle shot in MCU of the maid reaching the door, opening it and seeing Sweetland standing there with a basket in his hand, beaming. Trepidation written all over her features,

Sweetland hands her his hat triumphantly as her title reads: "The party ain't begun yet, sir."

Cut to a MCU camera angled still further to the right, brightly designed wallpaper visible behind them. Harrumphing an impatient explanation, Sweetland condescendingly importunes the maid to announce his presence to the mistress of the house. Camera rapidly pans with the maid as she rushes up the staircase behind them. Quick cut to a CU shot of the maid knocking on her mistress's door. Cut to another intrusively voyeuristic CU of Thirza, sitting profile R and washing her feet in a bath pot. Without makeup and relaxing in the privacy of her own room, Thirza looks quite lovely in her simple beauty. But Hitchcock only allows us a short two-second glimpse of her like this. Quick cut back to a CU shot of the maid hurriedly explaining the situation through the door. Cut to a five-second CU of Thirza, now flustered and looking like her old biddy self again. A foot flops into the bath, spraying her, and tension erupts all over her face. She calls out an order. Cut to a clever, sixteen-second closer CU of just the maid's shoulders and head, the camera panning with her as she hurries back down the stairs— our view, or possibly Thirza's imaginary POV — of her taking Sweetland's hat and asking him to please sit down.

The camera angle is precipitously steep shooting down onto his figure from the upstairs landing. He sits, anxious, and follows the maid with his eyes as she exits OSR. Glancing upwards towards the camera, he slowly relaxes in anticipation, picnic basket clutched under his arm. This is a surprisingly lovely, tranquil shot of Sweetland in the corner of the downstairs room at the foot of the stairs, brightly lit wallpaper and *objets d'art* all around him, and it affects us strongly because it's so contrary to both Sweetland and Thirza's feelings at the moment. Only Hitchcock could make such an unnaturally pastoral scene feel suspenseful (or a suspenseful scene seem pastoral)!

Cut back upstairs to the biddy frantically and spastically tearing on her tights— pathetic is the word for our viewing, not her action. Cut to a twenty-second shot of the farmer, same high angle but from a closer point to the bedroom door (reflecting more of the biddy's imaginings than a neutral camera's POV, thereby incrementally increasing the tension on the screen) as he argues over the basket with Minta this time. Finally hushing her away, he sits back down and gives a self-satisfied glance directly at the MD camera above him on the landing —*his imagination projected up to her now.*

Cut back to the biddy, finally successful with her clothing. She gets up, pulls close her robe, and hurries OSR. Cut to a CU of her back going to her plain bedroom door, reminiscent of the maid's movements earlier. Quick cut (two seconds) to the camera's POV, a CU of Thirza from chest level up sneaking a peek out her door, the camera asserting its autonomy by showing this private shot from its/our "neutral" POV. Now Hitchcock cuts to her *actual* MD POV of Sweetland, pacing and grinning far away downstairs. Cut back to another private camera shot of her, extremely agitated. Quick cut (two seconds) to her POV again, the farmer still pacing and glancing up. Very quick one-second cut to Thirza fearfully exiting her bedroom, shot now from a MCU lower angle (at hip height), suggesting her coming descent. Cut back to three more seconds of pacing. Very quick one-second cut to biddy afraid of being spotted as she rushes back into her bedroom. Cut to her POV, a MD shot of the farmer yawning. Cut to an *anticipated* farmer's POV (as we will see) in MD from below as the bid comes out, closes her door, and then realizes she's caught her robe in it, all shown SR. She pulls at it frantically. Cut to her POV, the farmer turning, seeing her (the camera had preempted this view), and starting to address her. Cut back to his POV, Thirza feverish. She finally yanks her robe free, then rushes OSL. Cut to the camera's POV, a CU of her back as she is seen presumably in another room to the left of the upstairs landing. She approaches a vanity table. Sitting, she throws a quick glance back at the camera. Cut back to more pacing downstairs, the upstairs landing's POV with the camera standing in for Thirza's and our own imagined view from that position. Images of the camera as alternating stand-in and autonomous neutral viewer have been accumulating throughout this film, more than in any up till now.

Cut back to an autonomous camera CU of Thirza, now frantic with her nylons and makeup. Release cut to a chest level CU of Sweetland becoming impatient, as are we. Once again, these feelings are being deliberately provoked in us. Sweetland puts down his basket and skulks about, petulant and little boyish. Quick three-second cut to a titillating AC MS of Thirza SL hurriedly pulling on her dress, the outline of a breast visible. Cut back to an AC CU of Sweetland, more impatient than ever. Cut to an AC MS from behind Thirza, working hard on her hair in a mirror and glancing fearfully back at the camera.

Cut to AC (stand-in) MCU of Sweetland almost considering leaving as he looks at the door. Turning suddenly, he erupts in ecstasy as Hitchcock cuts to his POV, a MS of Thirza miraculously appearing upstairs SR, her severe face firmly on as she walks stone-like to the head of the stairs and stares down at him. Cut to her POV, a CU in her/our face of a beaming smile plastered on Sweetland's mouth as he bows and innocently grabs his basket OSL to hide it, boy-like, behind his back. Cut to his MS POV of Thirza scurrying down to camera level, hard at work keeping her features immobile and expressionless. The geometric arrangement of the stairs and banister at right angles behind and to her left lends a powerful still life feel to this shot. Cut to an AC PAP CU of biddy (L) and farmer SR in profile, he bowing again (Hitchcock and Sweetland "trying on" this left-to-right marriage positioning for size, so to speak).

Glancing around, Sweetland notices that no one else is about. Quick AC cut to the open dining room door confirms this. Cut back to the farmer making some puzzling comment, biddy acting sly and stupid. Cut to an odd and most beautiful MCU, a new AC shot of the farmer backing up R and the biddy crossing in front of him, then turning DS and walking in front of him OSR. Sweetland's hands are clasped behind him in a gentlemanly manner, his chin is up, and Thirza's fingers are outstretched before her, lending the scene a touching, waltz-like quality that feels like a gentile courtship.

Cut to a reverse angle AC MCU as they enter another room, expanding our three-dimensional sense of this house in Hitchcock's typically marvelous way as Thirza looks over her L shoulder at Sweetland stalking her. Camera pans L with them, both remaining at an equal distance from each other, as the farmer yaps at her all the while (shades of old man Coaker's similarly annoying actions during the earlier wedding party). The basket is proffered. Cut to a CU of their profiles, more small talk. Thirza takes the basket and crosses in front of him to move OSR. Cut to his POV, a MS of her receding back through the front door seen in the background. Cut to an AC shot from the front door area as camera pans L to R with bid's brusque walk towards the pantry door, her back to the camera again. Cut to a CU of her back again passing along the corridor and entering her kitchen. Cut to a panning PAP MS of her moving R to L as she approaches her maid. Cut to a PAP CU of Thirza handing the basket over to her as the maid says via title: "Do you want me to do the plums before the ices, then?" Cut to a PAP MS — no answer — as Thirza crosses L to address Minta and Churdles, both of whom we now suddenly remember are working in the house, OSL in this scene. We had completely forgotten about them, actually, that's how engaged we were with Sweetland and Thirza.

Thirza's handed two plates full of food as confusion sets in all around, and the camera pans with her exit. Cut to a reverse shot of her tracks, but from such different angles that her movements cause us disorientation. With her back to the camera as she recedes (exactly like the maid's earlier movement towards the front door), Hitchcock cuts to a CU of her back entering the brightly lit living room.

Cut to the farmer's POV, a MS of her entering the room loaded down with food. Cut to her POV, a CU of Sweetland sitting and leaning against the piano, surveyor of his new kingdom. Reacting, he pushes himself off, oblivious to the seashell and two pictures that his action causes to fall down behind him. Grinning, he rises. Cut to a PAP MS of Thirza putting food onto the table and crossing behind Sweetland to replace the fallen items while he gestures dramatically, his back to the camera. Cut to a long, thirty-second, in-your-face two-shot CU of Sweetland haranguing Thirza. He's right on top of her as she hopelessly attempts to set up the table (flash on Coaker again). Pushed up against the frame of SR, we feel Sweetland's aggressiveness and her claustrophobia.

Finally, she begins to hear a little of what he is saying and stops to peer at him: "Now some men look for a bit of fat on a female..." he begins insolently. Interrupted (Hitchcock prolongs our payoff), they are startled by something from *behind* the camera (our eyes). Cut to a MLS of the maid, food in hand, acting querulous towards us. Cut to the maid's (camera's) POV, the farmer pissed off at being interrupted and Thirza placating. Cut to a new AC angle CU of the maid, camera panning with her R to L until she enters their frame, Thirza now US with the farmer glowering SL. The maid catches his eye and retreats, camera panning left to right as she looks over her right shoulder, aghast. By staying in CU with the maid the whole time—fifteen seconds—we feel *her* reactions, briefly identifying with her amazement over Sweetland. Backing up and still staring at him, she trips on the step of the doorway and stumbles out of the room.

Cut to an AC MS of Sweetland re-pursuing his catch. Biddy moves OSR to continue setting the table as Sweetland responds angrily to her retreat and, through proxy, at the camera's framing, which is denying us sight of her by putting some distance between them! He moves to the center of the table and leans over it. Cut to an AC shot of the *piano's* POV, a CU of Sweetland L leaning over the table with Thirza R, camera back tracking (a zoom out) as they both shuffle in profile toward the camera down table in a quick but clearly self-referential technical demonstration by the director. These are always fun to see. Cut to the previous AC POV, the biddy's back to the camera almost completely blocking Sweetland's figure. Not tolerating that scenario, he walks around the table, still forcibly restrained by frame L, to confront biddy in CU DS. We can feel the director's camera deliberately making Sweetland's proposal difficult by using the table and screen frames as obstacles, and we see Sweetland's resentment and frustration build. This further implicates the camera and us, since Hitchcock has been presenting more and more frequent autonomous shots for the last fifteen minutes or so.

Sweetland, irrepressibly importuning Thirza, plops his left hand on top of some food. In an almost full-frontal ECU, Hitchcock shows us a frazzled Thirza Tapper, nervously apologetic. Cut back to PAP profiles in MS, Sweetland fed up. Powerful, audacious cut to a full frontal ECU of

Sweetland's face screaming into the camera, one eyebrow arched defiantly: "Hang it, Thirza Tapper, *I'm asking you to marry me!*" [Second half of sentence in script.] Cut to a hysterically funny ECU full frontal of Thirza, blinking rapidly, totally unnerved as she shakes and jiggles a plate of jello she's holding at chest height — a blatant and humorously titillating stand-in for her own heaving breasts.

Cut release to a MS PAP profile of Thirza, now almost faint and backing up R to drop into a chair. Cut to a CU of Sweetland towering over her. At first he looks fearful, then triumphant. Cut to his POV, a CU of an overwhelmed Thirza in the chair nearly hyperventilating, eyes closed. Cut back to a CU of the real fox closing in for the kill, moving OS down L. Cut to an oblique lowshot CU of Sweetland taking the jello out of her hands, not knowing what to do with it (more deliberate distractions), and then patting Thirza's shoulder while she continues to gasp for breath, woozy. Cut to a MS of the same, Sweetland getting on his knees to propose, a vaguely familiar line beginning via title: "I'm a man a little child can lead, though a regiment of soldiers...."

Suddenly, Thirza dramatically rises. Cut to a two-shot CU of her on the *left* of screen above him now (the power spot in this film), him still kneeling R. Gesturing dramatically, she intones: "Rise, *dear Samuel Sweetland.*" He does, boyishly eager. He grabs her in one arm, but she shakes him off, and then we read her amazing title: "You are the first man who has accepted my sex challenge!" Astounded — stupefied is more like it, as we are — he shakes the comment off and grabs her anew. She cowers in his arms. "But I shall never seek the shelter of a man's arms— not even yours." Hitchcock cuts to a full frontal CU of Sweetland's now familiar mix of rage and disbelief right at us/Thirza. Cut to a CU of the still trembling Thirza, then eight alternating POV CU's of yelling and cowering between the couple (four shots each), Hitchcock pounding home the painful thoughtlessness and shy hopelessness of these two creatures.

Cut to a PAP CU of Sweetland continuing to belittle Thirza as the out-of-focus maid enters the scene between and behind them. Cut to an ECU of the maid's face crying, a tray of something spilling and dripping onto the floor from her hands. Cut to the maid's POV, a MS of Sweetland's face contorted in anger and Tapper's in fear. Cut to their POV, a MS of the maid with her tears streaming (they/we think she's crying for them, but...). Cut back to the maid's CU POV, Sweetland turning back on the attack to poor Thirza. Cut to an AC MS of Churdles appearing in the doorway behind the maid, then the camera pans R to L as she brings the tray over to them. Cut to a PAP CU of Thirza freaking out L, maid R, the tray between them. Maid thinks Thirza is upset at her, for she says: "How was

I to know the ices would melt if I left them near the fire!" Thirza waves her away. "Who cares about the ices?" we think, as Hitchcock laughs at all of us.

Cut now to an AC CU from *behind* the fighting couple, Sweetland still on his high horse, as Churdles enters the room US and between them (same kind of shot with the maid splitting their images). Sweetland now turns on him. Cut to Ash. He's about had it with Sweetland himself by now, and begins to defend himself, defiantly. Cut to Ash's POV of the farmer in CU, screaming. Cut to Ash, reacting. Cut to a crying Thirza. Cut to Churdles in CU figuring it all out. Narrowing his eyes, he shifts his gaze between the two of them. Cut to Sweetland, back at her. Cut back to Churdles, who sees this man as he really is—a blowhard crybaby. After all the earlier identifying with him as only a lowly servant, we suddenly rejoice in Ash's newfound awareness as we realize we've been secretly pulling for him to make some kind of assertive statement the entire film. He hasn't rebelled openly, but he has finally acknowledged, to himself and us, that he has a strength of character heretofore missing. Good for him, we silently acknowledge, as Churdles finds in himself some deeply suppressed dignity.

He and the maid slowly back away from the camera towards the kitchen door, our long-forgotten Minta again miraculously appearing. The maid trips on the step again, exiting. Cut to Minta and Churdles' POV, Sweetland still at it and Thirza beside herself. Cut to an AC MS of Churdles, glowering. Camera begins to pan with Minta as she crosses R to L, plums in hand (Sweetland's present). Cut to a CU of Sweetland, eyes following Minta. As he looks down, cut to a CU of the plums in Minta's hands. Cut back to Sweetland in profile R CU turning his head to the L to follow. Cut to a CU of the plums being placed on the table. Cut to a CU of Sweetland, still livid. Cut to a MCU of Minta coming between the two to comfort the sobbing woman. Sweetland SL heartlessly pulls out his list and scratches Thirza's name off it. He then stalks OS towards and past camera L. Cut to his retreating back—a powerful motif throughout this whole scene (in fact, the whole film)—towards the outside door. Hesitating, he storms out.

Cut to Churdles in MCU eyeing Sweetland's departure angrily. We're now led to believe he'll make some derogatory comment on his master, or show some sympathy towards Thirza. Thumb in fist waving, he moves SL with camera panning and gestures angrily to Thirza, Minta just behind her. His trousers need a belt, we notice, as his movements humorously reveal. Thirza, still visibly upset, is urged by Minta to help him out, and Hitchcock unexpectedly, improbably, yet believably veers the narrative off into new territory. Camera pans R following Churdles following Thirza. Cut to a sixty-second plus PAP MCU pan in the other room L to R as

Thirza arrives at a closet under the stairs. She pulls out a moth-eaten, dust-infested servant's coat. Ash shudders disapprovingly, feigning a sneeze as she shakes the dust off. He is dubiously helped into it after much harrumphing and fussing, then eyes it over somewhat proudly as he realizes he looks rather regal in its formal cut. Cut to a MLS, both of them SL, the diagonal line of the stairway SR — a geometrically strong shot. Thirza decides Churdles could also use some decent shoes, and heads up the stairs. Ash continues to adjust to his new accoutrements and shuffles over to the steps himself, not altogether undignified, I might add.

Cut to another long, thirty-eight second CU of Churdles humorously attempting to stitch his worn shoe with pieces of cord, frequently sliding off the step he is sitting on. Cut to a MLS, eighteen seconds worth, of Thirza coming down the stairs behind Ash with her sewing kit. Hitchcock's pace has slowed again. They descend to stand together, Ash reluctantly proffering his broken pants' button for her to sew. Cut to a twelve-second CU of her sewing, accidentally in position to see down Churdles' pants. They momentarily make eye contact. Ash turns his head R with a mixed look of satisfaction and grim approval. We can almost see him stifle a grin, but that would be too out of character (like John Whittaker's dropping of screen character in *Easy Virtue*), while Thirza turns her head L with a mixture of embarrassment and healthy curiosity written on her features. Cut to that earlier ECU of a bell ringing. Cut back to a CU of the couple, Thirza hurriedly through, but unfinished.

Cut to a PAP LS, fifteen seconds, of Thirza hurrying OSL and Churdles complaining about the unfinished job to no one in particular, flapping his oversized pants in mock anger. Cut to a rear MS of Churdles going to the door to let a family in: a boy, a girl, momma and poppa. Holding his pants up with one hand, Churdles waves away the father's proffered handshake in CU and says: "I ain't the party, George!" Dad gives him his hat instead.

Cut to Ash and Tapper ushering the family SR, camera panning in a MS. Cut to a door opening (AC from inside) in MS, guests entering — technical tour de force coming. Cut to an ECU of a fresh-faced, smiling boy facing the camera (two seconds). Vertigo inducing three-second *zoom shot* (NBS) of the boy's blurred view as he focuses in on an ECU of a cake on the table — the child's camera-enhanced POV. Cut to the camera panning R to L as the boy rushes over to grab at the confection. Cut to a MS from behind the boy, momma catching up and roughly handling him. Camera pans with the boy as he moves L to sit on a piano stool, where the farmer sat earlier. He laughs his mother's roughness off in a typical childlike manner, immediately negating mother's sternness. Cut to a MCU of the mother bitching to Minta about kids in general. We can almost hear Hitchcock say: "This child is what Sweetland was like when he was young."

Cut to a MLS PAP of Churdles opening the door (still obviously holding up his pants with one hand), slamming the door, and opening it again after forgetting why he'd opened it in the first place. He lets another guest into the living room. The man roams about introducing himself, looking lost. Cut to a MCU of Churdles opening and slamming the door again, then gesturing: "Here's the Doctor and his wife." Cut to a MLS as he lets them in, and he goes out of the door himself this time. Cut to a MCU as the camera pans left with the husband and wife as they approach the little boy's mother, already seated. Joining her, Hitchcock cuts to a CU of the Doctor having to suffer through nearly thirty seconds of the boy's mom amusingly running through her list of ailments: back, tooth, and knee. By now she's grabbed the harangued Doctor's hand, hiked her britches up, and vulgarly placed his hand on her leg so he can make a diagnosis. Quite used to such treatment, no doubt, at every party he attends, we can see that he is both embarrassed and fed up with this kind of attitude. All of Hitchcock's character actors, down to the smallest of parts, play their roles impeccably.

Cut to a MCU of Churdles again doing his thing with the door: entering, then closing it, then announcing the next guest, then opening it. Only this time (what else is new? Contrary to expectation) the maid rushes in with a samovar, pissing Churdles off. He slams the door closed, bitching that his job is now thrown out of kilter. Door opens and bangs against him as a guest opens it himself. It's old man Coaker from the farmer's party, who promptly exposes Churdles' pants before everyone and laughs in his face. Cut to a MLS PAP of Churdles splitting, Coaker eyeing the other guests. Spotting something near the camera, he trudges directly towards us in another of Hitchcock's self-conscious maneuvers, seemingly crossing the frame's threshold to stop just in front of us in CU. We realize that we can just make out a tableful of goodies in the foreground, overlooked as it was due to its close proximity to the bottom of the frame. This near crossing over the threshold, similar to an actor's crossing the fourth wall of the footlights in a theater, is all the more powerful because of its suddenness. In addition, the previous PAP shot gave us the wrong-minded illusion of a sense of camera neutrality from a distance. In that shot, all the characters literally kept their middle distance in the room, far from the screen's imaginary plane. Here, Hitchcock has the old man audaciously shuffle towards us almost out of the screen, further pricking our assumptions about film convention and subliminally making us feel uneasy as he approaches *our space*. In film reality all he does is go for the grub, but in audience reality he comes uncomfortably close to leaving the screen, like Jeff Daniels' character in Woody Allen's *The Purple Rose of Cairo*.

Cut to a CU left profile of Coaker sniffing and taste-testing the smorgasbord of delights, vulgarly bent over literally on top of the sweets. He's probably myopic, but his stance is also in a better-to-taste-you-with mode. His rolling eyes and smacking lips are shot with Hitchcock's typically voyeuristic intrusiveness, only the character and us involved in private indulgence. This implicates us in his feelings, of course —*we* are the rude pig. Turning his head and back on us to comment to the seated mother, he grossly puns: "'Tis all as perfect as a railway refreshment room."

Cut to a vertiginous reverse angle profile R shot as he rails forth, camera still in CU but now at standing (not bending) height above the mother, Doctor, and his wife (L to R). Camera pans into a CU as the old man spies someone OSR. He moves to say hello to this unknown man, seen earlier looking lost. Finished harassing him, Coaker spies something else further OSR. In addition to all of the movements and angles that we're generously granted by Hitchcock, all of this OS spying has cumulatively worked on our psyches to further expand the sense of space within and beyond the frames of the film. Cut now to Coaker's POV, a MD shot of Sweetland pacing outside as seen through the same crisscrossed windows we saw when Thirza's house was first shown onscreen, but this time from the inside out—more sense of space and three-dimensionality.

Quick cut to a reverse angle MS of him from the outside, unaware of being spied on from inside the house. Turning, a quicker one-second CU from yet another, slightly down frame right angle, Sweetland moves US to stare OSR. Cut to his MD POV of Louisa, Sweetland's first courted rejection—the independent woman—coming up the path. She waves and turns to go into the house L. Cut to a CU of Sweetland mulling that one over, revisiting their recent experience in his mind. Petulant and miffed expressions dart across Jameson Thomas's mobile features. Cut to his MD POV again—Mary Hearn, the third dance on his list still to be tested, waveringly prances down the path into the house, too. These are relatively quick cuts, particularly in contrast to the previous longish shots of the interior, so they have an amusing, almost mocking quality about them towards Sweetland as these two women dash in on his and our thoughts.

Cut to a right angle CU of Sweetland staring back at the camera. One suddenly realizes that this POV is of Sweetland's own imagined perception of *himself* taken from where Mary had just stood, but no longer is! What Hitchcock has done is given us a shot of Sweetland from his own projected POV of himself through Mary's eyes! Scheming, then smiling, he stares at his ever-present list and then back at us, willing to take up the gauntlet once more.

Quick cut to a fast pan in MD as Sweetland hurriedly follows Mary into the house. Cut to a CU from the interior as he opens the door, wild-eyed and calling her name. Quick two-second cut to his POV, a MS of a split-second's worth of her back disappearing through the living room door. In spite of my fear of overanalyzing this motif, it seems clear to me that backs are often seen *moving away* from the camera and people in this film, perhaps metaphorically representing the opposite paths we often take to get somewhere or find someone. Louisa is next seen momentarily sitting beyond the doorway. Cut to a MS new angle of Sweetland cursing his not being able to catch her alone. Churdles shuffles into view from OSR, gets harassed by the farmer for that mistake, and spits back at him.

Cut to a CU — a fresh, third angle — of Sweetland staring directly into the camera as if in a mirror, smugly and cockily straightening his tie in preparation for his third mating attempt. Cut to a two-shot MCU again as the farmer orders Churdles to announce him. Camera pans R following them to a now closed living room door. Churdles enters and closes door behind him. Quick cut to a fourth angle MS of the farmer waiting at the door. It opens directly behind him — our view. Cut to a reverse angle MS from the interior of the room, Churdles frowning his deepest frown up at him. Cut to a CU frontal of Sweetland coldly surveying the room. Looking left, Hitchcock cuts to his POV, Mary laughing with that ever-present, absurd hat in place. Cut to a CU of Sweetland smug as a bug in a rug. He's got his plan in motion now. Eyes R. Cut to his POV, Thirza jawing away with Louisa. We assume he's egocentrically thinking they're gossiping over him. Cut back to a CU of the farmer. He'll have his say to these ladies first. He enters the room. Cut to a new angle CU, Sweetland's POV of both women. He's now a bit closer to them and slightly to the left of his previous position and down one step, and a young girl can be seen in the background directly between the women reading a large picture book.

Thirza spots Sweetland. Visibly upset, she rises to greet him. Louisa notices her agitation, but hasn't yet seen Sweetland. Cut to a surprising, vertiginous reverse angle MCU of Sweetland and Thirza suddenly standing together L to R. The reason this shot throws us is three-fold: One, Sweetland's face faces the camera, so we assume he's looking at Thirza across the room, who had just noticed him; Two, we have just "stood in" for Sweetland, and so we expect him to be looking at Thirza — not so again, typical Hitch; Three, the reverse angle shows Sweetland looking down with a figure (Thirza) to his L (our R). Because we "were" Sweetland momentarily, we had no idea who that figure was until we (the camera) focused on it (it *was* Thirza), and our identification was so strong with Sweetland (we've been manipulated to and fro all film) that we just assumed he'd be looking at *Thirza* sitting down. In reality, the autonomous camera *itself* was gazing at her, not Sweetland, so we were startled to see Thirza suddenly standing next to him.

So ... who *is* he looking at? It must be Louisa, still sitting, as we regain our wits and bearings. Turning, he gives Thirza a short bow, then moves US, leaving her bewildered. Cut to a PAP MCU of Sweetland alighting next to Mary, his latest goal, and squishing himself into the crowded sofa. Trying to grab her hand in intimacy (no situation stops this egomaniacal man/boy), she slaps it away, instead grabbing a proffered cup of tea. Both turn left to look OS. Cut to their POV, a CU of Churdles (a new angle on him) entering the room to announce something to the hostess OSL: "His Worship the Parson, and his mother....the Hon. Missus," he squawks. Cut to a PAP MD shot (a solid and amusing sixty seconds worth) of the Parson entering, Ash going out the door, and with great difficulty dragging a huge wheelchair/carriage back in with the Parson's mother in it. Hitchcock defers our/Sweetland's pursuit again with this absurd shot, relentlessly building tension in our minds. Thirza gets jammed up against a wall frame L, Churdles backs into Sweetland and Mary US, the carriage end gets caught in Thirza's skirts, Churdles almost loses his pants again, and the whole circus goes on in the cramped frame of this part of the living room. It reminds one of the classic stateroom scene in the Marx Brothers' *A Night at the Opera* seven years *later*. Cut to a half-minute's worth MS of the right half of the living room, a PAP shot with more crashing, pants being lost, and the carriage swiveling wildly about. Cut to a twenty-second vertiginous reverse angle shot from behind Churdles of the same scene, everyone getting their tea and cakes and trying to settle down. Hitchcock is great at portraying human foibles through chaotic shots such as these of mindless millings about of crowds.

Cut to a MS of Coaker now standing next to Mary. The desperate Sweetland, no longer center screen, is still attempting courtship, but now our attention is being manipulated elsewhere. Old man takes the whole plate of cookies from the maid and, after spreading his own kerchief on his lap, sets himself the task of eating them all. Cut to a CU frontal of Thirza making some announcement. She looks down and OSR. Cut to her POV, a CU of the plate of cookies on Coaker's lap being masterfully gobbled down. Cut back to a CU of Thirza, frowning. (No one's listening to her, or apparently caring to. They only want to eat.) She looks OSL. Cut to her POV, the boy's mother importuning the maid to get her more tea, turning her back on Thirza and the camera. Cut to a CU frontal of Thirza (camera now standing in for the boy's mother, *if* she were looking). Thirza looks over her right shoulder OS. Cut to her POV, a CU of Churdles and his ever-present thumb in fist pointing out a new guest. Or is he? Just when we thought the room was full enough, the door bursts open onto Ash and a pile of bodies starts to tumble into the room! Churdles manages somehow to stem the tide and close the door again, losing his pants. Numerous points of view are now intermingling with humor in Hitchcock's Mad Hatter tea party.

Cut to a CU of Ash and Thirza. She says, "They must be the gleesingers!" The film has now become almost surreal. Ash nods his assent. "Oh, how stupid of me," his expression says. He opens the door and the four singers march in and through on out into the garden, camera panning with them. Cut to a CU of Tapper frowning at something OSL. Cut to her POV, a CU of Coaker still pigging out, profile L. Quick cut back to a CU of Thirza. Cut to the boy's mom demanding another cup of tea from the startled maid. Cut back to Thirza, vainly trying to stem her tide of overeaters: "Will all those who have finished, please pass into the garden." Cut to a MS of the guests en masse rising and moving to exit.

Cut to a new angle MS of the same, the huge carriage with the Pastor's mother in it foregrounded R. All exit through a door SR except wheelchair mom profile L and Sweetland, making his Mary-age proposal, as they move SL. Cut to a CU of Sweetland SL (where else?) importuning Mary SR as she giddily slaps his lascivious hand (15 seconds). Cut to a MS as she gaily trots outside. Cut to a CU of Sweetland from a right angle to the outside door, aware of someone back over his shoulder. (Backs, over-the-shoulder shots, things going on behind each other—all metaphors for missed, unseen opportunities to connect.) Cut to his POV, a gorgeously framed two-second shot of Minta giving him her knowing and loving look. He stupidly cannot see this, and we continue to feel just how unworthy he is to have such a woman love him. She nods her assent ("Go get her"), he nods his approval of her approval, and out the door he goes, his back to the camera (and her love).

Cut to a new angle of the living room door as it opens. Ash walks in, relieved to find the room empty. Pulling at his pants, the camera pans with him L as he moves towards the food table. Cut to the longest static scene of the film, nearly two full minutes of Churdles pigging out in CU at the table (shades of his similar actions in *The Ring*). Hitchcock completely trusts this actor Harker, the consummate ham, to keep our attention for so long. CU of Churdles in a LS partial profile R as he regally places a chair in front of the food in the foreground. Demanding the maid's own teacup, he exaggeratedly stirs the liquid, then dumps all his tea into the saucer!

Scalding his tongue and bitching, he slurps it all down (we can almost hear it) and then grabs a pile of food, rudely scarfing it all down. Ah, the royal life. No camera movements, just a straight pig-out parody of the rich on display in CU. Churdles is the entire Greek chorus of this film.

Still munching away, food literally hanging out of his mouth, he pulls out a length of cord, finally having time (though eating is most important) to tie up his trousers. The last image of this idyll shows both Ash and the maid surprised by Thirza, who is glowering at them from the outside doorway: "Fruit … *fruit* in the garden please." Cut back to Churdles hopelessly arguing for a respite. Cut back to Thirza storming out, her back turned. Cut back to a MS with Minta L, maid R, Ash center, still unable to finish tying up his pants. They each grab dessert plates and head towards the camera, arguing (Minta excluded — she quietly goes about her dignified business, everything in step).

Cut to a quick two-second fresh angle of them exiting the glass doors, taken from in front of them out in the garden, so it looks like an entrance instead. Cut to a new angle MLS of the garden set from the maid's POV, surreal in its outdoor yet claustrophobic atmosphere, chairs and people cluttering up the area. What looks like fake foliage covers the background at the top part of the frame. Cut to the threesome coming out (in) to serve, Ash still shoveling food into his mouth and hitching at his pants. Cut to a MLS of the party, servants seen entering and leaving the frame from behind while we catch a blurred shot of Mary being swiftly chased by Sweetland in CU from OSL to OSR. Upon closer inspection, the "natural" backdrop seems to be made up of numerous low-hanging branches from a tree, annoyingly banging into the rustling guests.

Cut to a MCU of Mary still being harassed by Sweetland, staring OSL towards a group to one side. The maid enters the frame carrying some fruit. Cut to a CU of Mary blathering on and taking a couple of plums, then handing one to Sweetland. He says no, he brought them for Thirza, but bitterly takes one anyway. Cut to a closer two-shot CU, Mary chomping away happily, Sweetland distastefully. They turn to notice something OSL. Cut to a MS of the barbershop quartet starting in on "I'm looking for a girl like you" *sung out loud* on this unknown composer's 1999 soundtrack! (I guess it's not officially a silent film anymore!) Cut back to the couple. Sweetland's not interested in the music, and he nudges Mary to go OSR with him privately. She couldn't care less. Cut to a 90-degree MS right angle as Sweetland heads to the house, gesturing towards Mary (and now us) to join him. Cut to a CU of just Sweetland, insistent. Cut back to a CU of Mary, stubborn and petulant. After six alternate cuts of CU's, Sweetland finally wins out.

Cut to a MCU of Mary from behind her, entering Sweetland's frame. Cut to a right angle shot from inside the house, Sweetland ushering her in and closing the doors behind him. Cut to an almost lovely (if it weren't for that hat) two-second ECU of Mary, quieting down just enough to seem tranquil. She is gorgeously lit. It is an intimate portrait, simultaneously voyeuristic and Sweetland's projected image of her—another of Hitchcock's singular cinematic gifts. Cut to her POV, the camera panning L with him as he goes to the living room door to check that they're alone. Cut to his POV, a MCU of Mary genuinely wondering what's going on. Hitch has been superb in delineating all of the exacting details of his characters' thought processes for us every step of the way in this picture.

Cut to a profile PAP M shot, Sweetland L entering the frame, Mary R. "Mary Hearn, I'm marrying again," he stupidly and arrogantly intones yet a third time. Cut to Hitchcock's by now familiar alternating CU's straight towards the camera. She surprises him and us by reacting with seeming support. He stupidly nods, knowingly. Cut to profiles. Mary: "That's funny, a fortune-teller told me *I'd* be married inside a year!" We know that'll tickle Sweetland's fancy, and if we didn't know or suspect the ending of this film, we might be duped into thinking he might actually be getting his wish this time with her. Cut back to his profile as Sweetland stupidly takes that one in, filling his breast with cockiness. As he struts out of the frame, Hitchcock cuts to a medium two-shot. Turning quickly, Sweetland triumphantly hurls: "I bet I can tell who he is!" "Go ahead, guess," she coos visually. He pulls her OSL with him this time, Hitchcock milking the phony suspense.

Cut to a new angle MS from behind their left shoulders as Sweetland plunks Mary in front of a mirror next to him, letting the reflection be his answer. Cut to a CU of their reversed images in the mirror on the mantle. Staring, Mary spits out: "You ... *you*, at *your* age!" Cut to a CU from the *mirror's* POV as she laughs in his face. Cut to a CU of Sweetland right at the camera, beyond incredulity: "Well, you don't want to marry a boy, do you?" Cut to a shot from over his left shoulder, a CU of Mary: "Why not? 'Tis a way with girls to marry boys, isn't it?" Cut to her over-the-right-shoulder shot of Sweetland, flustered. Pathetically insulting, he says: "Have you got the face to call yourself a *girl*?" Cut to a MS profile, Mary on the left in the power position, defiantly agitated. "What the mischief should I call myself, then?" Nastily, he retorts: "*Full blown and a bit over* ... that's what I call you!" Cut to a MS, then a MLS as Sweetland's rage knocks Mary back onto the sofa. Cut to a CU of him coming in for the kill, furious forever. Leaning over her (compare this shot to the one of the old man leaning over the food earlier), he shakes a fist and finger at her outraged expressions: "The trouble with you is, you are too fond of dressing your mutton lamb fashion"—a convoluted, clever, but cruel pun. He storms OSR.

Cut to a classic audacious Hitchcock shot, a CU of Mary wide open-mouthed staring directly at the camera. This one's for us and no one else, for Sweetland's not even looking. With a look that could either be total fright or laughter (it's absolutely impossible to tell which), her title screams: "Is this a nightmare?" Hysterical cut to her CU POV of Sweetland as he turns and gestures directly at us, "Your hat is." Cut to a profile MS as Hearn arises, shaking her fists in his face: "You old sheep ... [same woolly illusion] to come to a woman in all her prime and beauty." Now Sweetland's shaking his fists, too, in this absurd, animalistic confrontation. He yells: "Don't you think you were first, 'cause you wasn't!" Cut to a CU straight at the camera, no title, as Mary screams "Aargh!" She drops onto a chair in a cut to MCU. Cut to an over-her-left-shoulder shot of Sweetland leaning in, continuing his verbal assault. Cut to a horrible/hysterical CU of Hearn wildly flailing her arms at the camera and screaming. Cut back to the same over-the-shoulder shot, Sweetland pointing and haranguing. Cut back to Mary, flailing. Cut to an ECU of Sweetland, wild beastial eyes accusing. He suddenly turns his head to look OSR.

Cut to a MLS of Thirza and Coaker entering the room from the outside, Thirza freaking out. Cut to a CU of Coaker: "Guy Fawkes and Angels, what's Sammy doing to Postmistress?" He gestures to all the party guests to come see. Cut to a long shot of all the guests hurrying towards the camera. Cut to the crowd filling the doorway, staring. Cut to an interior PAP MS of everyone streaming around Mary, trying to calm her. Cut to a MS of Minta opening the living room door to lead the servants in. Cut to a CU of Samuel and Coaker in profile: "But what was you *doing*, Sammy?" Turning his back, Sweetland denies everything, pulling out his list again. Cut to a tight CU of all the bodies gathered around Hearn, Thirza whispering something to her personal maid Susan in the foreground. Cut to a behind-the-crowd MCU shot of her stumbling over the step leading out of the living room for the third time. Cut back to the hysterical Hearn in MCU still flailing away. Cut to a CU of her almost having a fit.

Cut to a CU of Thirza, reliving her own experience with Sweetland. She slowly backs away from the camera and the group, bumping into Churdles behind her. Throwing one arm round his head, she looks up at him and melodramatically faints. Cut to a 90-degree R angle shot of Ash catching her as she falls limp, one arm round her breasts and another desperately holding his pants up. He blows on her to try to rouse her as half the group now rushes to *her* aid. Cut to a MLS PAP of Mary's larger circle in

R foreground, Thirza's smaller group L background. The maid, stuck in the middle, drops her glass of water and starts screaming, too. Fade to black.

Fade up on a MS of a blazing hearth back at Sweetland's home, Minta faithfully listening to the farmer bitching about women. Both of them are sitting in the rockers framing the fireplace, right where they belong. Cut to a CU of Samuel complaining to the camera (Minta) and finally exclaiming: "I bain't be chasing any more women — shan't finish the list." Cut to a gorgeous CU of Minta patiently explaining something. Lilian Hall-Davis was a real knockout, and the 1928 audience must have really been laughing *at* Sweetland by now, and long before this, knowing what a dish she was. (In this regard, Hitchcock has always exploited his stars for their name/face recognition, frequently by casting against type and then constantly making us notice. And it's even more satisfying to view Hall-Davis in this highly sympathetic role this year, as opposed to her fickle, fair-weather gold digger part in *The Ring* the previous year.)

Alternate cuts of each other in CU, he ranting, she becalmed and radiant: "It's like that Mercy Bassett of the Royal Oak, will be the same as the rest of 'em." Cut to a MD shot from partly behind and to the left of Sweetland, anticipating both their heads turning to stare at the camera. *Cut to a shot of what their POV will be in just a moment*, a MCU of Churdles opening a door. What's so wonderful about this shot is not so much the angle of it, but its timing. By cutting to that shot at the moment just *prior* to their awareness of Ash's entrance, the camera visibly asserts Hitchcock's presence by standing in for their POV before Churdles even enters— before Hitchcock's audience, Sweetland and Minta even see what is going to happen next! This short montage is yet another extraordinary example of this director's experiments with time, space, and audience manipulation.

In truth, the camera is standing in for Churdles' *presence*, not his POV, for his entrance shows him to be in his perpetually downturned gaze. Churdles now does his other classic staring routine, this time with a knowing, accusatory tone right at Sweetland. Cut to a CU of Sweetland, not a little uncomfortable under that gaze. He knows what an asshole he's been. Cut to a LS PAP of the dining room as the farmer gets up and leaves the room. Ash shuffles forward with his ubiquitous thumb in his fist and gestures importantly at Minta. Cut to a CU of Minta. "I'm ashamed of Samuel Sweetland, offering himself at sale prices all around the country," says Ash. This statement certainly lightens the tone of what he may really want to say about his master's actions. Cut to a MCU of Sweetland's back, turning and listening out of sight from the bright outdoors. Cut to either his POV or his imagined one, a stunningly charged profile R CU of Churdles talking on assertively. Hitchcock's mobile camera is everywhere, constantly replanting itself for innumerable POV's. This one turns out to be Sweetland's *imagined view* (his ear's eyes, so to speak), for Churdles turns his head briefly to nod in Sweetland's (the camera's) direction with no change of expression — he knows Sweetland is out of eyesight (but not, perhaps, earshot).

Cut to a powerful, ten-second CU of Sweetland in the outside doorway, viewed sideways as he listens and reacts, wretched and ashamed. He is shot in semi-shadow, artistically placed within the darkness of the doorway of the main house, the bright wall of an outside building behind him starkly highlighting his image. Beginning with this powerful shot, and after all of his nasty deeds, Hitchcock seems to be granting him some redemption and sympathy in our eyes.

But Churdles remains harsh in his estimation. Cut to a MCU of Ash on SL, Minta patiently listening SR, as he continues: "It's a disgrace to us males that he can sink to go among 'em hat in hand ... only to be laughed at for his pains!" Cut to a quick CU of Sweetland, then a NBS LS of him taken from deep within the living room, through its door and across the kitchen — another marvelously unique perspective of this house. Beginning in this LS, we see Sweetland walk from outside into the living room, a small figure beginning far away in the distance until he arrives in a CU (reminiscent of the Girl and the barker's walk from a LS of the back of the church towards us into a CU in *The Ring*). In this way, I believe, Hitchcock demonstrates through a purely cinematic metaphor the distance and thresholds Sweetland's heart and mind must travel in order to begin to emotionally grow up. The shot is palpable for us, and it works. As Sweetland comes to a stop in CU profile L, Hitchcock cuts to his POV, a surprised Churdles and Minta left to right in MS. Cut to a CU of the threesome, the farmer eyeballing Ash. Cut to a closer CU as he moves in. He eyeballs both of them, then suddenly demands: "Get my horse saddled!" Moving across and OSR, Churdles is brought down a peg. Minta leans in, expectantly. Sweetland orders: "My other coat!" Good idea, Samuel. It's time you changed your look and actions. But will he, really?

Angrily gesturing, he barks his orders at the now frightened Minta. Cut to a LS PAP as she hurries upstairs in the background, a shot not seen since before the wedding. Cut to a new angle CU of the farmer pulling out his list and ripping off his overcoat. Cut to a LS again with the stairway in the background as Minta brings down his long coat. Camera pans with them as they cross to the outside door, Minta hovering, straightening and brushing off the coat. Both are back to their master-servant relationship.

Cut to an exterior MS of Ash reigning in the horse as Sweetland and

Minta come outside. He mounts and leaves. Cut to a longish, fifteen second CU of Minta waving goodbye, wistfulness turning to hopelessness on her features. She turns her back on the camera and walks towards the door, both of their backs facing each other (missed connections again). Cut to a starkly photographed four-second MS of her back as she heavily walks inside through the outside entranceway.

Cut to a CU from inside as she comes to a pensive stop inside the door, looking about and daydreamily fiddling with her blouse (10 seconds). Quick two-second cut to her CU POV of a rocker at the fireplace, Sweetland's empty coat in it. Cut to a PAP MCU seven-second camera pan of her as she trudges resignedly over to the chair. Cut to a ten-second, MCU, 90-degree angle L shot keeping her in profile (for she's had to walk around the dining room table, giving us a stronger sense of real time and space) as she draws her hand along the rocker, thinking of her life and love. Cut to a long, fifteen-second frontal CU of Minta caressing the top of the rocker and dreaming, lost in her thoughts. Quick cut (2 seconds) to her CU POV of the other rocker, empty and "staring" back at her. Cut to a MCU profile R of her breathing deeply. Cut to a sixteen-second CU from the *empty rocker's POV* of Minta as she silently slips into her chair, staring back deeply into our eyes—and her imagined husband's—with breathless hope and palpably visible desire. Fade to black.

Fade up on a long shot of a village street with houses framing the screen and an imposing hill looming in the distance. Suddenly, Sweetland and his horse's back come riding in from behind the right side of camera, cantoring off into the background. Cut to a MLS of the same subjects moving DSR to DSL. Cut to a CU of Sweetland now moving SL to R. Cut to a CU of his POV, a sign stating "The Royal Oak Inn" with the name "John Tarr" below it. Oh no, poor Mercy Bassett's chance. Cut to the *sign's* POV of Sweetland peering into the camera, not quite so confident as with his other three attempts. Cut to his new POV, a LS of a huge crowd of men on their horses, literally dozens of hunting dogs milling about. Cut back to a CU of Sweetland and his horse. Cut to a disorienting yet artistically framed reverse angle LS of a huge tree trunk SR with a man leaning against it and a crowd to his left. Cut to a MCU of Sweetland, stationary on his horse, in profile R as riders pass on both his L and R—behind him and in front of him by our view—giving us the feeling that everyone's passing him by and he's going nowhere. Sweetland uncomfortably twists every which way saying hello to a few of them as they rush by. Louisa Windeatt is the only one we recognize, and he frowns her a quick hello.

Cut to another reverse angle profile L of Sweetland, a closer CU of him staring straight ahead. Cut to a MS of his POV, Thirza Tapper and some other woman gabbing in a corner. Cut back to the same right angle CU of more frowns on Sweetland's face. He looks L and down past the camera. Cut to a MS of Mary Hearn gabbing off in another corner. The gang's all here. Cut back to a not overly thrilled Samuel, full of more frowns. He turns to look further L. Cut to a CU of Mary Hearn on her horse barking instructions to someone. (Hitchcock's women in this film are fiercely independent, however quirky they may look.) Cut back to a CU of Sweetland fed up with finding all his strikeouts here in one place and trying to figure out a ploy. Cut to a new angle MS as he turns his horse around, disembarking, other horses bustling about him everywhere. Cut to a lower angle shot from behind him as he ties his horse up.

Cut to a CU of his entrance from the inside of the inn as he looks around, his hat visually breaking up the strong, sharp line of the doorway behind him. Cut to his POV, a MLS of a crowded bar with piles of people milling about and drinking. Cut back to a CU of Sweetland whetting his whistle, game. His figure approaches and veers L of camera, looming momentarily in our eyes. Cut to a 90-degree right angle MS of his saunter through the crowd. Cut to what can only be a *hand-held*, NBS camera shot following and keeping him in CU as he pushes his way through the bodies as they shuffle out his the way to accommodate. One fellow eyes him suspiciously. Camera keeps Sweetland's moving back in CU focus.

He finds the ubiquitous Coaker at the bar and begins a chat. Camera zooms in a bit for a closer two-shot. Cut to the farmer's POV, a MS of the bar SL. Mercy Bassett, the barmaid, waves. Cut to her POV, a CU of Coaker and Sweetland. Though by now she's certainly back to serving drinks, Hitchcock gives us a long, thirty-five second shot of these two from her position (if not her continuing POV) of Coaker babbling on, while a big, phony, shit-eating grin freezes on Sweetland's face, a new and somewhat horrible expression we've never seen before on him. Obviously he's steeling himself for one final foray towards marriage with the barmaid.

Sweetland saunters directly towards the camera, looming larger and larger and looking goofier and goofier. Cut to a new angle, 45-degree L MS of his approach to the bar. Mercy is OSL and just out of sight (and reach) of him. Cut to over a minute's worth of a seriously flirting two-shot CU of Mercy and Samuel. This shot would be interminable if not for the fact that Ruth Maitland (as Mercy), another of Hitchcock's wonderful stage actresses, didn't burst from the screen with a natural *bon vivance*. After a brief frowning fit by Sweetland, she marvels: "Get on with you, I believe you're in love!" and brusquely shoves his shoulder playfully (a truly robust woman). Cut to a MLS from behind the bar of a quartet of drinkers, restless to be served. Cut to their POV, a CU of Samuel and Mercy ignoring them and chatting it up.

Quickly turning their heads SR, Hitchcock cuts to a long shot of a man in the smoky doorway gesturing behind him. Cut to a LS of the hordes of hounds following a lead horse and rider over a tiny bridge past the camera and OSL. Cut to a reverse angle ELS of the same scene, all profile L. Cut to an ELS from further down the road, in front looking back, as they head towards the camera.

Cut to a new angle MLS of the inside of the pub as the drinkers start to exit R. (Ah, there's nothing like a bunch of drunks out on a hunt.) Cut to a CU of Coaker badgering Sweetland from behind, Samuel staring OSL at Mercy as he tries to ignore the old man. Cut to a quick CU of Mercy crossing L behind the bar, then back. Cut to a two-shot, Coaker going on and on, Sweetland uncaring. A lot is spoken in this film (and all of Hitchcock's films), but far from all of it is listened to. Cut to a quick shot of Mercy going back and forth from SL to SR. Cut back to the two-shot, Sweetland getting kind of used to Mercy's comings and goings.

Coaker raves on while Sweetland thoroughly tires of him. After blathering on to no one in particular and everyone in general throughout the entire film, Coaker finally gets one of the film's funniest title: "Us be drawing turnips a' ready. Proper masterpieces—so round and white as a woman's bosom!" Ah, the pre-censorship, 1920's dialogue—so racy, politically incorrect, and alliterative!

Cut back to the two-shot of the men. Sweetland heard that one. Or did he? His face says, "Hold it. Do you hear that?" Cut to an ELS of horses and hounds out in the countryside. Cut back to a two-shot, Coaker intrigued. It worked! He leaves to go out and perhaps catch a glimpse of the hunt. Cut back to a two-shot of Bassett and Sweetland trading affectionate chatter during another leisurely thirty-second shot. Now Hitchcock *fades to black.* After explicitly showing us how each of his other failed conquests fared, the director deliberately withholds the results of this one. If anything, the fadeout on the happy, chatty couple gives us a kind of false hope for them, doesn't it?

Fade in to a CU of a heated discussion between Thirza on R and Mary Hearn on L, the postmistress's office mesh window behind Mary. Thirza: "After your outrageous behavior I wish to hold no conversation with you ... other than *official.*" Mary: "No man would even trouble to get you into hysterics, you pinnicking little grey rat!" Thirza cattily retorts: "Know this—I might have been a wife ... the wife of a high-minded and most worthy man, Mr. Samuel Sweetland." Mary: "Prove it Tabby Tapper." A cat by any other name smells like a rat—or some such. Fade to black as Mary dons her horrific hat, simultaneously purposeful and malevolent. No characters ever escape Hitchcock's sense of black comedy.

Fade up on a MS of Samuel in R profile on his horse, back home and outside his door. Cut to a CU of him from the inside looking straight at the camera from behind his crosshatched window. Cut to his MS POV, the out-of-focus window hatches in ECU foregrounding Ash still badmouthing Sweetland, Minta in a huff. Ash: "...and I'll lay if he 'aven't got her he'll come back in a proper tantrum, mark me!" Cut to the same CU profile L of Samuel, registering Churdles' comments. Affecting a self-satisfied air, he moves left and opens the door. Cut to his entrance from the inside, a CU. Cut to his CU POV, Minta L, Churdles R, a reaction shot straight up a bit at us. Minta's response shows us that she thinks he's been successful wooing Mercy Bassett, and her hand goes up to her blouse above her bosom as she turns her head away. Churdles frowns doubtfully. Cut back to a CU of a seemingly triumphant Sweetland, and we *almost* believe the same thing as Minta. Cut to a heart-rending ECU of Minta breathing heavily, almost faint from heartbreak. Backing away from the camera, she comes to rest behind her rocker, hands caressing its top.

Cut to a CU of a nastily smug Sweetland as he struts towards the camera, looming. Cut to a two-shot profile CU, Churdles on L and Sweetland R, as he nods Churdles away. Cut to Sweetland's POV, Churdles' back as he shuffles out the door, flabbergasted. Cut to Churdles' POV, Minta nervously rubbing her hands along the rocker as Sweetland tosses his cane and coat away. Cut to her POV, a CU of the thinly smiling Sweetland. Cut to his CU POV of Minta simultaneously uncertain, upset, loving, and vulnerable. Cut back to Sweetland, still sweetly and sickeningly smiling. He turns to make sure Churdles is gone, then looks back at Minta. Hitchcock milks it for all it's worth. We cannot tell what he's thinking, for once — the first and only time in this film. Deliberately. Hitchcock's earlier fade out on the happy conversing couple in the bar set these feelings up in us. Cut back to Minta, dying. Cut back to Sweetland.

Hitchcock now takes a full twenty-three seconds to show Sweetland's expression go from a triumphant sneer to one ... totally bereft. He cannot perpetrate or perpetuate his lie any longer on this woman. Swallowing hard, his head droops—a crestfallen and broken man. Cut to Minta, hope hardly daring to spring to her eyes. Cut back to Sweetland, near tears. We can hardly see his face, his head hangs so low. Cut back to Minta, elation barely suppressed. Cut to a MCU of Sweetland that includes the chair behind him to his L; but he turns and sits at the table. Beneath hooded eyes, he peers up at the camera with his hangdog, little-boy expression. Cut to a neutral, 45-degree angle, beautiful CU shot of Minta looking lovingly at Sweetland off DSL, her heart pounding. Cut to her POV CU, Sweetland wringing his hands on the table, just the top of his head visible. Cut back to the gorgeous CU of Minta, her hands wanting to reach out and comfort him, a tear welling up in an eye. But she knows her place.

Cut back to a closer CU of the farmer as he slowly pulls his cursed list from his pocket, saying: "'Tis all over, Minta — I'm done for!" A completely blind fool — yet, yet ... sympathetic, not partly because he is loved by someone, but also because we hope that he's finally going to learn something. Our sense of convention is approaching its necessary fulfillment.

He throws the list on the table, hopeless. Minta shakes her head "no." "Every time I've had to creep off with my tail between my legs." Sighing, his title pronounces: "The whole power of the female sex be drawn against me. They have taken away my self-respect." In point of fact, his lost self-respect is more closely allied to his shallow, thoughtless ego than to anything else. Only a purely narcissistic man would blame Woman's autonomy and integrity according to his own definition of power, and the deepest irony in this film is that he really doesn't deserve this woman's love. But people love who people love.

Minta, the light full upon her face, finally speaks up: "Don't say that, Sweetland — I won't hear a strong sensible man talk like that." Cut to her POV, a MS now as he stares wonderingly at her, then rises to cross two steps to his left. This at first acts as a tension reliever (giving us a bit of distance on his pain), but we suddenly spot his rocker SL, a visual channel connecting his movements. He sits in it. Cut to a MCU of Minta as she presses the offensive, coming from behind *her* rocker to lean on the table closer to him, her rocker still visible SR: "What be women made of nowadays?" she queries. Cut to her POV, a CU of Sweetland *looking up at her now from his seated position* for the first time in the film as he mulls that one over, agreeing: "I've got a lot of faults, but there's good in me yet, Minta."

Titled dialogue in the twenties could move the story along when necessary, and had healing powers. In his POV CU, Minta suddenly becomes an apologist for her gender — politically incorrect in the 21st century, but appropriate for her time — and says with soothing tones: "'Tis enough to weaken your faith in the whole pack of us." Cut to her POV, a closer CU looking down on him as he speaks: "You'd think being mistress of the farm might tempt them, if the farmer can't!" The next shot shows him offering this up in CU directly into our eyes.

Turning his head, he glowers at the empty rocker across the way. One by one, he superimposes the independent Louisa, teary-eyed Thirza, hysterical Mary, and vehement Mercy (Hitchcock sums up her rejection in five ghostly seconds), dissolving in and out of the chair for five seconds each, immediately followed by the very real Minta taking their places. True to cinema's rules, Hitchcock not only walks us through these thoughts but hammers home Sweetland's lessons. Will he see what we see? Will he really see — comprehend — who he's looking at now? She looks back at him and us, wondering herself.

Cut to her imagined POV, for now she's looking away, insight beginning to dawn in his eyes. Alternating cuts now occur back and forth four times, Minta acting unknowingly and Sweetland gaining in understanding. Cut to a MCU of Sweetland, who looks down and spies the carnation Minta put in his lapel. He starts to smooth his moustache, then gets up, turns his back on the camera, and stands behind the rocker, stealing a glance in the mirror and fixing his tie vainly — old habits die hard. Cut back to a CU of Minta, acting oblivious.

Cut back to Sweetland, the camera panning as he paces a bit and tries to figure out how to approach her. He moves in a little closer to look down on her. Cut to his POV, a CU from above and to her right. She faces the camera and says: "There's that nice woman, Jance Cherry, the huckster's sister." Her POV is a CU looking up, him shaking his head strenuously no. He swallows hard, screwing up his courage. "There *is* a woman ... one woman...." Mock surprise and swallowing hard herself, we see her mouth, "Who?" Cut back to her POV, a MS of Sweetland (a CU is unnecessary because we are watching so carefully for his reaction). He's on the spot now, and *still* doesn't quite know how to ask. Turning, he spots his phony list on the table. Having a brilliant idea, he reaches for his pencil. For the first and only time in the film *he* writes a name down on it, not her. Staring down right into the camera's eye, he shyly moves towards it and hands the paper to me.

Cut to his POV, a gorgeous CU as Minta takes the list from our hands. Hitchcock places us/the camera directly between the two, making us the mediating character of this drama. *We can practically feel him hand the paper right through us!* Cut to an ECU of the list in Minta's hands, all names crossed off and "Minta's" at the top. She turns to gaze back at him, speechless. Finally, she grabs her bosom. He, expectant but now humbler, nods assent. Cut to his POV, an ECU of Minta as she looks OSR and downwards, then into the hearth. Cut to a CU of Sweetland looking down on her, truly humbled. "Don't think you'll make me angry, if you say *no* — I be tamed to hearing *no*." And he has quite literally been tamed for, if we look carefully, we can see a stuffed deer head hanging on the wall behind him (Hitchcock's macabre sense of humor rearing its riotous head)!

For once in this film, finally, his manner of asking proves he's beginning to learn his lessons. Furthermore, the love welling up inside of him is transcending all class boundaries, an important moral Hitchcock would return to again and again. Truly repentant, he continues: "I'm offering myself so humble as a worm. Hope's gone, but I'd like to mention one thing in my favour … a little child can lead me." Minta has, not coincidentally, been caring for this little child even before his wife died — probably both of them — so, if we care to think about it, another strange and unsettling point is being made about the master-servant relationship.

Cut to his POV, a CU from above Minta looking back at us: "Be sure you mean this? 'Tis fearful sudden." The irony of this question is thick and humorous as her breast visibly rises and falls. ECU of Sweetland right in the camera: "The Lord works the same as lightning and don't give warning when He is going to wake sense in a man's heart."

Finally—finally—Hitchcock cuts to the two-shot we've been waiting the whole film to return to: *Minta on the left and the farmer on the right.* Cut to a CU, she turning to him, both faces close together. "I'll be proud to enter in, Samuel—I'll enter in with trust and hope." He pulls her head ever so delicately to his chest and then, still holding her tenderly, religiously intones: "If you repent this bit of work, then may I lose my salvation." Gotta think on that one a moment, as Hitchcock draws on Phillpots' Victorian novel, but well said, Sammy. Cut to a MCU — no kiss— but very warm feelings seethe out across the screen towards us from their profiles as they glance up above the mantle to his first wedding picture.

Sweetland says: "And now to mark the change, you must blossom out this very minute." Rather than closing the film on a clinch (the great film dancer and choreographer Fred Astaire also avoided them like the plague), Hitchcock explores our sense of afterglow by sustaining the foreplay. Cut to a MS from under the stairway as Sweetland peruses Minta from head to toe. "Where's that brave party frock my Tibby gave you?" Shyly she refuses, but Samuel waves her on and she happily heads to the stairs, *ever the servant.*

Cut to the kitchen door as Ash waves her over from his dark perch. Cut to his POV, a MS of her brightly lit. She hesitates and then moves toward him/us. Cut to a MCU two-shot profile, Ash L asking: "'E's catched a woman after all?" She nods her assent. Bemoaning, Churdles responds: "God befriend you and me then … to think of another female in this house!" Cut to his POV, a CU of a smiling Minta. Her CU of him shows amazement suddenly appear on his face. Cut to his CU, Minta tapping her chest "'Tis I." Churdles, thumb above fist, almost faints directly into the camera. Cut to a medium two-shot profile as Ash quickly collects himself. "They do say that the next best thing to no wife be a good one. He has come out on top at last." Churdles triumphantly redeems his cantankerous self—at last. Cut to a CU of Churdles at the camera: "I be on your side, Minta—*I'll* help you manage him."

Cut to a medium two-shot profile. She heartily pats him on the back. Ash leans in: "Don't forget to tell him I'm cruel under-paid." Before she can answer they turn to look OSL, where their POV reveals a MS of Sweetland entering the kitchen doorway in a rush. Cut to his POV, a MS of Minta answering his call with Churdles still incredulous in the background. Cut back to Sweetland grinning ear to ear at Churdles as Minta goes on upstairs OSL. Cut to a MS of Churdles' mouth hanging all the way open, staring back. Cut to Sweetland, genuinely ecstatic, as he hurries with the camera following in a pan to a window to look outside. Turning back, he looks at us, smiling.

Cut to his POV, a CU of Thirza and Mary in the doorway! He bows his head towards them/us. Mary pushes Thirza away and approaches camera/him, looming. Cut to a medium three-shot, L to R, of Thirza, Mary and Sweetland. Cut to a two-shot of Mary on L and Sweetland on R. Mary, flatteringly: "I've changed my mind, Samuel."

Cut to a CU of Sweetland. Now *he's* incredulous, mouth ajar. He can't believe it (and neither can we). He thinks a second and then smiles at us again, eyebrow raised. Cut back to a two-shot. Cut to a three-shot. Mary moves OSR. Cut to a two-shot. Thirza whispers in Sweetland's ear, no title. We know what she's saying, anyway. Another smile creeps onto his face.

He tilts his head to look somewhere and Hitchcock cuts to a CU of Mary, expectantly smiling back. Cut to a two-shot as Sweetland says to Thirza: "I was just going to tell Mary something interesting." Hitchcock milks the payoffs with great pleasure all around. Thirza, either thinking he's going to tell Mary off or propose to her (it's impossible to tell, she's starting in on her crying jag again), turns her head away. Cut to a goofy looking Mary grinning like a fool, turned sideways in a PAP staged stance. Mary cattily spits, "Don't forget to let Tabby Tapper hear it." Claws extended, she comes over into a medium three-shot, Sweetland stuck between them.

Cut to the doorway. Now *Coaker* enters. We can't ever be rid of this blabbermouth, can we? Cut to his POV, a disorienting three-shot due to this sudden change of angle. Cut to a four-shot right angle view. Cut to a two-shot, Coaker and Sweetland: "I've heard tell of your sad tale, Samuel, and I've found one for 'ee … worth her corn at a feast or a funeral." Temptation arises swiftly in this silly stage play. Unfazed, the farmer shakes his head smilingly and says: "I've made my selection, and you shall stay and drink to her." Coaker looks over at Mary, an ECU of a grinning idiot beneath a new and even uglier hat than her earlier one. Cut to a four-shot, Thirza far L, whimpering.

Cut to a NBS LS of Sweetland ushering them all over to the table as shot from the *stairway*. Cut to Sweetland bending down to get drinks. He spies Mary waddling over to the rocker by the hearth and sitting down. Oh no, he says, over here. Long four-shot has Thirza artistically playing with her bag in the foreground and pathetically staring into space. Cut to a CU of Sweetland pouring drinks and casting a quick gaze up above us (the stairs, the stairs). Cut to a LS of the empty stairs, then back to an ECU of Sweetland, who suddenly registers rejoicing. Hitchcock cleverly shows *his* face before we see Minta, making us anticipate her arrival even more.

Now he cuts to a long shot of the stairs, Minta standing at the top in a lovely dress, noticeable even at this distance. Cut to a medium four-shot, clockwise from the background: Mary, Samuel, Thirza, and Coaker all around the table looking above the camera. Cut to Minta descending, still in LS. Cut to Minta's POV as they stare back up at her in a closer MS (Coaker and Mary open-mouthed) to the left and above the camera, a reaction shot to where she was a moment ago, which gives us a jolt of disorientation and a powerful sense of movement. Cut to a full frontal CU of Mary, for the first time in her life speechless. Cut to her MS POV as Minta finishes her descent and takes her place next to Samuel. Churdles enters the background. Cut to the happy couple in CU profile in front of the hearth, one tea kettle visible between them on the mantle. The most beautifully lit ECU yet in the movie is now shown of Minta in profile L, radiant, a full five seconds of this gorgeous portrait of her by Hitchcock. The director finds ever more lovely ways to allow our eyes to drink in his women.

Cut back to a proud two-shot. Cut to a medium five-shot from Mary's POV, Churdles centered. Cut to a MCU of a screaming Mary, black wine bottle aimed at her bosom as she starts to wave her arms in hysterical reaction to the proceedings. Cut to a PAP M six-shot from behind Mary's R shoulder. Sweetland gestures for Ash to calm her; he takes off his hat and blows air onto her SL. Thirza and Coaker go to congratulate Minta in the background.

Cut to the happy couple in a two-shot CU. Minta glances at Samuel's coat, and the camera pans with her as she heads back up the stairs to get something. Cut to a three-shot, Coaker, Sweetland and Thirza chatting amiably. Cut to Minta coming down towards the camera, Sweetland's original coat open in her arms. Cut to a two-shot CU as she puts it on Samuel. He raises his glass and toasts: "And if anybody knows a woman with a gentler heart and a straighter back and a nobler character, I'd like to see her." (All qualities that we have yet to see Sweetland demonstrate himself.) Cut to a two-shot MCU with Minta happily brushing off Sweetland's coat. As the farmer raises his glass to toast, two disembodied hands with glasses filled reach in from off L and R frame. Fade to black.

Yes, it's the end of the film, but a typical Hitchcockian question begs to be answered — and, as usual, it cannot: "What, if anything, has actually changed by the end of this film?" Minta is still serving Sweetland!

Eight

Champagne

First screening August 1928

Six of the eight referenced film review compendiums critiqued *Champagne* with ratings ranging from two-and-a-half stars (LM) to two stars (VH, BB). Martin and Porter found it so bad that they went to the bottom of the barrel and gave it their dreaded "turkey" rating. The comments in the reviews generally reflect these average to poor ratings: "Tedious comedy with very few of the master's touches," says *Halliwell* (p. 151), which even goes so far as to quote Hitchcock's own assessment of the film in one word: "Dreadful" (although that source is unnamed). Martin and Porter followed their "turkey" rating with this comment: "Alfred Hitchcock regarded this silent feature as one of his worst films, and who are we to disagree?" (p. 187). *Blockbuster* was no kinder: "Even Hitchcock disliked this film. Flat champagne indeed" (p. 186). *VideoHound* at least claimed it was "brilliantly photographed" (p. 155), and the often-gracious Leonard Maltin said: "Overlong silent Hitch is moderately entertaining with the usual quota of striking visuals" (p. 229).

Of course, I agree with the positives and completely disagree with the pans, finding the film slight but full of extraordinary scenes and all of the director's wonderful themes and experiments constantly on display. London's *Time Out*, always more thoughtful, detailed, and incisive than the other compendiums, closely reflects my own perspectives on the film:

> Hitchcock's five not very happy years at Elstree produced a crop of ten films, most of which are now unfairly neglected. Saddled with a clichéd story from studio rival Walter Mycroft and an ebullient, assertive star, he still managed to imbue this light romantic melodrama with an air of sinister menace. The champagne-drinking sophisticate who clouds the destiny of [the] millionaire's daughter Balfour more than makes up for the weak 'cake-hound' hero, and Balfour herself proves remarkably adept at parodying her lost-little-girl image. Hitchcock's sly blend of fantasy,

game-playing and frightening lechery, and his continually inventive visuals, make for an intriguing exploration of '20s high-life [p. 200].

Hitchcock simplified all the names for this film (even more so than in *The Ring*), using generics such as The Girl, The Boy, The Man, and The Father for the characters played by Betty Balfour (1903–1977), French actor Jean Bradin, Theo Von Alten, and our old friend Gordon Harker (in his third of four appearances for Hitchcock), respectively. The film opens with Harker's face, The Father, angrily twitching away as he reads through newspaper after newspaper accounts about his daughter's shenanigans. Headlines such as "Street Magnate Defied by Headstrong Actress Daughter," with a subtitle stating that she's off on a "flight to join [her] love [on an] Atlantic liner," particularly irk him.

Cut to an extraordinary series of shots in just twenty seconds: From directly above and looking straight down, we first see a CU of a bottle popping its cork right at the camera, champagne gushing into our eyes! Dissolve into a side view ECU of a champagne glass filling up with liquid, tilting towards us, and being completely drained just below the frame. Through the bottom of the glass we view a LS scene of skewed looking ballroom dancers moving about a dance floor.

Cut to a reverse angle CU of a man's face lowering the champagne glass, black moustache and dark eyebrows highlighting a probing but inscrutable gaze. This person will turn out to be The Man, played by the adroit Theo Von Alten. Cut to a LS of his POV, a dancing couple whirling towards him across the dance floor as the woman's skirt swirls closer and closer to the camera with dizzying effect. The Man slowly looks around, at one point spying a woman staring back at him as she ignores her fawning partner. Juxtaposed with the wild dancing, his languorous looks charge the screen with high energy. The Man surveys everything as if he sits above it all, making us ever more curious about his character, motives and interests. Such will be the case with him until the very end of the film, when all will be revealed.

Suddenly, through several long shots from a variety of angles, we see hordes of people get up and rush the ballroom's stairway, Hitchcock shooting them in a frenetic, quick cut manner that further grabs our attention. What's happening, a fire? The Man doesn't run with everyone, either, but calmly follows along behind the crowd's manic impulses. Does he know something that we do not? For the first time, while we've never been explicitly shown the ocean liner until now, Hitchcock cuts away to a LS of the boat from the outside. We suddenly remember The Father reading headlines about just such a scene not two minutes ago.

The Girl (Betty Balfour) arrives via seaplane, flown by herself, yet another of Hitchcock's many headstrong, assertive female characters. In this film she will also turn out to be a rich, foolhardy, unsympathetic romantic who will learn very little from the opportunities her director throws in her path. Even in so simple a shot as The Girl climbing up the ladder onto the ship, Hitchcock turns it into a playful cinematic experiment. He shows us three different POV shots of her ascent. The first is from what can only be the camera's neutral (AC) POV — a LS encompassing the rowboat and entire side of the ship as Betty begins her climb. The second, ever so brief, is a CU of *her* view looking up the ladder — a wonderfully audacious, disorienting shot of the ship's dark side and bright, open door above. The third is a cut to an AC MCU of her final steps upward — the three shots juxtaposing from long to closeup to medium closeup, heightening their power — with a view of a man looking out of a porthole up her dress! Hitchcock always could find spots for throwaway humor, especially of the sexually titillating kind.

In retrospect, we realize that Hitchcock never gave us any time to realize that we wrongly assumed a fire or some other emergency had caused the mob to rush out of the ballroom, for we hadn't consciously comprehended that we were on an ocean liner in spite of the fact that Hitchcock had alerted us to The Girl's plans. What *did* cause the hubbub, of course, was the typically absurd, rich people's desire to be the first ones to spot celebrities (and be seen in their company). Once again, Hitchcock's plant in the first scene of The Father reading the headlines provided us with the clues we just did not use.

> *[P]eople confuse what I do with mystery. I don't believe in mystifying an audience. I believe in giving them all the information and then in making them sweat. It's no good devising a film to satisfy only yourself* [AH, in "Alfred Hitchcock" interview, by Charles Thomas Samuels; SG2, 2003, p. 131].

Revealing a dirty, windblown face, we see The Girl powder her nose after removing her pilot's glasses. Looking about amid a sea of pressing onlookers, we see excitement flash across her features as she recognizes someone partially hidden in the crowd. Cut to a CU of The Man. Is he the one she spies? No, but this is what Hitchcock wants us to think. The camera then cuts to a CU of The Boy in the crowd, surreptitiously acknowledging her.

So, who *is* The Man? Upon recognition of all three of these characters, The Girl walks off frame L and looks to her left for her lover to follow. The camera travels with her briefly (the first such panning shot in the film), ostensibly seen from her lover's POV. We suddenly see her walk past

The Man, who is smiling devilishly down on her, but she doesn't give him even one glance, confirming his anonymity in her eyes and, more importantly, ours. Seeing the two of them suddenly juxtaposed in the same frame, a charged feeling of uncertainty and curiosity creeps just beneath our consciousness. Hitchcock lets this pass, though, and The Man steps aside.

Dissolve from a CU of a steward's finger pointing to a map of the ship's quarters and The Girl's stateroom, B46, on the actual door of the room. The Girl enters, putters about, and closes the door. Cut to a long shot of a man coming down the hallway. We can't tell at this distance but he looks like her lover. He bangs into a stewardess as they both round a corner, and we see that we're wrong again. It's our Man, Theo. *Now* Hitchcock shows us The Boy coming down the hallway looking for her room. The Man doesn't hide his presence as he approaches, either, but just stares off frame R as the lover passes, giving him more of a glance than The Girl did earlier. Who *is* this guy?

The Boy knocks on B46. Cut to The Girl's face, hesitant, and we are shown her imagination at work. Is it the stewardess again? Why doesn't she rush to the door? Two reasons: One, she's being careful not to give herself away; Two, Hitchcock is shamelessly bringing attention to the art of the camera by inserting this shot, deliberately slowing the action down and temporarily delaying what we want to see, the conventional clinch of happiness between two lovers. He also may be saying that love is not always a safe haven but must occasionally be sought after furtively.

The staginess of their efforts to achieve privacy is replaced by the tremendous emotional power of their upcoming kiss. Hitchcock shows them both rushing towards the camera in CU, immediately intoning a third presence between them — us. They clinch, hold each other tightly, and peck happy flurries of love-kisses all over each other's faces. Then it gets serious as they realize they've actually succeeded in their little plot to run away, and now, finally, they are alone. Hitchcock treats this moment in an extraordinary way. As they go in for the big one, he focuses in CU on The Girl as her face is a bit more turned towards the camera than The Boy's. It is a private, privileged view for us and us alone, for The Boy cannot see what we see from his angle. Written all over her face is a somber and very intimate expression, as she begins to expose the depth of her being to this Boy. But *we* see this, not him.

Suddenly, she gazes directly at the camera as if she feels *our* presence. She first gives us a sly look, then accusingly stares at the camera with a brief glare that seems to say: "Shame on you for spying on our private union. Who are *you* to intrude on us so?" Then, immediately turning back to her lover, she deeply and passionately kisses him in spite of us, despite our voyeurism. A strange and unnerving sense of implication runs through us with her kiss, and this feeling turns a little bit to shame as Hitchcock cuts to a rear shot from behind The Girl at the end of their kiss as they both break out into fits of laughter. The Girl turns her head L and awkwardly (still in his arms) arches around to continue laughing hysterically at us, staying in character but further alluding to our complicity. "Ha, ha," she seems to say, "you can't feel this. You're trapped in a movie theater (or your home) watching and you cannot really share in our wonderful feelings."

> *As for me, the content of the story, the plot, does not interest me at all. It's the manner of recounting that fascinates me. What attracts me is to discover what will provoke a strong emotion in the viewer and how to make the viewer feel it. Moreover, I think that in all artistic domains we attempt to create an emotion. The importance of a work of art, no matter what sort, is to evoke a reaction* [AH, "Hitch, Hitch, Hitch, Hurrah!" Nogueira & Zalaffi, 1972; in SG2, 2003, p. 120].

Shortly, in polite society, the tables are turned. The Boy and Girl are soon found kissing in an elevator, a crowd of cackling women laughing shamelessly at *them*. Hitchcock has now allowed us to feel some small (but still guilty) recompense at their expense this time.

Through a "chance" meeting between The Man and The Girl, a fresh, unexpected element enters the picture as he begins to flirt with her. Engaging her in superfluous but easy talk, he immediately engenders jealousy in The Boy, much as Corby did to Jack early on in *The Ring* with that film's Girl. Exploiting and flaunting his obviously more mature skills, the Man plants the seeds of apprehension in The Girl even before she consciously realizes it.

The next scene bears this out as the lovers continue to encounter minor obstacles to their "perfect" union. The wind up on deck almost blows them overboard. The Boy's attempt at a mock wedding ends on a typically Hitchcockian, blackly comic note as his ring ends up fitting only the Girl's thumb (more *Ring* allusions). And when they try to seal it with a kiss, her boa's feathers get caught in both of their mouths.

"Cupid at the prow — but Neptune at the helm." The title card is typical of Hitchcock's love of *le bon mot*, or double entendres. The boat is rocking and both our heroes are dizzy and sick, as if from too much champagne. The doubly nauseating sight of a sumptuously laid-out buffet (and, appropriately, several CU's of a stuffed pig's head — another of Hitch's little jabs at the fat cats), along with the very real lack of manly integrity in The Boy's character, propel him back to his cabin rather than confronting his competitor (who, once again, is "innocently" flirting with the lady in question).

We see The Man as the only really stable person on board, for, as the wait-
ers and guests all lean in unison to the right and left with the ship's tilting, he walks across the dining room in a straight and sure line — pure,
silent cinema at its finest and funniest.

In fact, the rocking of the boat and the physical reactions of the pas-
sengers become humorous motifs for this absurd little parlor play being
acted out. A wonderfully simple and effective special effect in The Boy's
stateroom prefigures by thirty years Hitchcock's masterpiece on vertigo,
when he/we see three bobbing and weaving superimposed images of the
concerned Girl swaying before him/us at the foot of his bed.

The exposition bogs down when Hitchcock is forced to employ cue
cards to explain their argument over money — The Boy's and The Father's.
In fact, it becomes somewhat painful to watch for Hitchcock's own feelings toward the hypocrisy of the rich; their empty, banal arguments are
clearly repeated throughout his canon. Our young lovers are having their
first spat, and we shall see exactly what — or if — they learn from such challenges to true love over the course of this film.

She offers his thumb ring back, petulant. Just as he reaches to grab
it, the boat lurches. The ring falls (shades of Harker's church search for
the ring in The Ring the previous year), and he gropes all around the floor
for it. She tries to leave the stateroom, more lurching, and grabs his hair
to steady herself, then sickeningly wipes his hair grease off her hand. The
humor, no less funny but tinged with a bitter taste, sticks in our throats.

The film's tone and the lovers' tenor take a turn for the better. The
Boy and Girl seem to be growing up somewhat past their puppy love and
towards a tentative appreciation and respect for each other as individuals.
There's the surprising touch of The Girl's hesitancy just outside the cabin
door when The Boy quickly opens it and finds her still there, pensive and,
perhaps, a little repentant. And there's his own entrance in the next scene
in Paris, timid and yearning, as he is careful not to infringe on The Girl's
good time yet wanting to reach out to her just the same. Hitchcock allows
us to see these efforts at emotional development, and we begin to hold out
some hope for them — as intended by the director.

The Boy's uncertain but formally tacit acknowledgment of The Man
at her party also points up his potential manhood. Ah, but our Boy still
has much more to learn. The innocent joy over The Girl's playing at dressing up annoys him and he rejects her luxurious outfits, claiming: "I've
always understood that simplicity was the keynote to good taste." She
replies: "If I've offended your good taste I must try to make amends."
Forthwith she exits into her boudoir and returns hilariously dressed in her
maid's simple black garments, a kerchief wrapped round her head (the

half-dressed maid in the background) and a look of mock poverty on her face. She then takes a step forward and stops a second for a melodramatic, pregnant pause, then her hand flings confetti over her head in a hysterical spoof. The party erupts into laughter, all except our now serious Boy, who is furious. Hitchcock has The Girl approach him in an ECU, and we palpably feel his anger hit us squarely in the face. She turns to ask the ubiquitous but still mysterious Man, "Which do you think the most charming creation?" He answers, most nobly and correctly, "the wearer, undoubtedly."

Cut to a CU of a doorbell ringing. Who could *that* be? Why, it must be...it is! Daddy! His reason for coming? Not to protect his little girl, as we assume — that would be too easy, the conventional solution, and not allowed, or at least always delayed, in this or any Hitchcock film — but to tell her that the market fell, and they're broke! Once again, as Hitchcock would later note concerning *Foreign Correspondent* and *Notorious*, his story predicts or prefigures a monumental catastrophe on a global scale — in the former, it would be the outbreak of World War II, and in the latter, the discovery and use of uranium to make bombs. We should realize in this film that American's Great Depression will hit the following year and bring all of the Western world down with it. At the mention of their loss of income, the room spins dizzyingly for our heroine. Now it's time for her to learn a few things (perhaps), for we suddenly see her imagining herself through the door of the party, her back to the camera, still wearing that poor dress on her body, which not five minutes earlier she had so savagely mocked facing us/the camera. Hitchcock's painful irony is telling indeed.

To fend off complete poverty The Girl decides to sell her jewelry, but is immediately robbed on the sidewalk, the thievery shown onscreen only through images of legs in CU walking, stalking, running, and standing, a wonderful and clever prefiguring of the opening of *Strangers on a Train* twenty-three years later. As we have seen throughout these silent films, all of the director's skills and techniques are firmly in place.

Back home Daddy does squat thrusts and pushups with a stogey dangling from his mouth, while daughter dearest tries to flip the bed mattress. As she airs out the spread, occasionally blocking the camera's view of The Father peering over his shoulder at her erstwhile efforts, we see an obvious but no less clever cut from the white sheet of the bed to a checkered kitchen tablecloth. The Girl is trying her hand at some real work for the first time in her life, but will fail miserably at it.

Another favorite Hitchcock theme, food, is next played for laughs (culminating in its most riotous, black comedy treatment in *Frenzy*). Even though he can't cut into her homemade muffins, Daddy is pleased, and his daughter begins once again to dream of her lover, Hitchcock superimposing his face over hers. But the director will not leave her dream alone, and so he then superimposes the mysterious Man's face over loverboy's, forcefully reminding her and us that we still haven't got a clue about him. Who *is* that guy, and what is his purpose — good or evil? Theo Von Alten's devilish good looks bear down once again on our fair maiden, and provide much of the real suspense in this slightly absurd film.

The next scenes parody the idleness, pettiness, boorishness and bored lives of the pseudo-rich with a nastiness that hits hard via Hitchcock's commentary. One shot of The Girl's doughy handprints on her lover's back (he has come for a visit to their hovel) stands out with that always fresh, typical Hitchcockian audaciousness. Have I mentioned the director's derision towards the incompetence and impracticality of the rich, too? The Girl's pathetically unfunny attempts at kneading dough highlight those characteristics. Hitchcock deliberately drags this scene out so long as to really make us sick at the sight of her inabilities.

Another in a seemingly never-ending line of technical tricks pops into view as The Girl dreams of returning to sea. We see her vision of another ballroom full of couples dancing, a woman sitting in the foreground at a table alone with her back to the camera. It's our heroine, right? Ha! Hitchcock quickly freezes the frame, and the camera pans back to reveal The Girl looking through a store window at that photo! She had imagined the entire scene for our benefit, yet another brilliantly created, fresh way for the director to toy with our cinematic assumptions. How could we have fallen for his trickery again? Because he knows that cinematic conventions and expectations are deeply imprinted on our psyches, and he will exploit those reactions mercilessly.

Hitchcock's throw-away dirty old man joke — you know, the one about the guy staring up The Girl's dress as she climbed aboard the boat earlier — is now revisited in a less innocent, more perverse manner. The Girl decides to finally get a real job (another jab at those idle rich), although all she can really think about is getting back to high society, we rightly suspect. An ad reads: "Wanted: Young girls with beautiful teeth to demonstrate the advantages of using 'Minto' toothpaste." The Girl storms into the agency, ignoring and rushing past all the women waiting their turns as if her needs are the only ones in the world — more typical arrogance. The fat ad man behind the desk says, via title, "Why are you here?" Girl puckers up to show him her pearlies. Card flashes "Teeth!" Ad man says: "We're only interested in legs here." (Flash on the earlier theft scene.) Cut to a skuzzy co-worker leaning against a wall behind The Girl, leering. Silently and surreptitiously, he raises The Girl's skirt a bit to have a peek with a lazy, the-world-is-my-trash-can foot.

Champagne, 1928: The frivolous Girl Betty (played by Betty Balfour) surreptitiously being checked out by an unknown actor as she hands the impresario (played by Clifford Heatherley) her letter of introduction in order to work at his "speak-easy."

The Girl gets the job, of course, but not for her pearly whites — it's for those lovely robbed legs of her, and the job is in a dime-a-dance romance sleazy cabaret club. Teeth, legs, and face — all are interchangeable parts in the selling of flesh.

It's time for another audacious camera montage. For four seconds, the Girl and the cabaret madam walk toward the camera as it pulls back, keeping both women in a MS, establishing a sense of continuous, smooth movement forward (compare to the similar shot in *Downhill*, Roddy and Tim's movement towards their headmaster). Sudden cut to a side view of The Girl in partial profile right alone in the frame and half-turned towards the camera's new position. With the barroom action now seen in the background, the shot is slightly disorienting.

We are now set up for the amazing shot, and so perplexed by the change in directions that, as usual, it almost goes by undetected. Rather than seeing The Girl continue to move forward (which is now towards

SR), Hitchcock directs her to walk *backwards* towards SL. For a quick two seconds we see her in a MS staring behind left of the camera as she walks backwards. Cut to a stunning *reverse angle* MS POV from The Girl's eyes, the camera now moving smoothly right (as if moving with her backwards walk), and we see her view of two lovers heatedly kissing in a hidden booth. The sexual content of this short, two-second shot startles us. Reverse angle cut again to *the booth's* MS view of The Girl as she stares directly into the camera's eye, a look of complete astonishment on her face. Suddenly real-izing the true nature of her job — not so thinly disguised prostitution, I would say — she surprises us by giving the slightest of shrugs and accept-ing her fate.

The next scene is the obligatory exposition break, which allows the director to unveil an extreme overhead, bird's eye view shot of the Girl walking toward the maître d's table. Wealth (or, more specifically, the air of wealth) has its privileges, as her classy aura momentarily mystifies him. He reads her letter of introduction, simultaneous expressions of respect and lasciviousness flickering across his plastic features. But her lessons are far from over, and she must truly come to understand how it feels to be treated like an underling, a servant, if she is to learn anything.

In the kitchen, we see cooks literally throw dinners onto plates. Some food misses its mark, is picked up off the floor, set back in place, and served as if nothing has happened.

Hitchcock's skill at approximating three-dimensionality onscreen (breaking the fourth wall of the screen itself) is nowhere more apparent than when The Girl stands at the bar and sees a woman, not unlike her-self in her heyday, exaggeratedly dancing and flirting. Suddenly, a shadow appears between our/her view and the camera. A couple of bartenders enter the frame, filling the space between The Girl and her parody. Because we've been shown the flirty dancer first, we're subconsciously annoyed at the bartenders' physical impositions on our view, and we strain to keep our attention on the background action (much like our frustration along with the Girl in *The Ring* as she peered through the crowd to see the fight). Hitchcock doesn't indulge our anger for long, though, because The Girl's attention, we quickly realize, has turned to the foreground and the bar-tender's punny "Maiden's prayer" drink being concocted.

The director stays a long time with this scene as we see The Girl's expressive eyes fascinatingly absorbed with the bartender's machinations. She's just like a little girl at a grownup's candy factory, and the drink takes on a life of its own (it's a plant, and will soon reveal its transitory pur-pose). The camera, stand-in for The Girl's POV, pans right and moves a little L to follow the waiter and the drink all the way around to the other side of the ballroom (a full fifteen-second track), past pillars and people. We see in an ELS the drink finally reaching its destination — The Man at a table! Hitchcock's quite mobile camera now gives us a reverse shot of The Girl, and it moves a bit left as she finishes her own panning gaze, heightening our sense of her eye's movements and recognition of him.

A double irony is shared with us when The Man spies her, too, and the camera shows him taking the same long way around to say hello. He points out how strange it is to meet her in such a place. The Girl answers that she used to pay to come to places like this, but now they pay her. How truly incorrect that statement really is— she's the one *really* paying now. The power of their comments is particularly strong, for Hitchcock has them both speak directly to the camera (each other, and us).

Hitchcock's fourth wall is once again effectively exposed during the Man and Girl's table conversation. This being 1928 (and no Hays censorship restrictions in evidence for another six years), the lewd and leering maître d' comes by and roughly pinches The Girl on the arm, expecting her to give him some "private" company. She promptly stomps on his foot.

Champagne (what else?) arrives as the dizzy mob of dancers crowds in all about their table. The effect is almost like a drug tempting our heroine, as Hitchcock insistently keeps the camera on the pulsing masses an extra second or two so that we feel the crowd's pressure pressing in on our identification with them.

The Man looks deep into the camera (here comes the payoff, we expect) and says to us: "Don't you realize that anything could happen to a girl like you, in a place like this?" Another double message, as it's really *our* warning from Hitchcock. Cut to the same CU of The Man looking through a champagne glass as at the beginning of the film. Cut back to an even closer shot of The Girl staring straight into the camera, dreamlike.

Suddenly we see them get up and move toward the kissing booths, ostensibly for more privacy. Ambiguity is heightened as The Man firmly urges her inside, dark shadows crossing their faces as they sit down (*à la* the shadows behind the beaded curtains in the pastry shop of *Downhill*). The Man aggressively takes her in his arms and kisses her. The Girl fights him off— it's suddenly become a powerfully violent scene — and runs back into the ballroom, then turns to scream at him through the mass of dancing bodies all around her.

A surprising cut back to the earlier CU of The Girl reveals her gazing dazedly at the camera, discernibly breathing a little heavily. She shakes it off and turns back to The Man at the table. *It was all a dream, a lie!* Hitchcock didn't even bat an eye (nor did we) perpetrating his most barefaced act of deviousness. The Girl laughs, and connoisseurs will flash on the lie

perpetrated by Jonathan (Richard Todd) to Eve (Jane Wyman) during the
first part of *Stage Fright*, the lie that was not revealed to be a lie until the
very end of the film, the lie that 1950 audiences just would not accept.
Frankly, I think we deserve whatever we get from this filmmaker, and this
early silent film fib, like the later one, is in any filmmaker's recourse.

Immediately The Boy enters, barely a moment's respite before Hitchcock further complicates things, just like in life. He joins the couple and
sits facing the camera between their profiles. Another glass is brought over
as we are shown what seems like the thousandth shot of The Man's dark
and mysterious, deeply penetrating gaze. The payoff we've been expecting, of course, still has not come. The Man writes a note on the back of a
card — "Always your friend if you are in need" — and excuses himself. Ever-
present metaphoric temptation of frivolity, a brightly lit Pleasure Garden-
type dancer suddenly appears directly behind the Boy and Girl.

The Boy starts to believe The Girl has begun to appreciate the value
of hard work, then realizes exactly what kind of work she is doing here —
thinly disguised whoring. But, like everything she does, The Girl seems
to find innocence in all walks. Boy, ever suspicious and critical, is the nar-
rower minded of the two. Who's at fault here? Which is worse, naiveté or
suspiciousness? Hitchcock won't tell us, for we must decide, as in all his
films.

More ambiguity is revealed, this time sexual, as we see a couple of
girls dancing together (at the earlier party, The Girl's maid had a decid-
edly butch look about her as well). The Girl, slowly realizing how critical
The Boy is of her new life, rears her solemn, self-righteous head in silent
protest. How dare he pass judgment on her? Slowly, she spitefully mimics
the dancing girls, and we can feel The Boy's revulsion at this perverse
expression of her own frustrations over his myopia and prejudices. Once
more Hitchcock has the scene go on and on, exaggerating its effects so we
have no doubts about their feelings. The Girl hesitates a moment, then casts
the camera that direct, accusatory glance she'd used during their other
most intimate moment earlier on board ship. "What are you looking at?"
she glares. "This is *my* life." Then, turning back to the boiling mad Boy,
she ups the tempo of her mockingly false rapture.

Cut to an oblique shot of a balcony where The Man, who apparently
had not left the cabaret, gazes down. Cut to his overhead view. The Boy
pours more champagne and The Girl guzzles it down, then stares conspiratorially at the camera again, which has now moved back down to her
eye level, this time from the position where The Man had recently sat.
Then, once we've acknowledged her contact with us, she glances sidelong
to her right back at The Boy. Subconsciously we realize she's completely

got us—Hitchcock's got us—involved in her scheme as co-conspirators! Another quick stare at us solidifies our role.

For this entire scene Hitchcock has wrung as much emotion as possible out of every facial expression, and we've been willingly glued to these peoples' features. The Boy gets up and leaves, and Hitchcock is so confident in his manipulations that he shows his departure just by having the camera record The Girl's eye movements. We imagine him standing up, turning, and starting to walk away, all as seen through her eyes.

But no, once again, we've been deceived. He has not left the cabaret at all (as with The Man) but only gone outside … to fetch her father! Her reactions are straight at the camera, naturally, so we first see her elated features over seeing him, then turning into fury at the humiliation. She runs up the stairs to the balcony, ostensibly for protection from The Man. The lessons of life just will not stick with this frivolous and frightened person.

Commotion below, as something is about to happen. We see The Father and The Boy hurry over to the dance floor, then flinch as we see a *body* hurtle down from above the frame behind them! Might it be The Girl jumping to—no, it's just another part of the evening's entertainment, a dancing girl *flinging herself* from the balcony into her waiting partner's arms far below. Hitchcock cuts to a medium shot of both of them spinning, spinning, spinning around, and the camera zooms in for another dizzying shot.

Now the film's exposition rapidly advances. Cut to the earlier business card saying, "Always your good friend if you are in need." Fade out and then in to a scribbled name on a door buzzer. It seems that The Man is heading back to America. The Girl begs him to take her with him. Cut to a train heading SL, cut to The Boy in a car facing SR. All aboard another boat, Hitchcock cuts to The Girl and The Man entering a two-bed stateroom SL. The Man goes out and locks the door behind him. Suddenly nervous, The Girl opens and enters the door to Hitchcock's favorite room, loosening a towel rod next to the bathroom sink for protection.

She moves past the stationary camera in an ECU and hides behind the cabin door, ready to strike. Someone opens it, and she bops the person who enters square on the noggin. Astonished, she sees it's her true love, and smothers him with kisses, her knight to the miraculous rescue. "What are you doing here?" they both ask each other. Explanations abound, and then they clinch, this time older and wiser (we hope); but the scene has a sad and eerie familiarity about it. They both seem to have at least a similar resolve now, and have grown to cooperatively stage a showdown with their mysterious interloper. Conspiring together, The Boy waits in hiding in said bathroom.

The Man returns and leaves the outside cabin door ajar, then leans nonchalantly against the wall. Suddenly, The Father enters, an erect cigar proudly protruding from his mouth. The Girl's head starts to spin again, and she crosses her eyes. The Father places an arm conspiratorially in The Man's arm, then says, "Meet my very good friend." The Girl says, "But father he's a ----." A what? Gigolo? Liar? She doesn't even know, but apparently he had been sent from the start by Daddy Dearest to protect her from herself.

All is forgiven in a laughable manner. Champagne is served all around and we view The Man yet again as seen through his glass darkly. Briefly spooked by this one recurring image Hitchcock has shown us/her throughout all the traumas of this long hour-and-a-half morality play, the Girl shakes it off, only to begin arguing immediately with her lover over their marriage arrangements. Nothing, apparently, has changed between these two, as The Girl says to her father, "And we'll have an aeroplane to meet us outside New York, won't we, daddy?" Cut to The Man looking through his champagne glass *again*, then a reverse angle so we can see the bickering couple arguing, then kissing, through the glass—a typical uneasy, tenuously happy ending to another Hitchcock film.

Unlike in *The Pleasure Garden* and *The Lodger*, both of which ended somewhat happily, but similar to *Downhill* and *Easy Virtue* and *The Ring* and *The Farmer's Wife*, *Champagne* ends ambiguously, no one knowing if the protagonists have really learned anything of value or grown at all emotionally. As we shall see with the final two films in Hitchcock's silent oeuvre, *The Manxman* and *Blackmail*, their denouements will also be more closely allied with the latter category.

Nine

The Manxman

First screening January 1928, released in 1929

As with *Champagne*, most critics were not kind to *The Manxman*. Of the eight concise film review compendiums referenced, the star ratings ranged from Martin and Porter's turkey again ("afternoon soap operas are nothing compared to this howler"; p. 695) to Maltin's two-and-a-half stars ("OK melodrama"; p. 879) to even three-and-a-half stars by *Blockbuster*, although the latter had nothing positive to say except that it was the director's last film, so one wonders whether that reviewer even watched the film. *Halliwell* found nothing good to say, either ("stern romantic melodrama of virtually no interest despite its director"; p. 531), and both *Variety* and *Time Out* could barely muster that Hitchcock did the best he could with the weak story.

There were, however, a few positive comments made on the film at the time, although one has to look far and wide for them. Mordaunt Hall of *The New York Times* loved it: "Enchanting scenes...as beautiful as anything that one would hope to behold on the screen" (December 17, 1929), and in London, where audiences also raved about it (Hitchcock, apparently, did not), *Bioscope* (January 23, 1929) said: "Cleverly directed, finely played human interest story.... Only a skillful director could have devised from a story of this kind a picture of such remarkable power and interest. The unflinching realism and masterly manner [make the spectator] oblivious to the drabness of the story."

As with the previous film, I, too, agree that while it may be a lesser effort by the director, there are more than enough points of interest to reward repeat viewings.

As the credits begin, we see that the film was adapted from the famous story by Sir Hall Caine (1894), itself based on Tennyson's narrative poem *Enoch Arden* (1864). Its fame as a film, apparently, was already legendary, for in the space of seven years during the 1910's it had been made into four movies: two by D. W. Griffith, in 1910 and 1911, and two by others in 1915 and 1916. If one could track them all down, a comparative analysis of the five would undoubtedly make an interesting book all its own.

The credits continue over a long shot of crashing waves near a shore, huge rocks blocking their advance. The film stars Carl Brisson as Pete Quilliam, the fisherman, who had played 'One Round' Jack Sander two films back in *The Ring*; Malcolm Keen, playing Philip Christian, the deemster (Isle of Man lingo for "judge"), had already played Fear 'O' God in *The Mountain Eagle* and Joe Betts, the jealous detective, in *The Lodger*; famed Polish-Czech-Austrian-German-French singer, film and stage actress Anny Ondra (1902–1987), here as Kate Cregeen, would play the self-defending murderess Alice White in Hitchcock's next film, *Blackmail*; Randle Ayrton (1869–1940) is her father, Caesar Cregeen; and Claire Greet is her mother, Mrs. Cregeen.

The Manxman holds a unique place in Hitchcock's oeuvre, for his

The Manxman, 1929: Boyhood friends and soon to be rivals Philip Christian (Malcolm Keen) and Pete Quilliam (played by Carl Brisson) stare out to sea on location in Cornwall, England.

classic touches and cinematic tricks are *almost nowhere to be found*. As Rohmer and Chabrol rightly state in their groundbreaking book *Hitchcock: The First Forty-Four Films*, "there is no pointless virtuosity here — just a simple and precise shooting script," which included

> a minute, complete, and unflinching description of the moral conflict opposing three people whose behavior is practically beyond reproach. Their failing is the failing of all human beings. Ordinary morality is helpless to resolve their problems. Each one is obliged to assume his own responsibilities and to forge a personal ethic [1957; translation, 1979, p. 18].

Hitchcock himself agreed with this assessment in conversation with those authors' countryman François Truffaut: "*The novel had quite a reputation and it belonged to a tradition, [and we] had to respect that reputation and that tradition. It was not a Hitchcock movie...*" (1983, p. 61). Still, *Time Out* rightly noted that Hitchcock's "frequent use of shots taken through windows anticipates the interest in voyeurism in his later work" (2003, p. 754). Also, even though there are some of the director's most beautiful location shots on display, ostensibly on England's Isle of Man, "it was shot in Cornwall" (*ibid.*).

The film opens on a title with a line from the Bible: "What shall it profit a man if he gain the whole world and lose his own soul?" Quite a question, and it is in keeping, really, with all of the director's films, to the extent that all his characters, as I've contended throughout this book, are on a quest that will test their soul-searching skills. The opening title dissolves into "a shot of the triskele (three-legged) symbol of the isle of Man, and proceeds to tell a story that perfectly illustrates how none of its three main characters sees — at least until too late — the whole truth" (Mogg, 1999, p. 14). Throughout the film, there are the occasional classic over-the-shoulder shots and a great many close-ups — Rohmer and Chabrol note that the "direction is deliberately centered on the faces, on their expressions" (1957, p. 20) — which keep the focus squarely on these characters' quandaries, but I think one reason Hitchcock keeps his camera so long on CU's of his characters is to allow the wonderful silent film actors time to register all the emotions they're struggling with for us.

Still, several scenes are truly noteworthy, and typically Hitchcockian. When Anny Ondra as Kate promises to wait for Pete to return from seeking his fortune in a fit of crazy, childlike passion, she immediately regrets her promise, and the isle's lighthouse repeatedly flashes its warning light in the background, illuminating her bedroom shade over and over again. Pete then extracts a promise from his best friend Philip to keep an eye on her while he's gone, but both Kate and Philip already know full well they'll fall for each other and will break their promises.

It's not surprising, then, that Kate shows no remorse when news of Pete's death arrives, for all she can selfishly tell Philip is, "We're free!" What she really means is *she's free* from her promise. Philip, in turn, seems at least initially sad over the death of his best friend, and a bit querulous over her response, but his own quandary over Kate's desires and his lust for her has now started and, as much as we might want to cheer (by convention) for Pete's heroic underdog fisherman, the real Manxman of the film is Philip, whose friendship and sense of honor will be truly tested. Another way of looking at this is to imagine that Hitchcock has reincarnated Tim Wakely and his cowardly friendship with Roddy Berwick from *Downhill,* who is now given another chance to redeem himself through Philip's deeply moral struggles. As in that film early on, we spy two young boys play-fighting outside amongst the adults, metaphorical harbinger of trouble ahead for the two friends.

Immediately after all of this melodramatic dramatizing, naturally, there is a quick, startling cut to a CU of a smiling Pete very much alive. The sad, romantic triangle has really begun now — another version of *The Lodger's* trio, perhaps.

As mentioned above, many of the best scenes in this film are of extraordinary location shots in Cornwall, standing in for the Isle of Man. There is one especially gorgeous ELS of Kate clambering over a craggy cliff line to meet Philip at their favorite beach spot, her passage foregrounding the sun's dazzling light upon a huge cloud. And the ELS of Philip waiting for her standing center framed on the beach, barely visible through a huge cavity carved out of the rocks from eons of breaking waves, is also breathtaking, as is the ELS immediately following, a reverse angle shot from the other side of the chasm as Kate runs towards Philip. Hitchcock's English landscape and seascape dwarf these tiny figures as nature springs to life with its own immense character.

Later, when Pete says they're to be married, Kate nearly walks right into the camera, so stunned is she by the news, barely veering off to the right at the last second to arrive in front of her fireplace. Unlike in *The Lodger* and *The Farmer's Wife,* this film's hearth will provide no respite for its protagonists. And, in a nod to her next role, Ondra accidentally slices a finger while cutting her wedding cake, *Blackmail's* murderous knife looming large in our minds.

But her love stays true to Philip, and her self-inflicted emotional pain begins to catch up to her. On her wedding night with Pete, the moment of reckoning nears as she sits by the fire searching for solace and support —

the hearth will not warm her deceitful heart, and she shivers in fear. Later, Kate mouths the words "I'm going to have a baby" to Philip, and we are allowed to experience her emotional trauma as her out-of-wedlock child — sown by another man — is taken by the wrong man as his own. A classic and potently charged Hitchcockian shot emerges briefly right after Kate says this same thing to Pete, for we see him in CU staring incredulous directly into the camera — Kate's face and ours — while Philip's back is seen sadly hunched over in an out-of-focus LS over Pete's L shoulder. Naturally, our naïve Pete thinks the baby is his, and his incredulity turns into elation.

A word about the actors themselves: Carl Brisson as Pete is the absolute antithesis of his character in *The Ring*. All delicacy and gentleness, here he plays a loving father and surrogate mother to a child not his own! Anny Ondra is quite photogenic as Kate Cregeen, and is clearly being primed for her next starring role in the brilliant silent and sound transition film *Blackmail*—in spite of the fact that her thick German-Czech accent had to be dubbed by British actress Joan Barry just off camera while on the set. In fact, in both of her films with Hitchcock, Ondra plays a guilty and conspiring gamine, unwilling and probably unable to take a direct stand on her own behalf. And Malcolm Keen, quite effective as the narcissistic and jealous detective Joe Betts in *The Lodger*, plays a similar role throughout most this film as the solemn cur.

All the tests of faith, loyalty, trust, love, passion, promises, and deception from *Downhill* are tested in *The Manxman* with a vengeance. As we will see, the characters learn only moderately more than their predecessors, for when Kate finally realizes she must tell Pete the truth, Philip takes up her reigns of deceit, fearing public shame, which just drives both of them deeper into the depths of their lies. People's hypocrisy over money — a strong Hitchcock motif in these silent films— pushes its weight around a lot, too, towards both the rich and poor, as Philip is urged not to marry beneath him like his father, and Caesar (Kate's father) rejects Pete early on for being a poor fisherman. Upon Pete's return from the dead, however, Caeser hypocritically welcomes him back with open arms once he's made his fortune.

I don't know how he did it, but immediately after Pete reads Kate's "Dear John" letter, Hitchcock cuts to a MS of Philip's baby in a rocker by the hearth — the kid can't be more than a few weeks old — and darned if the baby girl doesn't lift her arm and point with an index finger at him with a kind of "I told you so" look! I had to rewind it three times and repeatedly study the shot, but that is *exactly* what this little baby does, and that is exactly what her expression is! And they say never to try to direct animals and babies.

After skulking around Philip's office for weeks on end near the end of her rope, Kate finally demands: "Philip — the time has come when you must choose between your career and me." She tries but fails to assert her needs with Pete, too: "I've come for my baby," she says, and wonderful role reversals appear before our eyes as we marvel at the sturdy Brisson playing the outraged mother and a delicate Ondra fighting for her own child. Even after he is told, "She's not yours— she never was," he protectively screams back, "It's a lie!" Hitchcock must have loved directing Brisson in this scene, a macho, six-foot plus he-man who had just played a boxer, as he tenderly and lovingly lifts up the infant and takes her upstairs for protection. It's also a great role reversal and difficult part to play for a woman to be denied access to her own child by someone who is not even the rightful father!

As the characters' characters become more and more tested, the story begins to take on more and more emotional energy, which is where the real strength of this film lies, I believe. The only one to keep his promise in the film, director Hitchcock stayed true to the material.

Just before Kate throws herself into the sea in an effort to kill herself, Hitchcock gives us a final exceptional montage (of so few), beginning with an incredible CU of her wholly bereft yet beautiful face looking USR *à la* Marlene Dietrich, blond hair wind-blown to the right of her fully lit face framed by the darkness of night. Then, in LS, we see her limply fall into the harbor. Cut to a CU of her bubbles rising to the surface in the brackish, dark water. Hitchcock then dissolves to an ECU of a circular, black inkwell. The camera dollies back to reveal a pen being dipped in it. Cut to a CU of a hand now writing with the pen, and a further dolly back reveals the hand belongs to Philip at work at his desk.

Finally, honesty wills out in this film as old Caesar figures out what the secret was all along. In a highly charged scene in one of Hitchcock's favorite sets— no, not the bathroom, but a courtroom — Philip, too, finally redeems himself (and Tim Wakely?), personal truth and honesty winning out over politics, vocation, and friendship. On his first and last day as a judge and in a full courtroom, Philip admits that he is the father of Kate's child, and will work hard to undo what has been done.

Growth, Hitchcock tells us yet again, is never easy, and the last shot we see in the film is of a rather stunned, if finally sober, Pete Quilliam, heading back out to sea, alone.

Ten

Blackmail (Silent Version)

First screening of the silent version August 1929,
sound version released June 1929

Blackmail was Hitchcock's last fully silent film and also his and England's first talkie, the latter being released before the former and the silent, just in case sound didn't take off, released two months later. Thinking most of the succinct film review compendiums would laud the film, both sound and silent versions, I was surprised to see that, even though their ratings ranged from a low of three stars (HA, LM, MP, VH) through three-and-a-half stars (SS) to a high of four-and-a-half stars (BB)—all excellent marks— their comments were far from wholly positive. Here are just three excerpts:

> *Blackmail*...remains famous for its innovations in [the area of sound, but] it's now more stimulating for its experiment with narrative structure: an efficient, impersonal police investigation that elides into a messy, personal story of attempted rape, murder in self-defense, blackmail and a chase to the death [TO, p. 121].
>
> *Blackmail* is most draggy. It has no speed or pace and very little suspense. Everything's open-face.... In performance the standout is Donald Calthrop as the rat crook. He looks it. Ondra is excellent as the girl. Dialog is ordinary but sufficient. Camerawork rather well, especially on the British Museum [in the chase finale] and the eating house scenes. A bit of comedy here and there, but not enough to be called relief [VA, p. 85].
>
> Hitchcock's first talkie is now a very hesitant entertainment but fully bears the director's stamp and will reward patient audiences in several excitingly staged sequences.... Hitchcock's ending was to have been ironic, the detective seeing the cell door shut on the arrested girl, going home and then being asked if he was going out with his girlfriend that evening. His answer: "Not tonight." This was unacceptable commercially and a happy ending was substituted [HA, p. 93].

The lengths of the various sound versions reviewed, typically, range from a low of 78 minutes (HA) through 82 (TO), 85 (my version) and 86 (VH, LM, MP, BB) to a high of 88 minutes (VA), with only Leonard Maltin mentioning the silent version length as being 75 minutes long. The silent version I watched, though, was a solid 121 minutes long, more than thirty minutes longer than the longest version of the sound feature, and almost 50 minutes longer than the shortest sound version! Truly, the silent film provides the viewer with much more bang for the buck!

Adapted by Hitchcock himself, the credits show that Anny Ondra, fresh off her role as Kate Cregeen in *The Manxman*, is back as Alice White; Sara Allgood (1879–1950), who will play Mrs. Boyle (Juno) in *Juno and the Paycock* the following year and a cameo in *Sabotage*, here plays Alice's mother, Mrs. White; Charles Paton (1874–1970) plays the father, Mr. White; John Longden (1900–1971), who will play Charles Bentham in *Juno and the Paycock*, Charles Hornblower in *The Skin Game*, and make a cameo appearance in *Jamaica Inn*, here plays Frank Webber, the Scotland Yard detective who turns out to be just as guilty of blackmail as the original blackmailer; Donald Calthrop (1888–1940), who will play Ion Stewart the following year in *Murder!*, and will appear in cameos in two other Hitchcock films, here plays Tracy, the first blackmailer; and Cyril Ritchard (1897–1977), who sang in operas at the Metropolitan and would win a Tony Award for Best Supporting Actor as Captain Hook in the 1955 production of *Peter Pan*, here plays Snidely Whiplash, uh, The Artist Crewe, the gentleman-cum-would-be-rapist-cum-murder victim of the film.

I don't remember quite such a detailed search and arrest in the sound version, as we see everything in semi-documentary fashion from the police stalking their victim through to him being thrown in a jail cell, and even the aftermath as the detectives wash up in the boys' room. There's also a nifty bit of camera work from the POV of the robber being caught in his bedroom, as he and the camera slyly pan SR to a very small mirror on the furthest wall. The camera (robber's gaze) zooms in to pick up his private view of the reflection of the officers standing in the doorway, immobile icons of the law. Deliberately melodramatic (for him and us), Hitchcock telegraphs the robber going for his gun in absurd slow motion, and the camera immediately cuts to a privileged CU of both officers' overcoats from behind, a sliver's eye view between them permitting us a three-inch window onto their scuffle with him. One of the officer's hands (it's Frank's, our soon to be "hero") pockets the gun, another private shot just for us, and his actions subliminally prefigure his palming of Alice's damning glove as evidence after the artist Crewe's murder at her hands.

The whole arrest and booking scene, a full twelve minutes worth, has been rightly analyzed by a number of critics, but there are also some wonderfully angled expressionistic shots in the montage, similar shots of which occasionally appear throughout Hitchcock's early British period, as well as the above-mentioned stretching of time and privileged shots, that are used for maximum audience impact. It's also worth mentioning that, in this pure-cinema silent version, Hitchcock did not use — nor need to use — one title card throughout this entire section. At its denouement, there's a neat little fade from a CU of the robber's face staring directly into the camera to an ECU of his fingerprint, oval matching oval.

Our introduction to Alice is rather expository, but does hammer home how bored she is with both her life and her Scotland Yard investigator boyfriend Frank, as she tiredly allows him a quick and cold peck on her cheek in the station house after work. Bitching right away over his being a half-hour late to pick her up, Frank, too, has nearly had it with her mock snobbish lack of appeal, barely repressed exasperation covering his face. And to his face Alice flirts openly and unabashedly with the other detectives. Anyone at this point in the film could easily wish her some kind of comeuppance for such childish behavior, which Hitchcock surely intends for us to feel towards her. But, of course, no one would wish the trauma she contributes to eliciting upon herself shortly. Wasting no time, Hitchcock is establishing his audience's conflicting emotions towards Alice.

Soon we are on the train heading towards dinner, where we see for the first and last time in a Hitchcock film a full twenty-five consecutive seconds of Sir Alfred himself "acting," in his funniest and longest cameo ever. And we so enjoy his tussle with the annoying kid, who pulls Alfie's hat down over his eyes and generally bothers everyone around him. It's easy to miss the continued difficulties our struggling lovers have together during this brief scene, or the moment they almost drop out of character to laugh at Hitchcock with us! Look fast, or rewind a couple of times! Two things are certain: Frank's a repressed stuffed shirt, and Alice craves excitement. It will take a lot out of them, but they will both work very hard shortly to get past these juvenile problems (and move on to more serious ones). Sadly, as a fitting ending to Hitchcock's silent period, they, too, as with most of the director's characters up to this point, will not have gotten far emotionally.

The would-be lovers continue their snippy behavior in the eatery with each other as they frustratingly try to find a table and get waited on. By now, both of them have become less and less sympathetic in our eyes. "Who would want to date either of them?" we wonder — exactly what Hitchcock wants us to think. An early title is more than revealing, for when Frank repeatedly asks if she still wants to go to the movies, Alice says, "I've seen everything worth seeing." Just you wait, my pretty. You ain't seen nothin' yet.

As if her attitude up till now wasn't bad enough, it turns out that she's been scheming all along, too. A note surreptitiously glanced at from her pocketbook states: "I'll be here on Tuesday at 6:30. Will you?" Having made another date already and now twenty minutes late for it, we better understand at least some of her previous fretting — though, rather than alleviate our disrespect for this conniving adolescent, who is playing at love, this new revelation only aggravates it. We're now prepared for powerful Hitchcockian audacity at its finest.

Just as we've about reached our limit over her deceptions and unpleasantness, Hitchcock undermines our animosity towards her by cutting to a lovingly rendered, full frontal CU of Alice's face, radiant. The director *always* finds ways to highlight contrasts onscreen and in our minds as strongly as possible. Recognizing someone, she smiles enchantingly. In spite of all the negative feelings we've built up in ourselves towards this young woman, we cannot help but be mesmerized by her beauty at this moment. The scene is all the more powerful because it has been so suddenly juxtaposed against the previously tedious, four-minute, static MD exposition of profile shots of Alice and Frank arguing. Here, we suddenly have a privileged, intimate moment with a woman's hopes all aglow on her face. The contradictory emotions at work in our hearts towards this young woman have been perfectly manipulated.

Quick cuts ensue back and forth between Alice's face and the artist Crewe's approach; her date has now also spied her. Not surprisingly, Hitchcock shows Crewe in a most favorable and sympathetic light — debonair, well dressed, and gentlemanly — all the things that Frank is not. Their sexual chemistry is palpable across the eating establishment and the screen. Needless to say, wholly unawares, Frank reaches his breaking point as Alice bows out of the movies after changing her mind a third time. He storms out. She leaves with Crewe almost immediately afterwards, which Frank notes surreptitiously as he stands outside, concern and amazement fighting on his face.

Outside Crewe's apartment, we see an ECU of someone's face, angled SR, watching the two arrive. Crewe's shadow animatedly converses with what turns out to be Tracy the Blackmailer's shadow, Alice looking on in the same frame — a powerful composition. She makes her second fatal error when she willingly enters the house with Crewe, who's still affecting a fairly good gentlemanly air. Hitchcock forebodingly shoots Crewe's vertiginous stairway from below in darkly expressionistic shadows for a quick two-count, clear precursor to the more famous shot thirty-one years later in *Psycho*.

Their two-and-a-half flight climb arm-in-arm is a stunner, for Hitchcock makes it feel like a walk to the gallows. In MS, the camera smoothly follows them on a vertical dolly up the stairway, which, from our perspective, reveals a missing banister on our side. At each landing, the camera slows down a bit and almost hesitates, waiting to keep both figures centered in a full-bodied MS as they turn each corner. Then, all three resume their foreboding climb to the top. Even more powerful than Roddy's *Downhill* descents in the escalator and elevator, thirty seconds and twenty seconds of real time respectively, Crewe and Alice's *ascent* lasts a harrowing forty seconds! Quite a powerful scene, it's a clear precursor to Bob and Bab's similar ascent up a stairway towards Rusk's flat in *Frenzy*, before that film's justly famous reverse track back down the stairs and out into the street.

We enter the artist's loft—error #3 for Alice. It, too, is strangely reminiscent of Roddy's expressionistically lit Marseilles flat. Crewe clicks on the lights, though, and the space comes alive and cheery. Alice goes to the window, and Anny Ondra's skillful acting briefly allows us to see Alice for who she really is: a frightened and naïve young girl way in over her head. She looks outside and down, and is temporarily bolstered by what she sees—a policeman strolling far below under a street lamp. Still, she hasn't yet seen everything worth seeing. Smiling to herself and briefly relieved, she glances back up into the apartment in the direction of the camera/us, and gasps. Cut to an ECU of the first of many shots of a large, painted clown (see the cover photo) derisively pointing and laughing at her and us. Quickly composing herself, she foolishly shrugs it off—error #4—and takes up flirting again—error #5—but we still feel the clown's ironic laughter ringing in our ears.

As Alice explores the flat, she childishly starts to paint a nondescript face on Crewe's blank canvas, which he completes, guiding her hand, into a curvaceous woman's naked body. Getting herself in deeper still, she asks Crewe how she would look as one of his models, as she fondles a dancer's tutu hanging on a hook. In a foreboding LS moving directly towards the camera, Crewe brings over two glasses of red wine he's just poured, miraculously remaining a model of reserved gentlemanliness. He asks her to put it on. With Alice still flirting like crazy, we see Crewe finally getting turned on as he ogles her from behind. She starts to protest about modeling but he convinces her, both of their excitement overcoming her trepidation. As she begins undressing and changing behind a screen just OSR, we see Crewe's back as he moves away, still seen in that foreboding LS. He downs a glass of wine and quickly pours himself another.

Alice reappears half-naked in the costume, flits about mock balletically, and "accidentally" falls into his arms. Still somehow restrained, Crewe plays along, but we know he is only "playing" the mock gentleman now. In a burst of gratitude for catching her, she gives him a quick peck squarely on his lips. We not only realize that this is farther than she has ever gone with a man, but is more intimate that Frank's pity peck back at the station house. This is when Crewe finally crosses the line of no return, and goes in for a real kiss. She struggles, pushes him away, and retreats behind the screen to start to change back, but he steals her clothes when she's not looking, leaving her in just her slip. Hitchcock's next audacious shot is ready to appear.

Up until now, throughout the full ten minutes of this scene in Crewe's flat, we've been watching it transpire from mostly a medium or long perspective, much like the earlier expository montage between Frank and Alice at the café (right before *that* audacious shot, too). Hitchcock now cuts to an *ECU* of Crewe's face, angled somewhat SR just like Tracy's face had looked earlier (Hitchcock loved to plant images that didn't make sense until later). We see Crewe mouth the title "Alice!" Cut back to a CU of her still looking for her clothes behind the screen, getting desperate. Quick cut back to the same ECU of Crewe's face, saying via title "I've got it," as he flings her clothes OSL. Cut to the director's most audacious shot of all, a MCU *reverse angle shot* from directly behind Crewe's left shoulder, focused on that shoulder and beyond to Alice, who is cowering partly behind the screen about fifteen feet away from him. As he walks ominously towards her, recapitulating the two earlier LS walks towards and away from the camera, the camera dollies forward to keep his back in MCU, as Alice's figure looms larger before us (as do her eyes). This shot lasts a frightening thirteen seconds, about one foot per second.

Over the next more than two full minutes, Crewe's attempted rape, Alice's murder of him, and the "silence" afterwards all occur in dark expressionistic shadow, and mostly behind the bedroom curtains out of sight. Except for the camera slowly zooming in for a CU of some bread on a table and the bread knife beside it (Alice's murder weapon), all we see is their struggle in shadow (harking back to the argument between Crewe and Tracy's shadows), the curtains ruffling SR and Alice's hand groping for help past the curtains SL (a clear precursor to Grace Kelly's three-dimensional hand reaching towards us out of the screen in *Dial M for Murder*). At the end of her fight for life, Hitchcock holds on the slightly rustling curtain for a tense ten-count, and then we see Crewe's dead arm fall out from behind the drapes to hang limp in front of the little side table.

With everything building up to this powerful montage, we really need nothing else for our imagination to fill in the gory details—neither titles nor the actual figures. The scene is almost as horrible as Gromek's murder in *Torn Curtain*, or Mrs. Blaney's in *Frenzy*. Minutes seem like hours, and Alice finally leaves the apartment, Hitchcock giving us one of his wonderful

Blackmail, 1929: As with Hitchcock's comment that murder (or the editing of films) is best done with scissors, a killer's next-best weapon of choice ought to be the common household bread knife.

overhead shots down onto the stairway for five vertigo-inducing seconds, precursor to our privileged view of Mother charging towards Arbogast with her knife raised in *Psycho.*

Stair iconography recurs almost immediately at the White's residence, and is shot exactly like the ones in *The Lodger.* After Alice barely sneaks into bed (she's been walking the streets all night in a daze), her mother opens her door with the morning tea to say that a murder has just been committed round the corner. Cut to Hitchcock's trademark overhead shot, this time a stunning CU down onto Alice's horrified yet beautiful face.

Later, when Tracy comes in for the blackmail, Hitchcock zeroes in on his hand reaching into Frank's pocket and pulling out Alice's damning glove that Frank had stolen from the crime scene. Holding the glove loosely, Tracy's hand hangs limp for a second, mimicking Crewe's dead hand in our minds. But Frank finds out shortly that Scotland Yard suspects Tracy of the killing, and the tide turns. For the first time in the film, Frank comes to life (as Joe did when stalking the lodger), and Hitchcock's camera privileges him from above and behind right, Tracy dwarfed SR (also for the first time). Overmelodramatically, humorously, and just right, Frank leers at Tracy while tipping a corner of his hat down, his own blackmailer's smirk deeply etched in a cheek.

As Frank shifts the blame onto Tracy, Hitchcock cuts to a reaction shot of Alice, disagreement yet hope fighting within her. She wants to admit to the murder but Frank won't let her, for he is paying her back in spades for her earlier fickleness; in a way, he is blackmailing both of them, Tracy for the murder and Alice for her love! Tracy walks out of camera range SR and we see his right arm reach back to point at Frank, harking back to Crewe's dead arm in yet another clever cinematic way. As Frank and Tracy argue over who will be believed, a blackmailer or a Scotland Yard detective's girlfriend, Hitchcock shows us a CU of Alice in even more turmoil. Frank and Tracy's hands are shown in the background directly to the left and behind Alice's head as Alice's hands nervously wring themselves in front of her face in the foreground. Frank points repeatedly at Tracy's hand, his finger mimicking a knife pointed right at Alice's head. (Note also Hitchcock's fascinating use of hand iconography in the underrated *Torn Curtain*, one of his worst films that are so good, as discussed in my other book.)

Finally, Alice cannot sit still and allow this blackmailer to take her place no matter the cost. She has come a long way emotionally in a very short time, and reminds us of young Charlie growing up just as quickly in *Shadow of a Doubt*. She gets up and walks behind Frank to whisper over his shoulder that he cannot blackmail this blackmailer. Cut to Tracy, looking hopeful. Frank's got them both where he wants them, though, Tracy consciously and Alice emotionally, and he tells Alice via title: "Don't interfere, Alice. I know what I'm doing." This is far from the truth, though.

Just then the cavalry arrive, and Scotland Yard rushes in. Hitchcock cuts to another first in the film, an audacious *low angle* CU up at Tracy, who is framed in front of the window Hitchcock has planned for him as an escape. In a sudden reverse angle MS from outside the building, Tracy bolts through the window and past the camera, and we see Alice turn to look directly into our eyes—the very spot from where Tracy had just left the screen, as if his back were looking back at her with us—with a bereft and helpless expression on her face.

Cut to an ECU of the wheel of justice, the very first shot we saw at the beginning of the picture, which was really a wheel of a police car spinning madly. As Tracy approaches the British Museum in his flight, we view him in a typical Hitchcockian ELS dwarfed by its pillars (another precursor to Michael Armstrong's similar flight through a museum in *Torn Curtain*). Running through its cavernous galleries, Tracy briefly hides in front of a glass case, his reflection and a couple of mummies black humorously staring back at him. He will soon join them in the next world.

Cut to the justly famous— and completely absurd — ML shot of Tracy climbing down a rope (how did *that* get there, one wonders) SL of a giant Egyptian head SR, both perfectly framed by huge arch in the background. During Tracy's flight, Hitchcock has constantly cut back to the same CU of Alice sitting at a table in front of a window wringing her hands— a more compact and oppressive version of her standing in front of Crewe's loft window earlier. Cut back to the chase through a labyrinth of book lined shelves in the upper dome of the museum. Audacious, extremely ELS of the top of the dome is now seen from the outside, three tiny figures running along its curvature. Suddenly, one of the figures falls behind the dome, out of sight.

In CU, Alice makes another decision and writes her confession note. She doesn't feel it, but we sense her redemption nearing. She rises from her chair, still in CU by the window as shadows pierce the light from the outside, and her head suddenly enters and is encased by a shadowy noose! Closing her eyes, repentant and free, sunlight streams in on her radiant face.

At the station house, due to a slew of accidental interruptions, Alice can only confess her guilt to Frank. Both gritty from bad love and two murders, and stuck with these secrets for the rest of their lives, Hitchcock's camera dollies backwards for a full fourteen seconds, keeping them centered in the screen in MS as they walk towards the camera down the hall. Cut to a reverse angle MS from behind them as the camera now dollies forward as they walk away from it/us, just their backs visible while still centered in frame. They are unable to escape the cell-like frames of Hitchcock's screen.

After a silly joke about female detectives, Alice begins to half-heartedly laugh out loud, trying to release some of her tension, but she is cut off in mid-breath as we see that frightening CU of the clown painting crossing in front of her as it is brought in for evidence. It laughs its hollow laugh, pointing at her complicity.

Blackmail is a brilliant film, worth repeated viewings in the sound version but richer, longer, and purer cinema by far via silence. It's difficult not to take lessons of cynicism from it, for these two characters will no doubt remain separated emotionally from each other for the rest of their lives, carrying their horrible secret around with them. There are certainly better and safer ways to grow up, Hitchcock tells us.

Conclusion

What have these silent films shown and taught us?

Most important, I hope that it is clear by now that, far from amateurish and untested in his first features, Hitchcock had already developed his technical, thematic and visionary skills to an expert pitch. Beginning to direct with *The Pleasure Garden* in 1925, Hitch had already worked with some of the best directors in Germany and had apprenticed in a variety of roles in England — including assistant director, art director, title writer, cameraman, and director of the unfinished *Number Thirteen* — throughout the first five years of the twenties.

Right from the start of his first film, it is obvious that his talents are already fully developed. Densely populated screen frames full of carefully placed, artistically staged actors and objects fill these early films, thrillingly challenging viewers to see everything there is to see in them. Fascinating experiments with perspective, camera movements, camera speeds, camera positions, camera distances, screen frame sizes, lengths of shots, speeds of shots, subjective POV's, *objective* POV's, actors' movements, and especially his extraordinary manipulation of the audience's emotions, all prove themselves ubiquitous and tantalizing throughout these nine features.

I do not believe we should blame anyone — early critics or reviewers in particular — for not bringing these extraordinary films to light prior to today. It has taken nearly a century to even find decent copies of these films, to be pored over in the closely critical way necessary for such analysis. For the same reason, the critics that have touched on these films to a certain extent already (I think especially of Rohmer & Chabrol, Durgnat, Yacowar, and Truffaut, among others) have had to rely more often on memory than extended access.

With Charles Barr's recent *English Hitchcock*, with the book you hold in your hands, and with newly insightful studies undoubtedly in process as I write these words, Hitchcock aficionados can continue to mine ever deeper the seemingly bottomless well of fascinating cinema that fills this director's oeuvre.

Bibliography

Barr, Charles. *English Hitchcock*. Moffat, Scotland: Cameron & Hollis, 1999.

Brill, Lesley. *The Hitchcock Romance: Love and Irony in Hitchcock's Films*. Princeton, N.J.: Princeton University Press, 1988.

Condon, Paul, and Jim Sangster. *The Complete Hitchcock*. London: Virgin, 1999.

Durgnat, Raymond. *The Strange Case of Alfred Hitchcock, or the Plain Man's Hitchcock*. Cambridge, Mass.: MIT Press, 1974.

Gottlieb, Sidney, ed. *Alfred Hitchcock Interviews*. Jackson: University Press of Mississippi, 2003.

_____. *Hitchcock on Hitchcock: Selected Writings and Interviews*. Berkeley: University of California Press, 1995.

LaValley, Albert J., ed. *Focus on Hitchcock*. Englewood Cliffs, N.J.: Prentice-Hall, 1972.

Leitch, Thomas M. *Find the Director and Other Hitchcock Games*. Athens: University of Georgia Press, 1991.

Mogg, Ken. *The Alfred Hitchcock Story*. Dallas: Taylor Publishing, 1999.

O'Connell, Pat Hitchcock, and Laurent Bouzereau. *Alma Hitchcock: The Woman Behind the Man*. New York: Berkley Books, 2003.

Rohmer, Eric, and Claude Chabrol. *Hitchcock: The First Forty-four Films*. Trans. Stanley Hochman. New York: Frederick Ungar, 1957 and 1979.

Rothman, William. *Hitchcock — The Murderous Gaze*. Cambridge, Mass.: Harvard University Press, 1982.

Ryall, Tom. *Alfred Hitchcock and the British Cinema*. Urbana: University of Illinois Press, 1986.

Sarris, Andrew, ed. *Interviews with Film Directors*. New York: Avon Books, 1967.

Sharff, Stefan. *Alfred Hitchcock's High Vernacular: Theory and Practice*. New York: Columbia University Press, 1991.

Sloan, Jane E.. *Alfred Hitchcock: A Filmography and Bibliography*. Berkeley: University of California Press, 1993.

Spoto, Donald. *The Art of Alfred Hitchcock: Fifty Years of His Motion Pictures*. Garden City, N.Y.: Dolphin Book/Doubleday, 1976.

_____. *The Dark Side of Genius: The Life of Alfred Hitchcock.* New York: Bal-
    lantine Books, 1983.
Truffaut, François, with Helen G. Scott. *Hitchcock.* Revised edition, English
    translation. New York: Touchstone/Simon & Schuster, 1985.
Wood, Robin. *Hitchcock's Films.* New York: Castle Books, 1965.
_____. *Hitchcock's Films Revisited.* New York: Columbia University Press, 1989.
Yacowar, Maurice. *Hitchcock's British Films.* Hamden, Conn.: Archon Books,
    1977.

Index

213